Microsoft BizTalk Server 2010 Patterns

Create effective, scalable solutions with Microsoft
BizTalk Server 2010

Dan Rosanova

BIRMINGHAM - MUMBAI

Microsoft BizTalk Server 2010 Patterns

Copyright © 2011 Packt Publishing

All rights reserved. No part of this book may be reproduced, stored in a retrieval system, or transmitted in any form or by any means, without the prior written permission of the publisher, except in the case of brief quotations embedded in critical articles or reviews.

Every effort has been made in the preparation of this book to ensure the accuracy of the information presented. However, the information contained in this book is sold without warranty, either express or implied. Neither the author, nor Packt Publishing, and its dealers and distributors will be held liable for any damages caused or alleged to be caused directly or indirectly by this book.

Packt Publishing has endeavored to provide trademark information about all of the companies and products mentioned in this book by the appropriate use of capitals. However, Packt Publishing cannot guarantee the accuracy of this information.

First published: October 2011

Production Reference: 1181011

Published by Packt Publishing Ltd.
Livery Place
35 Livery Street
Birmingham B3 2PB, UK.

ISBN 978-1-84968-460-6

www.packtpub.com

Cover Image by Sandeep Babu (sandyjb@gmail.com)

Credits

Author
Dan Rosanova

Reviewers
René Brauwers
Steef-Jan Wiggers
Randal van Splunteren

Acquisition Editor
Dilip Venkatesh

Development Editors
Swapna Verlekar
Pallavi Iyengar

Technical Editors
Manasi Poonthottam
Ankita Shashi

Copy Editor
Laxmi Subramanian

Project Coordinator
Leena Purkait

Proofreader
Bernadette Watkins

Indexer
Monica Ajmera Mehta

Graphics
Valentina D'silva
Nilesh R. Mohite

Production Coordinator
Shantanu Zagade

Cover Work
Shantanu Zagade

About the Author

Dan Rosanova is a two-time Microsoft BizTalk Architecture MVP with over twelve years of experience delivering solutions on Microsoft platforms in the financial services, insurance, banking, telecommunications, logistics, and high-tech industries. He specializes in high volume and low latency distributed applications. He has served as both a technical and strategic advisor to clients ranging in size from startups to Fortune 500. Dan has extensive experience with .NET, XML, services, and queuing, as well as evolutionary computation.

Dan is a Senior Architect in the Technology Integration Practice at West Monroe Partners, an international, full-service business and technology consulting firm, focused on guiding organizations through projects that fundamentally transform their business.

About the Reviewers

René Brauwers started his IT career at the end of the last century as a web developer/designer and was primarily engaged with building websites using classic ASP. Soon, his focus got more drawn towards developing client/server applications using the 3GL language Centura/Gupta Team Developer. Around the end of 2002, he got involved with the EAI/B2B/B2C/BPM world, starting off with WebMethods and did this for the next three years with an occasional side step to .NET development. This occasional side step got him in touch with BizTalk Server in 2005 and, since then, he has been involved with BizTalk Server and general .NET programming. Currently, he is employed as a senior BizTalk consultant for Motion10 (Motion10.com) in the Netherlands and can be contacted at rene@brauwers.nl.

> I would love to thank my parents, brother, and soon-to-be sister-in-law for supporting me and allowing me to become the person I am today; my girlfriend, best friend, and soul mate Miranda (let's move to Australia), and last but not least, Leena and Pallavi for finding me and giving me this opportunity.

Steef-Jan Wiggers, architect for Ordina (www.ordina.com), has built a strong foundation of experience as a technical lead developer and application architect, specializing in custom applications, enterprise application integration, and web services. He has experience in architecting, designing, developing, and supporting sophisticated and innovative software using many different Microsoft technologies and products. Steef-Jan has been awarded the Microsoft Most Valuable Professional (MVP) award (2010) for his contributions to the world-wide BizTalk Server community. He maintains a blog on his exploits, pitfalls, and musing with BizTalk Server and Windows Azure-related technologies at http://soa-thoughts. blogspot.com/.

Microsoft BizTalk Server MVP: https://mvp.support.microsoft.com/default. aspx/profile/steef-jan.

Randal van Splunteren lives with his wife, daughter, and son in the Netherlands. He works as a consultant for a Dutch consulting company. His focus is on implementing integration scenarios using Microsoft products and technologies. He has real-world experience with all versions of BizTalk Server and was awarded Most Valuable Professional (MVP) for BizTalk Server by Microsoft in 2010 and 2011. Randal is an active BizTalk community member and maintains a blog on BizTalk (http://biztalkmessages.vansplunteren.net). You can contact Randal at: randal.van.splunteren@hotmail.com.

I would like to thank Dan Rosanova for writing this book and giving me the opportunity to review it. I think Dan has succeeded in writing one of the best BizTalk books available today.

www.PacktPub.com

Support files, eBooks, discount offers, and more

You might want to visit www.PacktPub.com for support files and downloads related to your book.

Did you know that Packt offers eBook versions of every book published, with PDF and ePub files available? You can upgrade to the eBook version at www.PacktPub.com and as a print book customer, you are entitled to a discount on the eBook copy. Get in touch with us at www.PacktPub.com for more details.

At www.PacktPub.com, you can also read a collection of free technical articles, sign up for a range of free newsletters and receive exclusive discounts and offers on Packt books and eBooks.

http://PacktLib.PacktPub.com

Do you need instant solutions to your IT questions? PacktLib is Packt's online digital book library. Here, you can access, read and search across Packt's entire library of books.

Why Subscribe?

- Fully searchable across every book published by Packt
- Copy and paste, print and bookmark content
- On demand and accessible via web browser

Free Access for Packt account holders

If you have an account with Packt at www.PacktPub.com, you can use this to access PacktLib today and view nine entirely free books. Simply use your login credentials for immediate access.

Instant Updates on New Packt Books

Get notified! Find out when new books are published by following @PacktEnterprise on Twitter, or the *Packt Enterprise* Facebook page.

This book is dedicated to Jennie.

Table of Contents

Part 2

Preface

Microsoft BizTalk Server 2010 is an exciting platform for developing middleware and integration solutions. As our computing ecosystem moves ever further away from monolithic mainframe style applications, we find ourselves spending an ever increasing amount of time integrating existing systems. This trend continues and increases as more of these systems move to the cloud. The book is broken into two major sections: an introduction to Microsoft BizTalk Server 2010 from a detailed technical perspective; and the story of a realistic enterprise embarking on the process of adopting Microsoft BizTalk Server 2010 to build solutions. Through this unified story line that mimics how many real-world development initiatives flow, readers will walk through creating solutions according to best practices that will expand and grow with the enterprise that they serve. The same patterns and practices presented here apply to any middleware or integration platform including the upcoming AppFabric ServiceBus.

What this book covers

Part 1

Chapter 1, Introducing BizTalk Server 2010: This chapter introduces the reader to BizTalk Server, its capabilities, and internal architecture in an abstract manner. It introduces fundamentals of BizTalk Server 2010, the components that make up the platform, and how BizTalk fits into most enterprise environments.

Chapter 2, Introduction to BizTalk Development: This chapter introduces the developer to the BizTalk development experience, first through structure and architecture and then through the IDE and tool experience. It concludes with coverage of Business Activity Monitoring.

Chapter 3, BizTalk Development Guidelines: This chapter describes the best practices development guidelines for the most common areas of BizTalk development including maps, orchestrations, adapters, and pipelines.

Chapter 4, Operating BizTalk: This chapter introduces operational concepts of BizTalk that are important for both the developer as well as the administrator.

Part 2

Chapter 5, Basic Messaging Solution: This chapter introduces messaging in BizTalk Server at a basic binary level, and proceeds to build upon the concepts at each stage, until demonstrating how to make expressive and powerful message-based solutions.

Chapter 6, Unit Tests and BAM: This chapter introduces critical concepts to make every solution complete: monitoring and automated unit testing. This will show the reader how to create and deploy basic monitoring profiles and also how to create automated unit tests.

Chapter 7, Leveraging Orchestration: This chapter introduces the reader to orchestration and shows them how to model their current solution with orchestration (and why not to). It then introduces the true purpose of orchestration: service composition.

Chapter 8, The WCF-SQL Adapter and WCF Services: This chapter introduces the WCF-SQL Adapter, as well as how to expose WCF services from BizTalk. The user will learn both polling and query approaches to working with the WCF-SQL Adapter and how to expose different services in different manners from BizTalk.

Chapter 9, Expanding the Solution with Services and Rules: This chapter demonstrates how to use the previously defined WCF-SQL artifacts to make our processing solution more expressive and rich. The reader then learns how to use the business rules engine (BRE) to create powerful rules-driven solutions for decision making that are decoupled from our core solution.

Chapter 10, Envelopes, Flat Files, and Batching: This chapter extensively covers the concepts of flat file processing in BizTalk. It introduces the reader to both consuming and creating flat files, as well as providing guidance for working with flat files. It then covers envelope processing for XML documents, to handle message assembly and disassembly.

Chapter 11, Completing the Order Processing Solution: This chapter covers completing the order processing solution by exposing the existing solution to WCF clients, creating build scripts for deployment packages, and expanding the current monitoring solution to provide rich self-service interactive reporting capabilities to business users.

Chapter 12, Asynchronous Solutions: This chapter introduces advanced asynchronous concepts that scale well and address common challenges in the enterprise. The WCF-SQL Adapter is used with query notifications to provide alerts to changes in a database that do not rely on polling. Continuations are introduced and explained; then used to integrate with InfoPath documents (or other sources) to provide human workflow capabilities.

Chapter 13, Performing Parallel Processing and Branching: This chapter introduces methods for parallel processing in BizTalk server, and how to use them to shorten processing time and increase scalability, as well as when not to.

Chapter 14, Processing Message Convoys: The final chapter of the book introduces convoy patterns in BizTalk Server. These patterns are often used to overcome large impedance mismatches between systems in an enterprise, such as batched systems connecting to real-time (non-batched) systems.

Appendix: The appendix provides an introduction to XML presented in a BizTalk context. There is also troubleshooting guide that provides common problem solution approaches for use in BizTalk applications. Finally, there is an introduction to the concepts of loose coupling in software systems.

What you need for this book

Windows 7 (or Windows Server 2008 R2)

Visual Studio 2010

BizTalk Server 2010 Developer Edition

SQL Server 2008 R2 (Developer or Express Edition)

BizUnit 3.0.1

Who this book is for

This book is targeted at software architects, solution architects, and developers of BizTalk solutions. The technical focus will make the book less applicable to managers unless they have a fairly deep technical background, but it will still be useful for them to assure that their teams stay on track to developing effective BizTalk solutions according to time tested patterns and practices.

This book does not expect any level of experience with BizTalk. It is targeted at the beginner or intermediate BizTalk developer who has previous experience developing on the Microsoft platform in .NET and Visual Studio. If you have absolutely no experience with Visual Studio, then BizTalk will likely be more of a challenge to you and I recommend working with C# or Visual Studio a little on your own, ahead of time, to familiarize yourself with the IDE experience.

I strongly believe even advanced BizTalk developers will learn very much from the book, as it presents patterns and practices that are ideal for BizTalk solutions, but are largely not common knowledge in the BizTalk developer community. Cursory knowledge of XML, although useful, is not required. The book does include an XML primer in the appendix, so if you're new to XML you may want to read through this. The material in this book has successfully trained dozens of .NET developers as well as Fox Pro, Java, and iSeries programmers who have no .NET experience at all.

BizTalk is a departure from almost any other platform most of us have worked on, but it is largely a step up into a more abstract level that allows us to focus more on the business solution and less on the infrastructure involved.

Conventions

In this book, you will find a number of styles of text that distinguish between different kinds of information. Here are some examples of these styles, and an explanation of their meaning.

Code words in text are shown as follows: "We can include other contexts through the use of the `include` directive."

A block of code is set as follows:

```
public MyMessage SomethingInteresting(XLANGMessage message)
{
    MyMessage myMessage = message[0].RetrieveAs(typeof(MyMessage)) as
MyMessage;
    return myMessage;
}
public XmlReader SomethingElse(XLANGMessage message)
{
    XmlReader reader = message[0].RetrieveAs(typeof(XmlReader)) as
XmlReader;
    return reader;
}
```

When we wish to draw your attention to a particular part of a code block, the relevant lines or items are set in bold:

```xml
<?xml version="1.0" encoding="utf-8"?>
<Order xmlns="http://wmp/schemas/quote">
  <Number>1234</Number>
  <Date>2011-06-11</Date>
  <Item Number="4432" Quantity="1" />
  <Item Number="5532" Quantity="2" />
</Order>
```

Any command-line input or output is written as follows:

```
gacutil /i PRP.OrderProcessing.Library.dll
```

New terms and important words are shown in bold. Words that you see on the screen, in menus or dialog boxes for example, appear in the text like this: "If you click the **Parameter Name** dropdown, you will see that the **Products** variable is already specified. Select it and click **OK**".

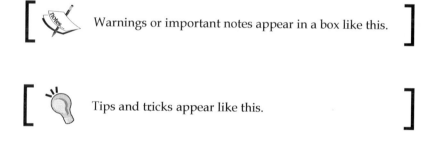

Warnings or important notes appear in a box like this.

Tips and tricks appear like this.

Reader feedback

Feedback from our readers is always welcome. Let us know what you think about this book—what you liked or may have disliked. Reader feedback is important for us to develop titles that you really get the most out of.

To send us general feedback, simply send an e-mail to feedback@packtpub.com, and mention the book title via the subject of your message.

If there is a book that you need and would like to see us publish, please send us a note in the SUGGEST A TITLE form on www.packtpub.com or e-mail suggest@packtpub.com.

If there is a topic that you have expertise in and you are interested in either writing or contributing to a book, see our author guide on www.packtpub.com/authors.

Customer support

Now that you are the proud owner of a Packt book, we have a number of things to help you to get the most from your purchase.

Downloading the example code

You can download the example code files for all Packt books you have purchased from your account at http://www.PacktPub.com. If you purchased this book elsewhere, you can visit http://www.PacktPub.com/support and register to have the files e-mailed directly to you.

Errata

Although we have taken every care to ensure the accuracy of our content, mistakes do happen. If you find a mistake in one of our books — maybe a mistake in the text or the code — we would be grateful if you would report this to us. By doing so, you can save other readers from frustration and help us improve subsequent versions of this book. If you find any errata, please report them by visiting http://www.packtpub.com/support, selecting your book, clicking on the **errata submission form** link, and entering the details of your errata. Once your errata are verified, your submission will be accepted and the errata will be uploaded on our website, or added to any list of existing errata, under the Errata section of that title. Any existing errata can be viewed by selecting your title from http://www.packtpub.com/support.

Piracy

Piracy of copyright material on the Internet is an ongoing problem across all media. At Packt, we take the protection of our copyright and licenses very seriously. If you come across any illegal copies of our works, in any form, on the Internet, please provide us with the location address or website name immediately so that we can pursue a remedy.

Please contact us at copyright@packtpub.com with a link to the suspected pirated material.

We appreciate your help in protecting our authors, and our ability to bring you valuable content.

Questions

You can contact us at questions@packtpub.com if you are having a problem with any aspect of the book, and we will do our best to address it.

Part 1

Introducing BizTalk Server 2010

Introduction to BizTalk
Development

BizTalk Development Guidelines

Operating BizTalk

1
Introducing BizTalk Server 2010

This chapter introduces the reader to BizTalk Server, its capabilities, and internal architecture in an abstract manner. It introduces the fundamentals of BizTalk Server 2010, the components that make up the platform, and how BizTalk fits into most enterprise environments. It also presents some of the internal design patterns used within BizTalk. The material in this chapter may be a little in depth for the beginner, especially if you are also new to middleware. Feel free to come back to it later if necessary.

This chapter covers the following:

- What is BizTalk Server
- Goals of BizTalk Server
- When to use BizTalk
- Where does BizTalk fit in the enterprise
- Architecture of BizTalk Server
- Design patterns used internally by BizTalk
- The BizTalk runtime environment

Understanding what is BizTalk Server

BizTalk Server is quite possibly the most advanced product produced by Microsoft to date. It offers scalability and reliability simply unrivalled on the Windows platform or, for that matter, any platform. According to Gartner, it falls in the leaders quadrant and has the highest ability to execute. It is now in its seventh version (2010) and has grown more robust and feature-rich with each release. It scales both up and out and is designed to meet the needs of even the most demanding enterprises, but also to work well for medium sized organizations.

At its core, BizTalk Server is meant to be a mediator or a conduit for information throughout an organization. BizTalk's primary focus is connecting systems and providing services. Yet it is more than just a middleware product, it is an entire toolset designed to help you build, run, and grow your enterprise's information systems. Today, more than ever, no software lives in isolation and BizTalk is the tool with which to break down the isolation that is still inherent in most existing software. Even cloud offerings like Azure or `Salesforce.com` no longer exist in a vacuum. Often these clouds are required to interact with other software systems in the enterprise, or with business partners, and increasingly with other cloud platforms. BizTalk is designed to bridge the gap between applications; to act as a mediator, broker, and router for business transactions. BizTalk is an integral part of Microsoft's future strategy, including their Cloud Strategy.

In addition to the core messaging server, additional tools such as Tracking, Monitoring, Business Rules, and a Visual Studio based IDE experience are provided to make working with BizTalk more familiar and powerful. Any developer having a background with Microsoft development should feel quickly at home with BizTalk. Developers from other platforms should also find the experience familiar when done correctly.

Through the use of BizTalk's core components (Adapters, Pipelines, Mapping, Orchestration, and Business Rules) BizTalk allows seamless integration with all major enterprise platforms such as SQL Server, DB2, Oracle, SAP, PeopleSoft, and many others. Beyond integration, BizTalk allows expressive and powerful business processes to be built upon the integrations it facilitates. Used in conjunction with human workflow products like SharePoint and InfoPath, BizTalk provides the enterprise with a variety of tools with which to create expressive, unique solutions that enable business and increase productivity.

In the past, BizTalk was referred to as a Business Process Management (BPM) product but that doesn't go far enough to convey the power of BizTalk. It is really more of a business enablement platform. As we will learn in the second part of this book, BizTalk can be a central component in the connected enterprise via enterprise application integration, SOA, or ESB.

Stating the goals of BizTalk Server

BizTalk is Microsoft's premier messaging platform. It was designed with many specific scenarios in mind and has evolved to work with others as well. Whether you are involved in integration, service orientation, business process management, or enterprise service bus, BizTalk's purpose is to enable the following goals:

- Increasing reliability

- Decoupling systems
- Providing reuse
- Decreasing development time
- Providing rich information to technical as well as business consumers
- Improving administration
- Providing a rich set of security options that can be controlled separately from the functionality of a solution

Used as presented in this text, it will deliver on all of these points. This is a lot to cover, so let's address each of these aspects individually and discuss how they are achieved.

Increasing reliability

The very core of BizTalk Server is a construct called the Message Box. Everything that goes in and out of BizTalk Server travels through the Message Box. We will cover this in greater depth later, but for now it is enough to know that even in a catastrophic outage, there is never a chance for messages to simply be "lost" in BizTalk. Distributed transactions while managing the input, update, and removal of messages from the Message Box are fully **ACID** compliant. BizTalk is designed as a distributed system and has resilience built into the product. Just as we have been able to abstract away details of processor architecture, BizTalk abstracts away details of durability and reliability. BizTalk recovers cleanly and often automatically from outages. This inherent reliability allows us to shift our focus to solving business problems rather than solving technical issues. BizTalk is also designed to work in a scaled environment; addressing both scale out and scale up scenarios in a simple manner.

Decoupling systems

BizTalk, when used correctly, provides unprecedented decoupling by allowing you to graphically map message formats to each other. This simple flexible mapping capability is critical to decreasing coupling as it enforces a barrier between chains of connected systems. Using the best practices presented in this text, changes in endpoints such as transport, encoding, timing, and format will have little or no impact on your internal solutions. Here again the Message Box achieves abstraction and helps by decoupling message senders from message receivers. As mentioned earlier, every message in BizTalk goes through the Message Box—so even a simple solution still uses the Message Box. This separation enforced by the Message Box allows us to decouple message senders (publishers) from message consumers (subscribers). For more information on loose coupling see "What is Loose Coupling" in the appendix.

Providing reuse

By using internal message formats that are known only to your BizTalk solutions, endpoints and adapters of existing solutions can be leveraged repeatedly over time. Other great candidates for reuse are infrastructure services such as logging or audit that can easily be provided by the ESB capabilities of BizTalk. Properly structured BizTalk solutions encourage reuse. By decoupling, format, transport, and time constraints solutions and their components can be readily reused to solve variations of specific processes. Some of these components, like the WCF Adapters, can even be used completely outside of BizTalk.

Decreasing development time

By leveraging the familiar Visual Studio environment, developers are quickly at home with BizTalk and can begin creating solutions almost immediately. We will see later how to make those solutions effective, scalable, and flexible. Perhaps the greatest time savers for developers are all the tools that are part of BizTalk. The Mapper, the Flat File Wizard, Business Activity Monitoring, the other wizards for various adapters, and all the robust infrastructure and service publishing tools make BizTalk a complete toolset to address the vast majority of issues facing the enterprise. Very few of the tools involved in BizTalk will be completely new or unfamiliar to developers who work on the Microsoft platform. Great care has been taken to make the transition to BizTalk as easy as possible. Further, because BizTalk does not focus on code and libraries the way most programming environments do, the amount of time taken to create a solution is greatly decreased.

Providing rich information to technical as well as business consumers

As mentioned earlier, nothing is ever "lost" in BizTalk. By default, there is a tremendous amount of technical tracking for every message and workflow (orchestration) inside of BizTalk. As useful as this is, there is another level available via Business Activity Monitoring (BAM) that allows for the creation of tracking profiles to follow business processes at the desired level of granularity and to include data from within the messages (content) as well as metadata about the messages (context). Further, this data can be used in automatically created analysis cubes (via SQL Server Analysis Services) to provide nearly self-service BI solutions. With the addition of notifications on this monitoring information, what BizTalk offers in this area is currently unrivalled by any other platform.

Improving administration

Continuing in the line of messages never being "lost", BizTalk also provides a rich set of tools for administrators to deploy, monitor, and manage solutions. Using the MSI deployment package concept, there is also no compiling or scripting necessary for the administrator (although these features are available if needed). BizTalk enables the solid line handoff between developers and administrators that is increasingly required by regulatory compliance regimes. Further, BizTalk allows administrators to reallocate and partition processing over their servers to make solutions more scalable or allow for in-place upgrades requiring little or no downtime. IT administrators have more control over the runtime of BizTalk solutions than of any other platform in the Microsoft stack. Moreover, none of these controls require code to be implemented, freeing staff to focus on their primary jobs rather than learning new scripting languages. BizTalk is also heavily instrumented and uses familiar MMC and WMI tools that IT operations staff will quickly feel comfortable with. Additionally, other administration tools like SCOM have add-on packs for BizTalk that plug into this instrumentation.

After using BizTalk for a while (in accordance with the practices outlined here), I invite you to revisit this list and determine for yourself how relevant each of the points have been.

When to use BizTalk Server

Perhaps most strikingly, unlike a lot of other software, such as Office, Windows, and even SAP or PeopleSoft in the enterprise space, after installation BizTalk doesn't actually do anything yet. I think this really confuses people and a good analogy is in order. BizTalk Server is much like its close companion SQL Server. Once you install SQL Server, it doesn't actually do anything; you must build solutions that use a database before it does anything useful. The same is true of BizTalk. Both products are platforms on which solutions are built, not solutions in and of themselves. In fact, BizTalk is an application built on top of SQL Server and .NET. To a certain extent, the same can be said of SharePoint; SharePoint doesn't do anything, it allows you to do things with it and is also built on a similar platform.

There are two primary areas where BizTalk fits very well into an organization: integrated (or distributed) systems and high volume systems. BizTalk is ideal for solutions that involve inter-system communication. If you are building software systems that will interact with other external systems, BizTalk is a good fit. Bear in mind that external doesn't always mean outside of your enterprise. It could mean outside your department or outside your current ability to change. The more external interactions that take place the better the leverage from the investment in BizTalk Server as you replace point to point or direct connections with a hub and spoke or service bus architecture.

The other close fit is for high volume and/or mission critical systems. BizTalk provides scale up and scale out growth more easily than any other platform choice and can accommodate the loads of even the most intensive scenarios. It is also reliable enough not to lose any messages and to provide best in class disaster recovery while maintaining transactional integrity.

For all its features and the benefits it brings to an organization, BizTalk Server is not the right tool for every possible solution. The license cost is high by Microsoft standards; although it is extremely low compared to rivals in the space. Not all businesses need BizTalk Server, but many will benefit from it. If you don't need adapters to connect to the existing line of business systems, business activity monitoring to provide analytics and visibility, message format mapping, business rules, or iron clad reliability you may not need BizTalk. If your solution only does Web Services (or WCF) in a homogeneous Microsoft environment with limited need for tracking and monitoring, you may be able to simply use Workflow Services on App Fabric and build a good solution. It may even be possible to simply code services by hand.

Finally, if your solution is not meant to be real-time, but instead to handle large volumes of data on a scheduled fashion, such as ETL, there are other tools that are probably more appropriate. SQL Server Integration Services (SSIS) certainly comes to mind quickly. SSIS is a great tool, but it is meant for point to point ETL and does not offer the rich fabric of features offered by BizTalk.

It can effectively be argued that everything BizTalk Server does could be built into in-house applications and thus there would be no need for it. Although this is theoretically correct, it would prove terribly costly to do so. Imagine the amount of dollars and resources Microsoft has already invested into BizTalk to ensure that it is reliable, scalable, extensible, and easily manageable. It's probably billions of dollars at this point in the seventh version. I would consider that to be well beyond the budget of most projects, especially considering that the risk is really the infrastructure that sits below the solution, not the solution itself. The same argument can be made of database software. One could choose to write their own database, but they would have a very difficult time justifying the cost.

David Chappell addresses this very issue in his article, Introducing Windows Server AppFabric: "*One of the great truths of building software is this: Application developers shouldn't spend their time creating infrastructure.*" BizTalk is an infrastructure layer that provides us with messaging, reliability, durability, and scalability. To this end BizTalk is a force multiplier, in that it allows fewer developers (and operations staff) to accomplish more work in less time. This is a bold statement, but once you know the product and its tools, the results are unmistakable. Unlike many other platforms, the tools in BizTalk Server allow for rapid but robust solution development. WCF services, for example, can be created, exposed, and secured without a single line of code being written. For this very reason many programmers are put off by BizTalk, but make no mistake, code is being written and it is quite advanced .NET code. For now, it is enough to say that you can get a lot out of BizTalk without ever knowing much about .NET, but a deep understanding of .NET will help you get the most out of the platform over time.

Where does BizTalk fit into the Enterprise?

This is an important question that bears answering. For all its glory, BizTalk is not a panacea for the enterprise. It is not an ERP or human workflow system, nor is it an accounting, claims management, or inventory management system. In fact, out of the box, BizTalk inherently does nothing. BizTalk's value is connecting these types of systems within your enterprise and with your trade partners. BizTalk is ultimately middleware, used to bridge these disparate systems and replace costly, tightly coupled, point to point integrations with an ESB or hub and spoke architecture, that is able to deliver more value as a whole than the constituent parts individually. BizTalk enables business processing to happen faster, more easily, and more reliably. BizTalk empowers your enterprise to leverage existing assets and interact with the larger world of software more easily. In some organizations, this will make it a core and central part of the enterprise architecture. In other organizations, BizTalk may serve more of an edge role, bridging the gap between external trade partners or legacy systems. Either way it is important to find where BizTalk fits for you and I invite you to start small, convince yourself, and iteratively build up and out to find the right place for BizTalk.

Exploring the architecture of BizTalk Server

At its core, BizTalk Server is a .NET application built upon a set of SQL Server databases that enable it to be both reliable and scalable. It is a Publish-Subscribe messaging system built to achieve the loosely coupled, flexible design criteria of modern enterprise software systems.

Critical to understanding the product is understanding the Publish Subscribe design pattern, which will be explored further later on. Importantly, as most of BizTalk is indeed written in .NET, it really does demonstrate some very advanced and specialized programming techniques utilized to make it so powerful. From stream-based processing (the pipes and filters pattern) to design patterns like unit of work and transaction script; BizTalk really is an example of a well-designed, modern, enterprise software system implemented in .NET. So specialized is the skill that went into the product that the development team actually tuned SQL Server to run in specific ways to improve the performance of the product (which, by the way, is part of the reason why it is unsupported to change anything in the databases, which are carefully and specifically tuned for BizTalk Server).

Design patterns within the BizTalk architecture

In addition to being a great application server, BizTalk serves as a model in application architecture and design. The following sections explore some of the architectural features of the product itself ranging from core precepts to more subtle implementation details.

Messaging

Messaging has become an overloaded term in technical parlance these days. You can ask different parts of the technical (IT) community what messaging means and get very different answers. Almost all of them legitimate. To some, messaging represents e-mail and instant messenger or human communication. If this is the camp you find yourself in, I am afraid you have purchased the wrong book. Increasingly, messaging means an interaction between parts of a software system. Today these are generally distributed systems, but that need not necessarily be the case. A quick read of Grady Booch's seminal work, *"Object Oriented Analysis and Design with Applications"*, *Addison-Wesley Object Technology,* will show that, even in early OOP, the concept of a client and server were well understood; though they almost assuredly were parts of the same executable. Booch goes as far as using the term message to describe the call from a client to a server (client and server are also used in a different, but very appropriate, context from what we would understand today). In this way, we can see that what messaging and middleware are doing is not necessarily a radical departure from traditional programming paradigms, but an evolutionary step into a more robust and distributed incarnation.

As Phil Boardman once proclaimed to me during his journey deep into WCF: "*The message is the unit of work*". This is an important proclamation because it bridges a divide between traditional software design patterns and distributed computing. We'll dig deeper into this as we go on and see exactly how significant this statement is in terms of BizTalk, but for now it is enough to remember that a message is an encapsulated payload of meaningful data normally having associated metadata.

On this note, it is probably appropriate to explain how messaging in our context of modern distributed systems differs from messaging of old. Although Booch may have seen setting the properties of a class as messages, those would not be meaningful in a distributed software environment. These types of messages would be neither meaningful nor self-encapsulated. In order to be both meaningful and self-encapsulated, such a message would have to contain the entire object (which would violate some OOP principles including the Law of Demeter). This is an aspect where distributed/message-oriented development can appear to deviate from OOP practices. Most often, in practice, the Data Transfer Object is the pattern used to reconcile these differences.

Messages can be commands or CRUD operations or simply status updates, but as the definition says, they should be meaningful and encapsulated. A Purchase Order, let's say (in XML format) would be a great example of a message. In the service context, the Operation (or Action) to which the Purchase Order is sent would determine what is to happen to it. There are many schools of thought on message and schema definitions or designs, and it is important to strike the right balance for your organization between flexibility and control, but that is a topic for another conversation.

Publish Subscribe

It is important to point out that Publish Subscribe is predicated upon messages being published, that is to say, to external sources sending messages in. This is perhaps one of the more difficult concepts for many developers to embrace with BizTalk. BizTalk is not a proactive or imperative (procedural) environment like Java, C#, or most programming languages; it is a reactive one. BizTalk never starts processes on its own; it may start complex processes based upon specific messages being received, but it does not have the concept of a traditional application starting point. There is no "Hello world" in BizTalk. Frankly, "Hello world" is a concept best left to introductions to computer programming.

In a traditional procedural/imperative environment, the starting point of an application is often similar to the following:

1. Look for input.
2. Decide what to do with the input.
3. Send the data to whatever destination is determined to be the recipient.

This pattern is pictured as follows:

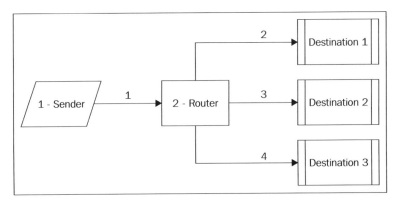

In most implementations, parts 1 and 2 are in the same process. This results in each sender (step 1) needing to be aware of each possible recipient. Even if implemented in clever ways, such as recipient list, the result is implicit coupling from the source to the destination. Also troublesome is the fact that the router is normally replicated in many places throughout the enterprise, often via unique implementations in each system that is being integrated. This is a colossal opportunity for reuse that is missed in most organizations. Some try to leverage this with home grown solutions or open source platforms that can fall far short in the long run. The previous pattern violates loose coupling principles for both service and object-oriented methodologies.

Publish Subscribe overcomes these limitations by almost completely turning this model around. In the Publish Subscribe model, the sequence of events is as follows:

1. Subscribers enlist (or enter) their subscriptions (what they're interested in).
2. The Subscription Manager tracks these subscriptions.

The sending system (Publisher) sends a message (it is now done) and the Subscription Manager matches the subscription list, forwarding each subscriber its own immutable copy of the message.

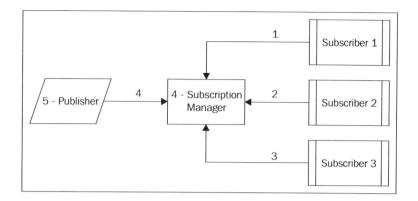

The Publisher (sender before) is now completely unaware of which systems are interested in the message it is sending. Further, the Subscription Manager not only abstracts away the recipients, it also abstracts away the state of those destination systems. Filled subscriptions can simply await their delivery long after the sender has completed sending its message. If there are no subscribers, it is really not the concern of the sending system, but of the Subscription Manager.

A primary goal of Publish Subscribe is to move away from point to point and synchronous architectures and towards loosely coupled asynchronous interactions. Publish Subscribe goes a long way towards making loose coupling a first class concept in software.

BizTalk embraces Publish Subscribe so fully that there is actually no such thing as a synchronous request in BizTalk. We can make services or endpoints appear to be synchronous, but they are in fact asynchronous.

Adapter

Adapters are a core concept of BizTalk. Adapters allow us to bridge different systems together through common experiences and tools. The adapter pattern has a readily understandable implementation in the wider software world: ODBC. Most developers have at least some experience with ODBC (or JDBC). These are adapters to the underlying database they connect to. Although connecting to SQL Server, Oracle, or MySQL are all done in a fundamentally different way, the ODBC driver (really it's an adapter) allows us to connect to all of these data sources and more. BizTalk uses adapters for all endpoints, in and out, of a solution. In this way, no matter the platform outside of BizTalk, inside everything is a common platform and is almost all XML.

Streaming

Streaming is another critical architectural principle in BizTalk, but thankfully it is one that many developers will never need to work with directly. With very few exceptions every component in BizTalk is a stream-based component. Pipelines and maps use streaming to handle messages in BizTalk. This means that stream classes are chained together in the framework so as to avoid large memory buffers. This is one of the concepts I struggled the most with early in BizTalk, but it is also so critical to the scalability of the platform.

Instead of loading an entire message into memory, BizTalk loads a piece of it—normally only a few kilobytes. Then, each class in the chain of classes involved in mapping and pipeline processing calls the Read operation on the next in the chain, passing this small buffer between them, making their requisite changes along the way. The ultimate motivation behind this is to keep a flat memory footprint for the process. Even with relatively small messages, a high volume system will quickly consume large amounts of memory if loading entire messages. The larger the messages, the faster this becomes problematic. For very large messages that have operations requiring large intermediate buffers, BizTalk will even stream to disk as needed, to save memory.

These stream classes are some of the most impressive parts of the BizTalk framework and something many in the .NET world have been eagerly awaiting.

Understanding BizTalk message flow

When a message is received by BizTalk, it is received via an Adapter; always. Adapters are the endpoints of any BizTalk system. They are the points of contact to the outside world; the gateways if you will, into the realm that is BizTalk. These endpoints could be File, HTTP, DB2, or any of the dozens of transports supported by BizTalk out of the box.

Upon arrival, all messages go to the Message Box, but to get there they must follow a specific sequence. The following is the list of actors involved in receiving a message listed in the order in which they process the message:

1. Adapter.
2. Pipeline: chain of Pipeline Components.
3. Map.
4. Message Box.

This flow is depicted in the following figure:

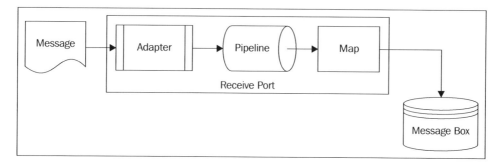

Before we discuss the Message Box itself, it is worth describing a little more of what these components do. The message is clearly what we are interested in receiving. The Adapter is the communication endpoint that does the physical receiving of the bytes. Pipelines process the stream of data received, so that it can be made more usable for later components. The pipeline contains components within it that can provide services like decoding (such as decryption), disassembly, validation, and party resolution (determining who sent the message).

This is almost like an international arrival when flying. The adapter is the airplane, the pipeline is the way you get to customs, with components of jet bridge and hallway, the signs and queues are the map, and the customs booth is the Message Box. The customs agent really doesn't care if you flew in a Boeing 777 or an Airbus 330, or even how you got to the booth; they care about letting you into the country.

As this chain of processing completes, the message is mapped and streamed into the Message Box.

The Message Box

The Message Box has been the central construct behind every version of BizTalk Server since 2004. The Message Box is the place where everything in BizTalk happens. Messages that are received from adapters are put into the Message Box. Messages sent out of BizTalk are retrieved from the Message Box in a pull fashion by send ports and orchestrations. These sent messages are pulled by their subscribers. Understanding this complex series of steps is very useful, but you can also skip this section for now and come back later, if you prefer.

The Message Box is based on the concept of queues. In fact, the first versions of BizTalk used MSMQ internally to organize their work queues. MSMQ is really a fantastic technology, but BizTalk's solution to queuing is far more scalable and appropriate for the type of work BizTalk performs.

Each queue consists of several tables that are as follows:

- Queue
- Suspended queue
- Scheduled queue
- Message Ref Count Log
- Dequeued batched

In a nod towards our future discussions, these tables exist for each Host in the BizTalk group; the significance of which will be addressed later in this chapter.

When a message arrives at the Message Box—during insert to the actual database—the Subscription Manager checks the subscription list to determine subscribers for that message. Then each subscriber gets a queued "work item" inserted into its queue. If there are many they each get a work item, but the message itself is not actually duplicated, they simply get a reference to the original message from which to perform their work. This reduces duplication and increases performance. It all works because messages are immutable in BizTalk. That is, you cannot change a message once it has been received. Even at times when it may look like you are changing an existing message, you are not; you're creating a new message.

Each subscriber then retrieves its queued work items, marks them as retrieved, and processes them. When they are completed (be they an orchestration or a send port) they are marked as completed and the reference counts are adjusted to reflect this. Other maintenance tasks perform the necessary clean-up later on.

If no subscribers are found, the message is still inserted into the Message Box, but as a failed message, which is a special type of message that simply stays in the Message Box.

All of this may sound a little complicated, and to some extent it is, but it is the key to BizTalk's scalability. As users of BizTalk, and I mean this as developers or administrators, we are completely unaware of all this going on. It simply works. It is an infrastructure provided to allow us to focus on delivering real value in our solutions. The Message Box construct is the core of BizTalk that makes all of this possible.

Other BizTalk databases

Beyond the Message Box there are quite a few databases involved in BizTalk. They each fill a specific role in the platform to enable it to be the scalable, distributed product that it is. The BizTalk databases are briefly introduced as follows:

- **BizTalkMgmtDb**: This is the management database that holds all artifacts that are part of a BizTalk solution. Ports, Maps, Schemas, Orchestrations; they all go into this database. Although some are actually loaded from the Global Assembly Cache (GAC: the .NET component registry), this is where BizTalk knows what to load from the GAC. If the Message Box is the heart of BizTalk, the management database is the brain to a large extent. The management database is also where runtime information and statistics are kept to allow BizTalk to self-tune or throttle itself.

- **BizTalkRuleEngineDb**: This database is for the Business Rules Engine, which stores and manages policies as well as vocabularies.

- **BizTalkDTADb**: This is the tracking database that records all events which take place within BizTalk.

- **BAMPrimaryImport**: This database stores all initial Business Activity Monitoring (BAM) data. BAM data arrives here from the Message Box and can also be offloaded to the BAM Archive database later on, in order to further reduce the burden on system runtime.

- **BAMArchive:** This database is an exact mirror, structurally, of the BAM Primary Import database. This database is used to offload Business tracking data that is outside the lifetime of online requirement, but is not yet able to be deleted. Custom reports, or even the BAM Portal, can be pointed at this data source to allow indefinite storage.

- **BAMStarSchema**: This database is used for the analysis services feature of BAM.

- **SSODB**: This is the Single Sign on Service database that holds configuration information for BizTalk groups.

- **BAMAlertsNSMain**: This database contains information on how notification services connect to BAM, such as the protocols used for notification delivery and the version of the BizTalk database.

- **BAMAlertsApplication**: This database is the real body of notifications. It stores subscription parameters as well as records of all notification deliveries.

Add to these the Message Box, which we've already covered, UDDI and the ESB databases and you are looking at almost a dozen databases that are part of the core BizTalk product. This may sound excessive if you come from a background of single large databases, but it makes perfect sense and is part of why BizTalk can scale so well. As a system administrator you're free and even encouraged to move these databases to different servers and instances. If your applications are tracking heavy, you can move all the BAM databases to their own servers so as not to interfere with live transactions.

Presenting the BizTalk runtime environment

Now we will examine the BizTalk runtime and its different constituent parts. This section is useful for developers and critical for architects and administrators. We will start by outlining the servers and their roles (services) involved in a BizTalk installation and then focus on the organization of a BizTalk environment; concluding with specifics of the runtime itself.

Servers and Services

All of the following servers fulfil a specific role in a BizTalk installation. They do not directly equate to physical machines (or virtual ones). They are servers in the sense of a role they fulfil. Each server provides a specific set of services for the platform.

Application Servers

BizTalk is an application server, but it is designed as a distributed system. There are several specific servers in a BizTalk installation and each runs specific services. The first is the BizTalk Application Server; this is what most people would think is a "BizTalk Server". The BizTalk application is a Windows service that runs in the background on the server, in a similar way to any other service like IIS or SQL Server. Each BizTalk Server can run multiple instances of this runtime that function independently of each other. It is these services (introduced later as host instances) that actually pull the queued work items from the Message Box for processing.

Database Servers

The second set of servers/services are the Database Servers. These host the databases for BizTalk that were covered earlier. They also host Notification Services for use with BAM. Because the Message Box is the heart of BizTalk, the database servers play a critical role in any BizTalk environment. They also run SQL Jobs that are a vital part of the BizTalk architecture. Finally, they run Analysis Services when using BAM Aggregations.

Web Servers

Web Servers also serve an important role in BizTalk. Two specific areas served are as endpoints for HTTP/Web Services/WCF and the BAM Portal; both of which run on IIS. Adapter endpoints must be on a server with the BizTalk Runtime installed, but the BAM Portal only needs the BAM Portal components installed and can thus be on a non-BizTalk Server.

Enterprise Single Sign-On Servers

The Enterprise Single Sign-On service provides secure credential storage for BizTalk solutions. This service is a mandatory part of any server hosting the BizTalk runtime. This is necessary in BizTalk because many applications require non-Active Directory authentication, such as the FTP, DB2, and Oracle Adapters. SSO allows BizTalk to securely store credentials for use by the Adapters. Many other settings are also stored here, which is how BizTalk is able to share credentials and configuration information between different servers in a collection of BizTalk Servers, known as a group.

Each BizTalk server runs its own instance of the SSO service, but one must be designated as the Master Secret Server, which is used to prime the pump, so to speak, for the other SSO servers, by hosting the encryption key used to make the SSO store secure. The other servers in the BizTalk group (introduced next) securely request the master secret from the master secret server and keep a cached copy, checking periodically to see if the secret has changed.

These servers comprise the core parts you would expect in a Visio diagram of a BizTalk environment. In fact, they also match what you would expect from a SharePoint installation or many other systems. Depending on the environment, they could all be on one physical server. This would not, however, be very desirable. They could also be spread over a dozen servers in a large, highly available environment. In *Chapter 4, Operating BizTalk*, we will cover more about specific topologies and how they might look from an infrastructure perspective.

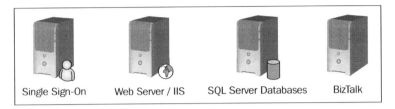

Single Sign-On   Web Server / IIS   SQL Server Databases   BizTalk

Understanding roles and relationships

In this section, we introduce the basic logical components of the BizTalk infrastructure and explain the organization of the BizTalk runtime.

The BizTalk group

This BizTalk group is the top level abstraction of BizTalk. It is a logical container for everything in a BizTalk installation. The group generally has an analogy to an enterprise, department, or division of the organization that it serves. Applications, servers, and the databases we discussed before belong to one, and only one, BizTalk group. The group is associated with a BizTalk management database, and when you connect to a group via the BizTalk Administration Console, you are actually connecting to this management database, which provides command and control for the entire group. The group itself is purely an abstract construct. It doesn't physically exist on a server; it is all the servers that are involved in a BizTalk installation represented as a collection or single container for ease of organization.

We use the BizTalk group to operate on BizTalk on a global scale, that is to say on all servers in the group at once. From within the BizTalk group, we can see all servers that are part of the group and all applications in the group, as well as their status, which we can also control. If we stop an application in BizTalk, which is done through the group level, it stops simultaneously on every server in that group. The best way to understand the group is to see it through the BizTalk Administration Console. When we look at the Administration Console, we can see the group displayed in a graphical format and this makes it more clear as to how it is structured, as shown in the following screenshot:

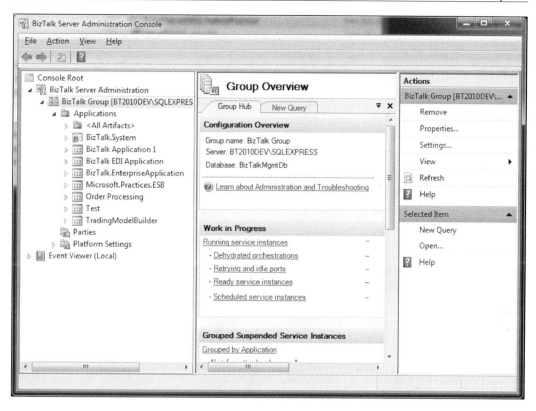

We can clearly see sections for Applications, Parties, and Platform Settings. These are all attributes of the group as a whole and are displayed as such by being directly beneath the BizTalk group to which they belong.

A typical enterprise will have several BizTalk groups, normally one for integration/ developer testing (used after individual developers check in their changes), one for UAT or user testing, and a production environment. Promotion of a solution through these environments is an important aspect of getting the most out of BizTalk and provides many opportunities for control and audit.

Hosts

Hosts are the next level in the abstraction and hosts are also a purely abstract concept. A BizTalk host defines a logical runtime component; it is an organizational unit for BizTalk that allows separate physical servers to be represented together as a single unit. Hosts are almost like a virtual machine in reverse; they represent a virtual process that can actually exist in multiple physical processes on multiple servers concurrently. That concurrent part is what makes BizTalk so much more powerful than typical clustering. Unlike in a cluster, hosts in a BizTalk group are meant to run concurrently, meaning that two or more servers running the same host instance will not only have automatic fail over, but they will run in an active-active fashion, fully utilizing their potential. Hosts allow us to create a single larger "virtual process" out of many different machines; hence the notion of them being like a virtual machine in reverse. Hosts are the organizational units that equate to the work queues we discussed earlier. Recall that when messages are delivered to subscriptions they are placed into work queues; these work queues are organized by hosts. This gives us the unique ability in BizTalk to tailor our runtime environments to the type of processing our solutions require. If we have solutions that are heavily involved in sending messages to a web service, we can distribute this load over multiple servers though host configurations.

Hosts are also the place where performance settings can be set for the specific purpose that the host is fulfilling. These include throttling, which can be resource, rate, or orchestration-based (covered in Operations Guidance). This is even more significant in BizTalk 2010, where settings that were once global across all hosts in the group are no longer; specifically the Message Box Polling Interval. This is the timespan that the runtime will query the Message Box to check for pending queued work items. Lower polling times allow lower latency, but at the cost of overhead that will reduce throughput. This means a specific host can be set up to be High Throughput or Low Latency, two opposing goals that were not possible to be balanced in a single BizTalk group in older versions of the platform. Fortunately, BizTalk 2010 remedies this and, if nothing else, it is worth the upgrade just for this feature. Because a server can only belong to a single BizTalk group and the licenses are not inexpensive, the alternative in older versions was to simply have two groups. Thankfully, this is no longer the case.

Host instances

A host instance is, as the name implies, the instantiation of a BizTalk Host. This is the executable runtime process that people generally think of as BizTalk. A host instance runs under a Windows user account and on a specific server within the BizTalk group. A host instance is the Windows service for a given host. Each host configured on a server gets its own Windows service, which is automatically created. This is where the processing is actually done; maps, orchestrations, pipelines, and business rules all execute in the context of a host instance. Host instances are powerful constructs different from many programmatic concepts that developers come across. They are indeed processes, but being in a .NET platform they contain app domains and thread pools all their own. They are heavy weight constructs capable of performing all of BizTalk's processing in a single one of them (which is the default upon installation, but not appropriate for a true server installation). Importantly, a server can only have one host instance for a given host, this is not the limitation it may at first appear in the context of the previous statement about their capability. It is a well-designed and thought out construct.

On a server that is running Host Instances, they will be visible within the Services MMC just like any other Windows service, as shown in the following screenshot:

ASP.NET State Service	Provides su...		Manual
Background Intelligent Transfer Service	Transfers fil...	Started	Automatic (D...
Base Filtering Engine	The Base Fil...	Started	Automatic
BitLocker Drive Encryption Service	BDESVC hos...		Manual
BizTalk Service BizTalk Group : BizTalkServerApplication	BizTalk Serv...		Automatic
Block Level Backup Engine Service	The WBENG...		Manual
Bluetooth Support Service	The Bluetoo...		Manual

This Windows service functions like most .NET applications and thus has many other settings that can be set at the host instance level. In BizTalk 2010 .NET CLR, orchestration and memory throttling settings are set at this host instance level.

The following is a figure depicting the relationship between the group, hosts, servers, and host instances in BizTalk:

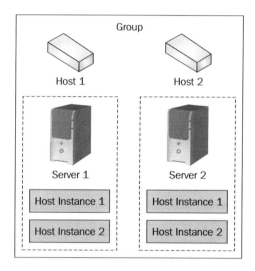

Isolated vs. in-process hosts

Finally, we have the concept of in-process versus isolated host instances. In-process host instances run the BizTalk runtime executable, which covers everything we discussed earlier about host instances. It is a Windows service running on the specific server within the BizTalk group. An isolated host instance is isolated in the sense that it runs in another process context, most often Internet Information Services (IIS). This is isolated, and called such, because it has a limited role that it can fulfill as it is not the BizTalk service executable we described previously.

It is generally a host specifically for receive adapter and cannot perform orchestration, tracking, or send operations. Because these host instances are not in the BizTalk runtime, their status will always appear as Unavailable in the BizTalk Administration Console, as they are not equipped with the same instrumentation that the in-process hosts instances have been.

Summary

In this chapter, we were introduced to Microsoft BizTalk Server 2010; its architecture, components, and runtime. We discussed how the Message Box is the core of the publish subscribe model and how this pattern allows us to have loosely coupled solutions that are asynchronous and scalable. We covered how BizTalk achieves scalability and reliability through the use of immutable messages in the Message Box and how streams are used to enable a flat memory footprint for the runtime under any load. We also set out the ambitious goals that we plan to accomplish with BizTalk. For more detailed coverage of the BizTalk runtime environment, see *Chapter 4, Operating BizTalk*.

2
Introduction to BizTalk Development

This section introduces BizTalk as a development platform. After a brief introduction to the developer experience, the remainder presents best practices for solution structure, and outlines the pieces of best practices in BizTalk solution.

The following topics are covered in this chapter:

- The BizTalk development experience
- BizTalk solution architecture
- Types in BizTalk
- Monitoring a solution

Developing BizTalk solutions

The developer experience in BizTalk largely revolves around Microsoft Visual Studio, the premier integrated development environment for the Windows platform. Visual Studio has set the benchmark for IDEs for a decade regardless of the platform. Many developers who work in the Microsoft space will be very comfortable with Visual Studio already, but even those who do not will quickly feel at home in it. Microsoft expends a great deal of effort to make this the case.

The general steps involved in creating a BizTalk solution are typically:

1. Creating schemas
2. Creating maps
3. Creating orchestrations
4. Deploying locally

5. Binding the solution

6. Creating visibility and monitoring

7. Testing the solution

Steps one through four are done in Visual Studio and are often aided by wizards and simple UIs. Step five is performed via the BizTalk Administration Console that we were first introduced to in *Chapter 1, Introducing BizTalk Server 2010*. Step six is generally performed in Excel and the Tracking Profile Editor (TPE). Step seven can be performed in a variety of ways, but implies a running solution; ideally this is through automated unit testing.

The primary components of the development process are outlined as follows in no particular order:

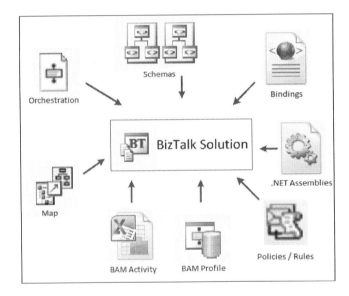

Let's discuss what all of these pieces actually are. Schemas represent our internal and external data types. File formats that we receive or send would be external data types; XML messages that we use inside our solution would be internal. Maps are the translation used to bridge internal and external formats. Recall these play a vital role in preserving our loosely coupled goal. Orchestrations represent message flows that are used to model more advanced scenarios. Bindings connect orchestrations, endpoints (ports), maps, and schemas together. The monitoring components (BAM) provide us with visibility and monitoring.

The artifacts we create in Visual Studio are compiled into .NET assemblies that the BizTalk runtime loads in a host instance to execute our application. This fully leverages the capabilities of the .NET framework for making extensible solutions and is the best implementation of these extensibility features I have ever seen. To make deployment and management easier, the assemblies and other artifacts of a BizTalk solution are then bundled into an MSI Installer package for deployment onto other BizTalk servers.

Before we begin to create BizTalk solutions, it is useful to know how we can partition and structure our solution to get the most out of the platform.

Partitioning the BizTalk solution

The structure of a BizTalk solution can be critical to its success and ease the development, deployment, and maintenance efforts required over its lifetime. In the years I have been developing BizTalk solutions, I have happened upon many tips that make the process much easier and many are related to solution structure and the build/deployment process. This section will describe some of these tips in detail and provide guidance for architects and developers.

In the context of a BizTalk solution, structure carries the dual role of enforcing the isolation of components through separation of concerns/loose coupling and organizing artifacts into manageable pieces that can allow for varying rates of change. A poor solution structure will allow changes to propagate uncontrolled throughout the solution and result in a more haphazard spaghetti code approach; this is a bad thing for any project on any platform. It will also slow development and the rate of change while increasing costs for both development and maintenance. Ultimately it can even lower morale and result in a less successful solution outcome and a perception that BizTalk and the team have fallen short of expectations.

The guidance for solution structure that follows will help you create a successful BizTalk solution by avoiding the common pitfalls many make with the product. (I know. I made them. This book exists to help you avoid them.)

Specifying the requirements of solution structure

Before we delve into how to structure your solutions, we should outline the basic goals we are trying to achieve from a development perspective. The solution structure for all but the most trivial BizTalk applications must support:

- Multiple concurrent developers (and robust source control)
- Building on any developer workstation

- Testing on any developer workstation
- Test-driven development (TDD)
- Automated functionality testing
- Continuous integration
- Automated performance testing

These bullets are all important for different reasons and all manifest themselves in different ways in the solution structure. If your application centers around one large orchestration with all the logic enclosed in a single giant file then only one developer at a time will be able to make changes to it safely. You could try shared checkout, but I'm not sure what results you'll receive when it comes time to merge. Newer tools are meant to merge these files better, but I am still not convinced. BizTalk wasn't meant to be used that way anyhow, good BizTalk solutions have more smaller parts rather than fewer larger ones. Furthermore, as in traditional development, large monolithic structures are not very easy to work with. They are one of the code smells that Martin Fowler wrote about nearly a decade ago. This is certainly an area where BizTalk and traditional software development have much in common.

Being able to easily build the entire solution on any developer workstation, and test it, is also critical. Every developer should be able to see the solution work, on their own, in a private environment where they can feel free to break things or tear things apart, as well as simply debug issues. There are several other reasons for this, including support, loss of the build server, and emergency fixes.

Importantly, component and functionality testing must be automated and should be done early. After only a few manual test runs you would already have saved time by creating automated tests at the outset. Further, automated functional testing reinforces the idea that first you identify the problem, then you devise the solution. This is the core of TDD and is a great fit with BizTalk. These tests should provide self-documentation for the solution so that a new developer can see what the solution is meant to do and then watch it work. If you take TDD to its zenith then you will build your tests first and they will simply fail until the solution works.

Once these tests are in place and working with your first pass solution, you are free to go change the internal implementation with the confidence that you are still solving the problem at hand in a predictable and expected manner. As solutions get more complex, this becomes even more imperative, as it is easy to lose details. We'll cover unit testing later, but I'll leave it now by saying all expected behavior, including error handling, should have automated coverage. It is simply unacceptable in BizTalk to do this any other way. Manual testing is a recipe for disaster as changes in one part of the solution may introduce errors in another. Manual testing makes finding these errors almost impossible and requires far more time than simply automating tests.

Continuous integration (CI) aids us further by allowing full test suites to be run after every developer checks in. This becomes crucial in larger solutions as the decoupling BizTalk encourages carrying a price that some errors will not be found until runtime. I have worked on solutions where one developer's changes in a completely separate application have caused failures across many applications. Using the same tests from TDD on your CI environment can greatly reduce the chance of side effect issues.

Finally, automated performance or stress testing provides insurance that your solution will scale and run as expected with realistic loads. Many who are new to BizTalk create solutions that will work perfectly well on their developer machine running a few transactions, but fall apart when they encounter production loads. Sadly this is often in production environments. This embarrassment is unnecessary and completely avoidable.

Poorly planned solution structure will restrict all of the abilities listed previously and can make the platform feel more like a prison than a liberator.

Understanding the layers of a BizTalk solution

Continuing our train of thought about partitioning a BizTalk solution, we now arrive at a very familiar topic in system architecture: logical structure. From a logical standpoint, a properly constructed BizTalk solution, like any good software solution, stresses the separation of concerns in an effort to control dependencies. This throws off a lot of people new to BizTalk because it involves concepts from both the object-oriented and message-oriented theories of software development.

The following proximity diagram depicts how the layers in a BizTalk solution should interact. Only layers that actually touch each other should be interacting in any way. The intention from this should be quite clear; it is to isolate the layers in the solution and minimize their interaction points so as to create a more robust solution that does not allow changes to propagate throughout the core.

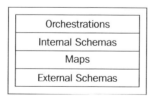

This layout will give us the ability to drastically change the solution, at its edges or in its core, without impacting other parts of the solution. A new external partner schema, say for a different vendor purchase order format, should have no impact on our orchestration layer or on our internal schemas. Conversely, a change to logic within an orchestration should be completely invisible to the outside world.

This same concept can also be expressed in a more detailed fashion with a UML diagram. The following diagram expresses the basic layers (or packages to use the classic term) in a BizTalk solution that follows these guidelines. This also allows us to further restrict the dependencies with relationships between layers expressed explicitly.

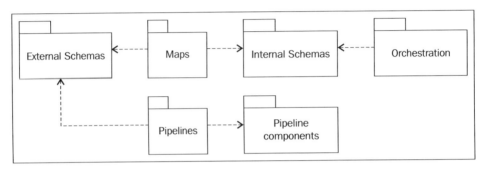

Again the goal is flexibility by tightly controlling contact points between different parts of a solution. Visual Studio can be leveraged to help enforce this architecture in your solution. Importantly, each of these packages actually represents a .NET assembly containing pertinent artifacts to that layer of the solution. For the rest of this chapter, package, assembly, and project will be used interchangeably.

Recall that at its core a BizTalk solution is really a specialized .NET application. Since these are .NET assemblies we are able to leverage the concept of references in the .NET framework and Visual Studio to enforce our layering pattern. This is done by creating separate projects in the solution for each of the layers presented previously.

If you're not already comfortable with the layers pattern, or you're already a little familiar with BizTalk solutions, you may be asking yourself 'So why do this?' Some would argue that you could just do a logical separation using solution folders and not need separate Visual Studio projects for each of the packages shown previously. While there certainly is some merit to this argument, it overlooks some very important capabilities inherent in this architecture.

For one, there is no chance of a dependency creeping throughout your solution, the Visual Studio references between projects will ensure that. Further, you can also now choose to deploy your solution in a variety of arrangements of tiers* derived from the layers presented above. Finally, and perhaps most importantly, this design allows you a much larger amount of flexibility when deploying, upgrading, and especially patching BizTalk solutions. Maps, for example, can have many mapping errors resolved and redeployed without requiring downtime in a highly available BizTalk group.

Tiers versus layers

I know it is subtle and often contested, but I believe tiers and layers to be two distinct concepts in application architecture. Layers exist in software at the design and development level, they represent abstractions and separations in that software whereas tiers exist on the deployment and operations level representing physical distribution of components. Although layers may be deployed on tiers that very closely resemble the same structure, there is no fundamental requirement to do so.

It is important to also note that not all solutions will follow this exact structure. A common variation I encounter is using pipelines from within orchestrations. If you must do this, be sure the pipeline uses internal messages and not external ones. You may end up needing both internal and external pipeline projects and that is perfectly acceptable, but they should be separate projects because they will reference separate schemas and this division is important to protect your architecture.

Visual Studio solution structure

Now we'll see how to use Visual Studio to implement the structure that has just been introduced. These suggestions are based on both my experiences as well as that of others within the BizTalk community. I always use this basic template presented in the following image for every solution and it has served me well for years.

First always start with a blank Visual Studio solution, as this will allow you to name the solution in a way that represents the functional area, the solution addresses, and the projects within the solution in a manner that reflects their purpose within that solution; such as Maps, ExternalSchemas, and so on. It is important to note that within the solution, the projects can have short names like Maps instead of MyIntegration.Maps. The name of the solution in Visual Studio is unrelated to the names of the assemblies or namespaces. Once you have your blank solution you can add new projects to it by right clicking the solution and selecting **Add Project**.

Generally, I like to break my solutions into the six projects as shown in the following screenshot. I find that this meets the needs of most solutions, but it is not a hard rule. Some solutions will have more, others less, but they will all be a similar variation of this concept. Each project is explained below. Importantly, only start with the projects you need and simply add others as the need arises. A Visual Studio template can be found here: `http://biztalk2010patterns.com/documents/templates/solutionstructure` and can be used to generate solutions with all these base projects already created, complete with references.

Projects

The following are the typical projects in a BizTalk Visual Studio solution and a brief explanation of the role that they serve.

External Schemas (.xsd files)

This project contains all of the schemas that are sent or received by the BizTalk solution. Port-level mapping, a later recommendation, ensures no dependencies are leaked into or out of the BizTalk solution. This project would include schemas generated by adapter wizards, SOAP, or WCF references, flat file formats that we send or receive, and EDI schemas. It is vital that these be treated as what they really are: external artifacts (that is external dependencies). Even if you own the source system, don't assume that the rate of change between two systems will be equal. You may end up with schemas that closely match internal schemas, but the flexibility you gain is certainly worth the very small cost. This project contains no references to other projects in the solution as it represents the endpoint or edge of our solution.

Internal Schemas (.xsd files)

The **InternalSchemas** project contains all the schemas used internally by a BizTalk solution. These are schemas that are never exposed to any other systems outside of BizTalk and define entities within the actual solution. Every external schema should have a corresponding internal schema or translate to part of a composite internal schema. These schemas are commonly referred to as **canonical** schemas. This project also contains no references to other projects in the solution. It represents messages that will be used internally by orchestrations, business rules, direct subscription routing, and so on. Property schemas would also exist here.

Maps (.btm files)

The **Maps** project contains all maps within the solution that translate internal to external schemas. It references the **InternalSchemas** and **ExternalSchemas** projects and nothing else (with the exception of custom functoid assemblies). This project is the guardian that prevents external dependencies from permeating a BizTalk solution. Critically, every external schema should have a map translating either to or from internal types as needed. Again, this ensures the flexibility that is so vital to successful distributed systems. The orchestrations assembly should never reference the maps assembly as it would require the orchestration package to now have an indirect reference to the external schemas project, and therefore bypass this carefully constructed separation we are trying to enforce. It is true that occasionally you need a map in an orchestration, but that map should exist in the orchestrations assembly or in an internal assembly of its own, perhaps named InternalMaps, not in the maps assembly, as this would violate our separation of concerns.

Pipelines (.btp files)

All pipeline components (assemblers and disassemblers) are grouped in this project to make testing and maintenance easier. This project should reference the **ExternalSchemas** project or the **InternalSchemas** project as needed. If you want to provide a very robust isolation, you could create internal and external pipeline projects, but I really only recommend this if you need to call a pipeline from within an orchestration to avoid leaking a dependency into your orchestrations layer. The **Pipelines** project will contain BizTalk pipeline files (.btp) and also reference any assemblies that contain custom pipeline components if they exist. Pipelines are perhaps the most underutilized and most misunderstood part of BizTalk.

Many useful and complex solutions can be created in BizTalk using only pipelines and adapters.

Pipeline components (.cs files)

Not all solutions will need a **Pipeline Components** project, but when they do, pipeline components, which are .NET classes, should be in their own project to continue our isolation paradigm. If the pipeline component being used is commonly reused throughout your enterprise, you can just put the component in third-party assemblies (covered shortly) and have a dedicated solution just for the pipeline component. Pipeline components should be flexible and reusable and thus be in their own solutions. This can also avoid assembly locking problems in Visual Studio.

Orchestrations (.odx files)

This project contains all orchestrations used in the solution. It references the internal schemas project and possibly the pipelines project (if you're using pipelines from within an orchestration). As depicted earlier, orchestrations are the top layer of the BizTalk solution layer model. They should generally be unaware of any outside systems or artifacts. Failure to preserve this isolation principle results in tighter coupling creeping into your solution. Even when you call a web service from an orchestration, you're not actually calling the service from an orchestration. The message box functions as an intermediary. Care must be taken not to tie your orchestrations to the specific endpoints that you will eventually connect them to.

Libraries (C#, resources, and so on)

Any custom classes or utilities that are used by your solution should also be broken into their own projects. It is important to not let these bleed dependencies into your solution. If you have some custom components to do processing in an orchestration and some for custom functoids or pipeline components these should be broken into their own distinct projects. Isolating functionality into separate assemblies gives us flexibility to make changes without having side effects on other parts of the solution. It will also simplify our versioning and patching options.

Testing (.xml, .dtd, .cs files)

This project hosts all unit and functional tests and their supporting data. The only direct references should be to the utility assemblies (libraries) and to the testing frameworks (for example, Microsoft UnitTesting/NUnit and BizUnit). This also ensures a clean separation of tests and artifacts from the other parts of a solution. Normally there is only one testing project in the entire solution and it can be used to test BizTalk as well as .NET artifacts.

Non-project artifacts

There are also several solution-level folders I like to use to organize my solutions. Solution-level folders in Visual Studio are logical folders, not physical directories, so I like to create physical directories that match them to keep everything more organized. These are generally:

- **Third-party assemblies**: For storing any external assemblies and components the solution may need to utilize. The BizUnit assembly used by the solution testing should go here.
- **Bindings**: To store deployment bindings used in each of the environments you will have in your solution. I generally have Local Development, Integration, Staging, and Production. You may have more or less depending upon your organization and its needs.
- **Build**: Used to hold build scripts and other build artifacts like assembly signing keys. I also put my CI scripts into the build folder for safe keeping and source control.
- **Policies**: This solution folder will hold business rule policies and vocabularies and will help you keep them organized and in source control.
- **Tracking**: This folder will hold all BAM-related artifacts like activity definitions and tracking profiles.

It is important to not only structure your solution correctly, but to ensure that the build is as self-contained as possible. Although some environments will have only a single BizTalk developer working on a solution, it is vital that solutions contain all the artifacts necessary to build them within source control. This is a time saver if your workstation dies or your team size grows, or better yet you win the lottery and decide to take some well-deserved time off. I would like to validate that I am accomplishing this by building the solution on another developer workstation to ensure the build is portable, repeatable, and reliable. The following tips will help you to achieve these goals.

Tip

Always use relative path locations for all artifacts including:

- **Keys** used to sign assemblies. Don't browse to these; that will hard code an absolute path to the key file and the chances of another developer's workstation being set up exactly the same are slim. Worse still the browse feature in Visual Studio will likely make a local copy of the key file in the project folder. You really only need one key for an entire solution:

```
<PropertyGroup>
<AssemblyOriginatorKeyFile>..\Build\PurchaseOrder.snk</
AssemblyOriginatorKeyFile>
</PropertyGroup>
```

- **References** to other assemblies and projects in the solution. Always use project references, not absolute references, when adding references to other BizTalk projects in the solution. After adding references to third-party assemblies (and if it is not compiled in this solution, it is a third-party assembly) edit the project file manually, it is simply an MSBuild file, and correct the absolute path. This is easy to test as your solution will no longer build correctly if the path is invalid.

- **Paths** of test files should also be made relative. For instance in BizUnit tests it is easy enough to simply paste in the path to the sample input file, but now that path is hard coded, use a relative path instead.

Tip

Bad idea:

```
D:\Projects\BizTalkPatterns\InvoiceProcessing\UnitTests\TestData\
PurchaseOrder.xml
```

Good idea:

```
..\..\UnitTests\TestData\PurchaseOrder.xml
```

This will make it easier to build the solution on multiple machines and also make it easier to use a CI server to perform automated building and testing of the solution. Not doing this will result in solutions that only properly build on one developer's workstation. A good guideline is that you should be able to compress a solution folder and send it to another developer (or Microsoft Support Services, should the need arise) and not have to spend any time getting the solution to build or deploy. I was once given what I consider to be a great complement by Microsoft Support Services when a solution I needed support for built and deployed cleanly with no changes at all directly from a zip file. Even the support engineer was amazed.

Remember not all solutions will have these projects listed above; some will have less, others more, but keep in mind the separation of concerns brought up in the discussion about layers in a BizTalk solution. Later on I'll cover some specific examples of when to combine which parts of this guidance.

Motivations for solution structure

It is natural and healthy to ask why we should go through all this trouble (ignore that creating projects in a solution is very simple; even more so with a template). Earlier we covered the need to control dependencies and this is a certain way to do that, but there are other reasons as well. You may find yourself needing to update in-flight orchestrations or maps in a solution with such in-flight orchestrations that you cannot terminate and cannot wait for completion. Perhaps it's a simple fix and you haven't quite worked out your versioning strategy, or the business demands an emergency resolution (a misplaced decimal point or rounding error would be good motivations). With separate assemblies you are free to deploy just the changes necessary, rather than all assemblies and artifacts at once as would be the case with a single project solution, which would also require a full stop and termination of any in-flight instances.

Building solutions in a separable manner is a good practice that allows administrators and operators more control over the solution once it is out of development. This is critical to the success of any enterprise software system and even more so to BizTalk solutions.

Understanding types in BizTalk

All good technology makes the complex look simple. BizTalk is no exception, but beneath this simple façade lie some fairly complex constructs. This section gets very deep into some complex parts of BizTalk and the .NET framework. Do not worry if you don't understand it, and feel free to skip over it, but be sure to remember where it is for when you need this knowledge.

The preceding compiled projects are actually .NET assemblies that will be used by the BizTalk runtime to execute our solution. All BizTalk artifacts become .NET types when they are compiled. Understanding types in BizTalk is slightly tricky at times and we'll walk through it now.

In most programming languages, types are the structures we work with to organize our code. BizTalk bridges a gap between messaging, which is often XML and .NET. This means that BizTalk has both messaging types and .NET types. Messaging types are for XML messages, but everything is a .NET type. If we look at the properties of any BizTalk artifact in Visual Studio we can see that they all have a section for Namespace and TypeName. This is a core concept of .NET. Namespaces are used to organize classes and types. A good example would be `System.Net` which is the collection of classes and types having to do with networking in the .NET framework. In this namespace, there is a class identified as `System.Net.WebRequest`; `WebRequest` is the actual class and it is in the namespace `System.Net`. Because our BizTalk artifacts are all compiled into .NET types for use by the BizTalk runtime, they must all be organized into namespaces and types. The best way to do this is to set the default namespace in the project properties in Visual Studio. Each project that we outlined previously should have its default namespace set before we start adding artifacts to them.

The typical naming convention for project namespaces would be as follows:

[Company abbreviation].[Solution].[Project]

An example external schemas default namespace for a company called Performance Racing Parts creating an order processing solution would be:

`PRP.OrderProcessing.ExternalSchemas`

In very large organizations, this can be expanded to include a division if necessary.

[Company abbreviation].[Division].[Solution].[Project]

The project portion of the namespace should match the name we give the project within the solution and helps us to organize our artifacts better. Each artifact will then have a fully qualified name organized by namespace. To complete our example a schema for a sales order in our external schemas project would have a .NET name (namespace+type) of `PRP.OrderProcessing.ExternalSchemas.SalesOrder`.

Message types

XSD schemas in BizTalk have .NET name type like we covered previously, but XML messages that conform to those schemas also have an XML message type. In XML, it is common to identify documents by their fully qualified root element name; this includes the namespace and the element name. Unfortunately in this case, the worlds of XML and .NET have collided and namespace is an overloaded term. In the following XML, we can see an example of an XML namespace: `http://somecompany.net`.

```
<order xmlns="http://somecompany.net">
    <number>1234</number>
</order>
```

The message type for this XML document would be `http://somecompany.net#order` and this is how BizTalk will identify the message and match it to a specific schema. It is this dual identity role that can be tricky for a lot of developers new to BizTalk.

For non-XML messages, as far as the messaging infrastructure is concerned, they are generally untyped. This means we cannot use data from within their content for routing or use maps on them, but we do still have context and internally BizTalk does use .NET types to represent them. As these types are internal to BizTalk, they are generally not too visible to developers.

Types in contexts

In BizTalk, there are not just different types of types there are also different types in different contexts. All messages in BizTalk's messaging engine, including pipeline components, are represented as an instance of the interface `Microsoft.BizTalk.Message.Interop.IBaseMessage`. Once in an orchestration a message is represented as an instance of `Microsoft.XLANGs.BaseTypes.XLANGMessage` and can be sent to or from a user component as such. Often this would be in a helper class. Interestingly enough, these types cannot be converted between each other, nor can they be casted. You'll generally use `IBaseMessage` in pipeline components and `XLANGMessage` exclusively in orchestrations.

If this is a little confusing at first you're not alone, but trust me, it makes sense once you stop fighting it. Look at it this way: a message arrives in BizTalk, goes through a pipeline (and its components) and a map then goes to the message box. It was represented by `IBaseMessage` this entire journey and its journey is over. Even if you have an orchestration that will receive this message, it will receive it as `XLANGMessage` and in a fresh receive, completely disconnected from the first operation (the adapter, pipeline, and map). In our minds as developers, this all looks like one flow and that is the catch with BizTalk. It is not one flow, it is two, and they are completely decoupled. Delivery to the message and then to the orchestration engine are in fact two distinct operations.

To make things a little more complicated, any message in an orchestration can also be declared as an instance of `System.Xml.XmlDocument`. It is not so much that these classes are all related per se, but they have both practical and historic reasons for this arrangement. Historically this is because the original versions of BizTalk used the DOM extensively to pass around XML documents; as a result the use of the `XmlDocument` class, which is the .NET DOM object, was included to make it easier for developers and solutions to be ported to newer versions of BizTalk. This has been a decision that has caused much confusion over the years. Another reason is that it allows you a simple way to deal with non-XML messages in orchestrations; you can specify their type as `XmlDocument` and handle just about any type of message, even binary. That said, if you have a non-XML message and try to use any of the members of `XmlDocument` on it, you will receive an exception from the orchestration engine at runtime. `XmlDocument` is very dangerous to use in orchestration and should be avoided at all costs. Its use was common in older versions of BizTalk, but should not be repeated. Further, `XmlDocument` is actually not what it at first appears. Although the language of the orchestration engine appears to be C# it is in fact a different language X#; the XLANGs language. `XmlDocument` in the context of X# is actually a wrapper around the real `XmlDocument` class from the `System.Xml` namespace which, even more inexplicably, is not serializable.

These different interfaces (or interface and classes) allow different types of interactions with messages in their own contexts which can sometimes be challenging until you understand the lay of the land so to speak. All will allow you to manipulate message bodies, but again, care must be taken here so as not to load the entire message body into memory at once, which is the real downfall of XmlDocument. Recall our coverage of streaming.

To sum it up, in these contexts, messages are of these types:

Messaging Engine: IBaseMessage

Orchestration: XLANGMessage or XmlDocument

Type resolution

Even in a messaging-only scenario where orchestration is not involved, BizTalk does a sort of two-phase type resolution. The first is to determine the message type via message inspection, which is performed by XML and flat file pipelines. This is where the namespace and root element name will be used to resolve the message type. From here BizTalk uses this message type to retrieve the schema information from a .NET assembly that actually contains the schema. This assembly is deployed with the MSI you install, or from Visual Studio, in the case of a workstation. This is an automatic resolution based on a BizTalk global catalog of namespace and root element name for all schemas deployed to BizTalk.

A conflict can and normally will occur if you deploy multiple schemas containing the same namespace and root element combination to BizTalk. This happens when one of these messages is received and run through a pipeline like the XmlDisassembler (that is, something that inspects the message to determine its type). The error will be very clear, normally including "Multiple schemas match the message type". This makes sense, because you have done something naughty and short circuited BizTalk's message type resolution mechanism.

A final note is in order here. The Pass Thru pipelines, as their name implies, don't inspect or modify messages in any way. They are almost like a null pipeline that simply lets a message flow unaltered through them.

Understanding the solution at runtime

Earlier we saw a package diagram representing a typical BizTalk solution and in the previous chapter we discussed how BizTalk uses the management database and the GAC to load solutions. How this all works is a fairly important aspect of our solution architecture and of BizTalk so we'll now have a quick stroll through this process. The actors involved are as follows:

- BizTalk runtime (.NET runtime)
- Message box
- Management database
- Global Assembly Cache (GAC)

Of these, the only one that we have not covered is the GAC. The GAC is a core feature of the .NET framework and was created to address the shortcomings of COM architectures. The GAC is a database or repository of .NET assemblies installed on a machine; hence the global part of the name. The GAC is responsible for making sure that we don't experience the pain of versioning and management that often accompanies COM DLLs (colloquially referred to as DLL Hell). To accomplish this, the GAC enforces several constraints on assemblies, the largest being that they must be Strongly Named. This is accomplished through the assembly manifest; metadata about the assembly itself; specifically a combination of the name, version number, digital signature, and culture.

This means that assemblies for BizTalk solutions must be strongly named. That's why we talked about keys before; we use them to strongly name assemblies. This mechanism gives us an explicit method for defining versions of assemblies. The default version for an assembly in .NET is "1.0.0.0". These four sections of the version number correspond to the following: [Major version].[Minor version].[Build version].[Revision version]. The idea is that the numbers will count up with the left-most numbers changing the slowest and the right most changing the fastest. The .NET framework itself reflects this in the v1.1 and v3.5 releases, where 3.5 was major version 3, minor version 5.

This whole apparatus allows .NET applications to load types at runtime secure in the knowledge that the types will be what they expect (or at least conform to the same interface). An added benefit is that this arrangement also allows for multiple versions of assemblies to coexist safely with each other.

The following diagram depicts the way this is used by BizTalk to load our solution. The steps are labeled in the diagram. It is intentionally a simple example:

1. When a message arrives in BizTalk, the host instance (BizTalk runtime) that receives the message inspects the message to see if it matches a known message type. The list of known types is stored in the management database.

2. After finding a matching message type, the runtime then loads the assembly containing this type from the GAC.

3. The runtime is now free to use the loaded .NET type which can be a schema, map, pipeline, or orchestration.

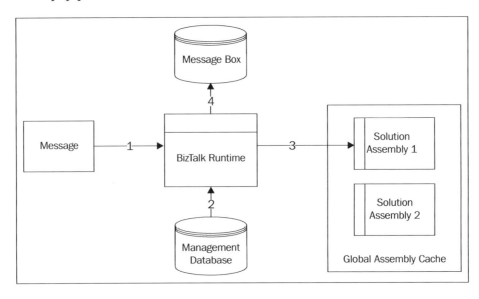

The diagram shows how BizTalk resolves the message type and loads the schema representing that message type from the Global Assembly Cache. A final note of importance is that this loading from the GAC only occurs one time for each type during the lifetime of a host instance. This means that after the first load, the process is considerably faster. This is a part of the cache portion of the name. If you restart a host instance, which is to say restart the windows service for that host instance, you have to shut down the old process and the types will again load on first use. Some assemblies in BizTalk will also unload after extensive periods of idle time.

Every .NET application that uses the GAC doesn't actually run the assemblies from the GAC, it copies them to its own working area so that the GAC can be changed and updated without interfering with running processes. This allows us to register replacement assemblies in the GAC without first stopping the processes that are currently using those assemblies. The drawback is that a replacement assembly will not be loaded until the application domain (a sort of lighter weight version of a process that lives within a process) is reloaded; this generally means restarting the host process; that is, the BizTalk runtime. That said, newer versions with different version numbers can be deployed and loaded without restarting the process in a side-by-side manner. This means that when planned carefully a BizTalk application can be upgraded in place without any downtime. Carefully planned is the key operative here.

Monitoring

Monitoring is a critical part of all software solutions, but even more so with Middleware, Integration, and Service Orientation. These types of solutions inherently do not have a user interface so knowing 'what is happening' becomes critical. The ability to view data and transactions as they happen becomes important both from a technical, as well as from a business operations standpoint. No solution is complete without monitoring. I repeat that point, no solution is complete without monitoring capability. Monitoring can generally fall into two types: technical or platform, which would be covered by tools like SCOM and commonly referred to as tracking and business or solution monitoring.

Unfortunately most solutions don't have good monitoring or instrumentation built into them in the first place. This, however, is one place where BizTalk Server really shines. The entire solution stack, all the way through the adapters and message box, support advanced monitoring centered on BAM — Business Activity Monitoring. In most cases, BAM can be added to a solution after it is completed without requiring code changes. This is actually the preferred method as monitoring is rarely an upfront requirement; though it certainly should be.

Why BAM?

BAM is a powerful set of tools that, when used properly, creates the infrastructure we need to gather, analyze, and present data about our business solutions without writing a single line of code. This can even include complex statistics and aggregations. The BAM tools in BizTalk will create the infrastructure needed to provide monitoring. This includes tables that BizTalk will then automatically populate with the tracked data analysis cubes used for more complex derivatives, and also maintenance of SSIS packages, to age or archive that data and to process analysis cubes. These are all designed to scale and built with a care and detail it would be very difficult to replicate on our own. That said, like most of BizTalk, they also represent a good model to be inspired by, if the need ever arises. In fact, BAM can be used without BizTalk at all and any WCF service can have BAM added without recompiling the service.

Importantly, although BAM has a lot of similarities to data warehousing, it is not a data warehouse and not meant to replace your data warehouse. Data warehouses are created for exploring your data. Generally speaking, in BAM you aren't exploring that deeply although you can to a certain extent. BAM is, however, a great way to feed your data warehouse and it is a great way to provide both business monitoring, as the name implies, as well as operational monitoring.

BizTalk also has its own tracking information in the DTA tracking database and this can be good for emergency operational tracking or viewing some information about running transactions. This data is really meant for BizTalk, however, and generally this type of tracking should not be relied upon as it encourages inappropriately tight coupling. A term I have often used, resulting in many giggles, is inappropriate intimacy. This data is also purged periodically and requires administrator permission to BizTalk (or at least operator) just to be viewed. It is also prone to bloat in even moderate volume environments if not purged often, which it is critically important to do. For this reason, BAM should be used for all tracking and monitoring wherever possible.

Understanding BAM concepts

There are several ways to work with BAM, including a .NET API, but I believe the best way is to keep it simple and as originally intended by the tools. I believe this approach results in a more loosely coupled solution than other methods such as the BAM API. Coupling is a slippery slope and it is something we must struggle to avoid all the time. There certainly are times when the BAM API is needed, but I've run into only two in all my time with BizTalk.

The best way to avoid coupling and produce excellent tracking is via the Excel Plug-In and the Tracking Profile Editor (primarily the TPE). This is covered in great detail in the second half of this text in the context of our development storyline, but I will briefly present the concepts here. Please refer to the appropriate sections for a detailed walk through of each concept.

Instrumenting a BizTalk solution is done in three steps: creating the structure of what you want to track (an activity), creating the way you want to present the data from this activity (a view), and binding the activity to the solution via a profile.

Creating a BAM activity

A BAM activity defines the base data that we wish to track. This is broken down into milestones and business data. Milestones are timestamps, points in time when events happen, such as a message received or sent. Business data can be any text, integer, or decimal that is in a message. Although something like Order Date in a received message is a date, it is not a milestone, it is actually business data; whereas Order Received would be a milestone representing when BizTalk actually received the order message.

You should track all pertinent information that you will need to report against in BAM, but do keep in mind that there is such a thing as too much information. BizTalk will handle this fine and the SSIS packages that are created to manage the data will help keep the database bloating to a minimum, but you should really track only the data you're actually interested in. The activity represents the database structure that will be created to hold our tracking data.

Creating a BAM view

Creating a BAM view allows us to select which activity data we would like to present in a display. We can combine data from multiple activities or display only some of the tracked fields. We may want to do this because IT operations staff may want to know things like the number of orders or time to process, while business operations staff may be more interested in the total dollar amounts of orders (that is, teams will be interested in different metrics and creating different views is a great way to provide each with what they need).

In addition to selecting what we want to see we can create durations between milestones, groups that allow any one in a set of milestones to represent a logical milestone (such as when a branch can be taken, but both sides result in a "complete" status), and create aliases so that specific user groups can see different labels for the same data. We can also make logical progression markers out of milestones so that we can assign labels to each milestone. This would be useful if we wanted to show the current progress of a long-running process that has multiple milestones.

Perhaps most extraordinarily, we can also create dimensions and measures with which to drive deeper analysis. These result in multidimensional analysis cubes from our data, for which the BAM tools will then create the infrastructure. All of this will be covered in detail later. Measures are data aggregations such as count, sum, average, maximum, and minimum values, while dimensions can be time, data, ranges, and the aforementioned progress. Taken together, these allow us to provide our users with complex and expressive views into business transaction data.

Creating a BAM tracking profile

The tracking profile is the glue that binds an activity (and its views) to a BizTalk solution. These are created in the Tracking Profile Editor (or implemented via the API, which I've already explained I believe is best to avoid). The activity and views define what we want to track, and the profile defines how we want to track it; that is to say at which points in our solution we want to connect data passing through BizTalk to our tracking profile. The TPE is a simple graphical tool that allows us to bind these components together. The complete figure if the BAM activity and profile in action is displayed before.

In this diagram, we can see how the profile ties the running solution to our activity, which represents the tables into which the data will flow.

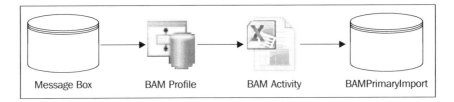

Message Box   BAM Profile   BAM Activity   BAMPrimaryImport

Advanced BAM concepts

Although all of these are covered in detail this is an explanation of some of the more critical, advanced BAM concepts covered in the second half of this book.

Continuation

A continuation is a way to connect disparate parts of a business process into a single tracking record. Suppose a business process involved receiving a purchase order that is sent to an ERP system, then receiving the order confirmation from the ERP later on, asynchronously. This solution involves two disparate steps, but they are both part of the same business process—processing a sales order. A BAM continuation would allow us to connect these two by the use of a common information token, like an order number.

Subtly and importantly a continuation is expected to continue at some point, so they should be designed with care.

Relationship

A relationship in BAM allows two different activities to be linked together. Suppose in addition to the previously mentioned "purchase order received" that we also have "purchase order cancellations" sent via a different mechanism. These are two different business processes, a sale and a cancellation, so they should be two different activities. They are, however, related because the cancellation is of a previous sale. This is accomplished via a BAM relationship that also uses a specific piece of data, like the continuation though in a different way, to perform its duty.

Document reference URL

The document reference URL is perhaps not an advanced concept, but it is useful and allows us to add links to file shares or better still to SharePoint to link documents into our monitoring profile. If these purchase orders were submitted via an InfoPath form a link to the archived original form within SharePoint could be provided for fast and easy reference.

Introducing the BAM portal

Another component of BAM is the portal that ships with BizTalk to allow us to view the data we are tracking and monitoring with BAM. The BAM portal is a simple SharePoint inspired website that installs as part of a BizTalk installation. It is a fairly light weight tool that allows us to build and run queries based on the tracking data that we have defined. It allows for sorting and also for saving queries and also creating alerts based on these queries. Finally, it has interactive charting capabilities built into it that allow users to drill down into aggregations we define in the activities and views. The portal is not the only way to interact with BAM, however. We can also access the underlying SQL infrastructure either through ADO or even via SharePoint's Business Connectivity Services.

Presenting BAM alerts

Finally after detailing all that we have here we get to the subject of BAM alerts. Alerts in BAM are user-created notifications that can be tied to simple BAM queries or even complex aggregations. BAM alerts (and BAM in general) really spearhead the concept of self service in IT. What specifics interest users will change depending upon who the user is, business conditions at the time, and often even the time of year. BAM alerts allow users to decide when they want alerts and give them an ability, through the BAM Portal, to configure them.

BAM alerts are either via e-mail or a file. I only use the file ones to trigger other BizTalk processes, as we'll see later, but the e-mails are very popular with users. Perhaps a user wants to be notified when a very large order (or very large check) is received (or requested). Or perhaps they want to be alerted by the result of an aggregation, such as a specific client orders more than X dollars within Y months. All of these can be linked to user-created BAM alerts. This frees our time as developers to focus on higher value tasks while still getting our users exactly what they want. Better yet, they still think we're rock stars because of it.

Summary

In this chapter, we learned about the steps involved in developing BizTalk solutions, how to logically partition and manage our solution, and how to use Visual Studio to structure our solution. We also covered details about how our solution is used by BizTalk at runtime. We finished with an introduction to the monitoring capabilities of BAM and how we can use them to instrument our solutions and provide visibility.

3
BizTalk Development Guidelines

This chapter will cover various best practice guidelines to follow when creating BizTalk solutions. Some will be abstract principles and others will be specific techniques. All will contain what I believe are ample justifications that I hope will convince you of their validity. Everything covered here is implemented in the second part of the book, but this chapter gives you the reasoning and the theory behind it.

This chapter covers the following:

- Determining where to place different types of logic
- Isolating our solutions
- Orchestration best practices
- Pipelines and pipeline components

Core guidance

This section contains core guidance principles for BizTalk best practices. Most of these will be a little on the abstract side and therefore serve more as recommendations than as best practices per se, but I strongly believe in all of them.

Determining where to place different types of logic

In *Chapter 2, Introduction to BizTalk Development*, we looked at the architecture of the BizTalk platform and the basic components involved in a solution. Now we will focus more on these components themselves and present suggestions and patterns for them. The first involves deciding where to place logic within the solution structure that we saw in the previous chapter.

A common problem that BizTalk developers face is determining exactly where in a solution to house different parts of their logic. This can be a fairly complex issue that can result in paralysis by over analysis. I wish I could say there was an easy answer, but finding the right balance is really more of an art than a science, and all I can do is offer some basic guidelines.

Maps

Maps are a common place to put a lot of logic in a BizTalk solution and it can be a good place. The problem comes, however, with scalability in terms of the growth of large maps and the extension of logic placed within them. It can be hard to track down where a logical decision is being made in BizTalk, when it takes place in a map. Appropriate uses of pages, notations, and documentation can alleviate this, but maps are mostly meant for translation, not for the embodiment of business logic. In fact, avoiding placing business logic in maps is really considered a best practice within the BizTalk community. One benefit to putting logic in maps is that fixes can be made by simply GAC-ing a new assembly and restarting the affected host instances. This can provide low (or no) downtime patching. This generally is not a good enough reason to place logic in maps. Maps are really intended only to perform translation between formats.

Orchestrations

Being graphical, workflows that have similarities to flowchart's orchestrations often seem very familiar to us as developers, even more so with Windows Workflow now in the marketplace, but stuffing too much logic into orchestrations is not a good practice. Orchestrations are focused on message handling, but the decision and looping shapes providing familiar programming constructs to work with and many programmers quickly, equate these with decision and looping constructs in programming languages. The greatest downside of overusing these is that your orchestration canvas grows very large very quickly and making changes becomes cumbersome. Even working in a team environment becomes more difficult in these circumstances. This is similar to creating large methods in C#; it's just not a good practice. Orchestration is not the programming language of BizTalk and should not be treated as a programming language; it is one part of the entire platform that is BizTalk.

Business rules

Not a lot of people use the Business Rules Engine (BRE) in BizTalk and I cannot say I know why, but it could be due to a lack of real world examples and cryptic documentation. I don't believe this tool ever lived up to its original promise of a business analyst friendly tool, but it certainly lives up to my expectations of an effective way to encapsulate logic into a solution in a loosely coupled manner. This is because the rules themselves are deployed independently from the BizTalk solutions that use them. This means they can be updated without changing the solutions that use them. If you have complex decision logic, this is a great tool to implement it. Used correctly, BRE can help you create extensible solutions that can be extended without recompiling your entire solution.

The BRE is an ideal place for logic that is used for routing, and business decisions such as pricing or discounts. There is also the classic example of credit scoring. The BRE is meant to address more rapidly changing logic than orchestration shapes would provide. My favorite way to use BRE is to call rules with XML documents; ideally providing them with all the information they will need, so that they do not need to make external lookups. This focuses the rules on business rule logic rather than on lookup or database logic.

Pipelines and pipeline components

Pipelines are one of the least understood areas of BizTalk, but deserve a lot more credit and attention than they often receive. Almost any .NET component can be called in a custom pipeline component such as BAM and BRE, but great care must be taken not to interfere with the memory model used by BizTalk. Pipeline components can also be used to promote properties or check for duplicate messages. Almost the entire ESB Toolkit for BizTalk is implemented via pipeline components. This allows the developer to use these already created components for a variety of tasks throughout BizTalk from mapping to itinerary processing. Even in the included tool set, pipelines can be used to determine parties and promote or demote properties. Pipeline components are a good example of real reuse in BizTalk, but unfortunately pipelines themselves often are not reused. The parameters for a pipeline can be set in the BizTalk Administration console and they can be set separately for specific receive locations or send ports. This allows us to create a single pipeline that can be reused in multiple places by simply changing the configuration. If less is indeed more, this is a great way to achieve it.

General concept

Ultimately, I believe the downfall of any part of a BizTalk solution is complexity. You should never try to put too much logic into a single place. This is a design tenant well known in OOP—Single Responsibility Principle—but it is one that is easy to lose sight of when working on any platform and BizTalk is no different. BizTalk's graphical focus can actually make this more difficult to avoid at first, as well as the fact that it is not as granular as OOP by nature. Often, if a design is too complex, it should be broken into smaller designs. This advice serves well for maps, orchestrations, rules, and even pipeline components.

Mapping at the port level

As we have seen in our solution architecture so far, it is important to isolate our internal, canonical formats from the outside world; that is external formats. This advice is extremely important, even if all the systems involved in the communication are controlled by a single development team. This is critical because any schema exposed by BizTalk is in essence a public interface. Public interfaces are a contract that may need to be supported for a long time. Any change to a public interface may break calling applications, and BizTalk will be unaware of these implications; yet, just as in traditional programming, we want to be free to change the implementation behind any interface.

The solution is to always map messages going into or out of BizTalk, so as to never let external dependencies bleed in, or internal details seep out of a solution. If your solution is very simple and will never have more than a single calling system and will never ever have to change over time, you may not need to use this technique. The effort required to use maps at the port level is indeed small and it is worth the extra effort to be prepared for the changes that inevitably come to all software programs.

To see this in action, imagine that we create a simple solution receiving a message, routing on some part of the content, and then transforming (mapping) this message as we send it out of BizTalk. If we now have to make this solution work with another inbound message format, we need to route on the new message's content and create another map for sending the message out. If our solution uses business rules or orchestration, this makes it even more work to add a second format; it would also affect our BAM.

What we're trying to do is isolate our solution from changes in other external systems, or requirements. Mapping on both the receipt and send of a message isolates our internal solution from changes in the outside world. The following is an example of the chain connected, travelling through BizTalk and being mapped at both ends of the chain.

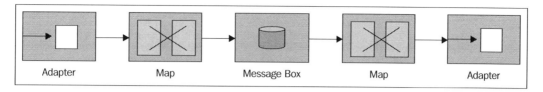

The isolation enforced by this pattern guarantees that no external dependencies will leak into or out of the solution. Our routing, orchestration, and business rules, and even our BAM tracking, are isolated from the outside world. They will be easier to manage and change as a result. Anything between the maps can be changed or implemented in a different way and the external interfaces and endpoints will not need to change at all. This is an effective example of decoupling.

Orchestration best practices

Orchestration is the technology provided by BizTalk to allow us to graphically model business processes and complex messaging scenarios. Orchestration is a powerful tool that allows us to build expressive solutions that can help us overcome coupling inherent in the systems we are connecting. It is also the tool we generally use for service composition.

Orchestration is a close relative to sequential workflow in Workflow Foundation (WF). In fact, the same team that built WF built BizTalk's orchestration engine; orchestration even predates WF. The two have many similarities and some distinct differences. The biggest difference being that in orchestration, like in all of BizTalk, messages are immutable; meaning that once assigned, their values cannot be changed. The two share the concept of **dehydration**—the saving of state—so that the workflow can be removed from memory. This is vital to the scalability and reliability of both, but in orchestration we do not directly control when dehydration occurs. Orchestration also has a concept of persistence related to dehydration.

To create an orchestration, we sequentially model the steps of our business process in the orchestration designer within Visual Studio. The toolbox provided to create orchestration resembles a flow chart from Visio, but it also includes more advanced concepts for constructs than most flow charts cover. These include delays, exception handling, compensation, branching, and role party links.

When we design orchestrations, they are actually stored as XML, much like WF, but are then compiled into a language of their own, X# (X Sharp), which looks very much like C#, but is a distinct language. The orchestration engine in BizTalk is called XLANGs; hence the X# language. In addition to a simple graphical flow, orchestration provides us with durability in our business processes thanks to the previously mentioned dehydration and persistence.

Developers and analysts tend to favor orchestration because it gives them a clear graphical representation of the process they are modeling. As a result, orchestration tends to be over utilized or not used optimally in BizTalk solutions. The following recommendations relate to best practices in the use of orchestration within BizTalk solutions.

Avoid overuse of orchestration

Orchestrations are a great tool in the BizTalk toolkit, but they come at a considerable cost. Many of these costs manifest themselves as round trips to the message box, which means crossing a process boundary and writing to and reading from a database; the message box. This is an expensive operation and one that should only be done when it is necessary. Early in their experiences with BizTalk, developers often latch onto orchestration because of its apparent simplicity and graphical design. Please try to resist this urge. You can do this on your development machine just to get comfortable, but for your first project, make your life easier and avoid orchestration for simple operations.

When I train developers on BizTalk, we wait until the fourth or fifth lesson to cover orchestration at all, which this book does as well. I strongly believe it is important to cover the fundamentals of messaging, mapping, and testing before one begins to create orchestrations.

The following figure shows a situation where orchestration was not the right solution for the problem:

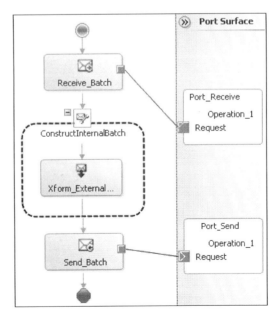

All this orchestration does is receive a message, map it, and forward it on to a send port. This can all be accomplished using a messaging only approach. The following steps explain how it would work:

1. On the send port, where you want to send this message, go to the Filters page and add a filter similar to the following: **BTS.ReceivePortName == <<Name of Receive Port>>**.

2. While still on the send port, change to the Outbound maps page and assign the map to use for transforming this message.

If your schemas and map already exist, these two steps can be completely accomplished within the BizTalk Administration console. The two solutions are functionally equivalent, so let's take a look at the runtime steps involved for each; in particular how they interact with the message box. Often in BizTalk, trips through the message box are called **message box hops**. These are expensive operations and should be minimized.

In the orchestration solution, the steps executed by the runtime are as follows:

1. Receive message via adapter and write to message box.
2. Retrieve work item from message box and start orchestration.
3. Write new mapped message to message box.
4. Retrieve work item from message box for send port.

Each of the previous four steps requires an interaction with the message box. If we now look at the messaging only approach, the steps are as follows:

1. Receive message via adapter and write to message box.
2. Retrieve work item from message box for send port.

Clearly, the second approach has half the trips to the message box. Your performance realistically will be twice as good in the second solution as the first. When you deal with high throughput or low latency solutions, these types of savings are critical. Even when you don't have strict performance requirements, remember that BizTalk is a global platform. Just because one solution does not have high performance requirements is not to say that another, running in the same group, will not. The aggregate demand of many poorly implemented low volume applications can adversely impact a BizTalk environment.

Always use multipart messages in orchestrations

Although most messages used in BizTalk solutions are not multipart, in the sense that they only have one body, using multipart messages in an orchestration provides the benefit of isolating schema changes from impacting orchestrations. In an orchestration, we must define messages at the orchestration level and these messages can be either schemas, .NET classes, multipart messages, or web message types (which makes no sense to me, as this represents tight coupling considering that, by their nature, they are external). The BizTalk IDE is trying to be our friend here by giving us choices, but you should really only use multipart messages. This is because the use of multipart message types gives us another level of indirection and also gives us a reusable type that we can leverage in all of our orchestrations in the solution rather than just in one.

Assigning a message directly to a schema message type is almost like in lining a type. It effectively creates a statement in the orchestration, declaring a variable and its type: `OrderSchema MyMessage`. This means that anywhere the message is used, the orchestration is essentially being coded to this in lined type.

This is significant because changing a schema without using multipart messages will require disconnecting all the port, send, and receive shapes within the Orchestration Designer. This is a tedious and error-prone process and it is not always easy to track down all of these affected shapes. There is also no automated way to do it ahead of time. If you think you'll never change your message types, imagine what happens the first time you have to version your assemblies (for a side by side deployment). If you guessed that you need to disconnect all the port, send, and receive shapes in your orchestration, you guessed right!

The solution is to use a multipart message type in the orchestration and then create a body part for the new multipart message type that is bound to the schema we want. We then assign the message to use this new multipart message type. This effectively translates to a declaration similar to `IMySchema MyMessage`. This is not a totally accurate translation because orchestration really doesn't care what the previous interface is, just that it is there. In a way it means we are free to change the implementation, just not the actual interface. This pattern probably has more in common with COM, or even the concept of a pointer to a pointer, or a reference to a pointer.

Multipart message types can be reused between orchestrations, so that we do not have to create as many message types, but be aware that this does introduce a small degree of coupling. Sometimes it is a good idea to put all multipart messages or shared types into an orchestration that contains no logic at all and is only used for such definitions.

Finally, this technique allows you to stub out your ideas more quickly in the development phase because you can always just convert everything into an `XmlDocument`. This directly contradicts my other advice in a later section, but we all do it at some time. Only don't let it get into production that way!

Avoid large orchestrations

This is the same as the OOP coding suggestion to avoid excessively long methods. As you build orchestrations, it becomes very easy to keep adding functionality to them by dragging more shapes onto the canvas. This can make the orchestration difficult to follow and lock all of the functionality deep inside of it. The **Call Orchestration** shape is a simple way to compartmentalize your orchestrations. This shape works just like a method or function call—it is a synchronous direct invocation. You can send parameters into it or receive them out; or both. Call Orchestration even supports reference parameters. Any orchestration that does not have an activating receive shape as its first shape is considered callable. One benefit to call is that, just like a function or method invocation, there is not a lot of overhead with the call. This is different from **Start Orchestration**, which asynchronously creates a new orchestration under a new context and does so via the message box. Start Orchestration is actually a specialized direct send.

Encapsulating reusable logic inside called orchestrations is a great way to leverage reuse and is something you should address the same way you do in traditional code. Generally, the second time that you need logic that already exists, simply refactor the original logic into a new orchestration and execute it using Call Orchestration. If you know at the outset that your orchestration will be big, and some are by nature, try to compose it from multiple orchestrations. This is clearly simple advice, but it took me a long time to take it to heart and realize the benefits of doing so.

Minimize trips to the message box (persistence points)

One of the great benefits of orchestration is that it provides us with robust durability automatically. This is very different from traditional programming paradigms. Orchestrations are process agile, meaning that they are independently able to change to a different process—indeed server—as needed; an example would be an outage. This is possible because at any point where an orchestration makes contact with the outside world, it saves its state in the message box. This is called a **persistence point** and it happens automatically. During this operation, all messages and variables used within the orchestration, including any artifacts that contribute to its state, are saved into the message box. Send shapes are the most common persistence point. The engine does this because once the orchestration sends out a message, it does not know if the response will be immediate or not. Remember, the message box acts as a buffer here, like always, decoupling the orchestration from the actual send and receive. This allows the orchestration to be unloaded from memory and to restart on any available host when it continues. Atomic scopes and send operations result in persistence points, but others happen automatically for other reasons. Most, however, are driven by a trip through the message box.

An easy way to determine if your orchestrations are resulting in too many persistence points is to use **Performance Monitors** to determine the runtime characteristics of your solution. I always recommend doing this. For orchestration in particular, the performance monitor's `Persistence points` and `Persistence points/sec` in the `XLANG/s Orchestrations` performance object category are particularly useful.

A simple tip to reduce persistence points includes, bunching multiple sends together in a single atomic operation. This will result in one persistence point instead of one for each send. This can be confusing at first but it works fine. Orchestration is not like C# or Java. A send shape does not need to be immediately followed by its corresponding receive shape. This is because the response is held in the message box anyway. If you have to call three web services that don't require the response from one to call the next, you can place all three send shapes in a single atomic scope and they will all go to the message box together; in one persistence point. Even if the responses arrive out of order, the orchestration will only retrieve them in the order you have laid the receive shapes in.

It is a good practice to design with persistence point counts in mind. Because persistence has a significant cost and can happen unexpectedly, there really is no replacement for stress testing of a solution to find where these points will emerge.

Avoid using atomic scopes to call .NET methods

Orchestration allows us to create .NET class variables and use their methods to assist our business process. This can be a great feature, but any class that is used as a variable in an orchestration must be marked with the `Serializable` attribute. This allows the orchestration engine to store the class with the running orchestration in the message box (the durability we talked about before). This is fine if you're creating your own classes and libraries, but not if you're using existing ones. The workaround most use is the atomic scope, which will allow us to instantiate any .NET class and call its methods. The atomic scope was designed to handle Atomicity, Consistency, Isolation, and Durability (ACID) compliant operations that must either all succeed or all fail as a group. This is a classic database transaction style. It is designed to carry an orchestration from one stable state to another. This is why you cannot both send and receive from an atomic scope, because by design the message box is not a lockable resource. To accomplish this atomicity, the orchestration engine persists the entire orchestration state to the message box before the atomic scope begins; it subsequently persists the orchestration again when the atomic scope completes.

Do not use an atomic scope to simply call a method of a .NET class that is not Serializable. If you absolutely must call a `non-Serializable` class, and can only do it in an atomic scope, try to combine this with other operations to make the most of the trip to the message box; like a send shape as shown in the following figure:

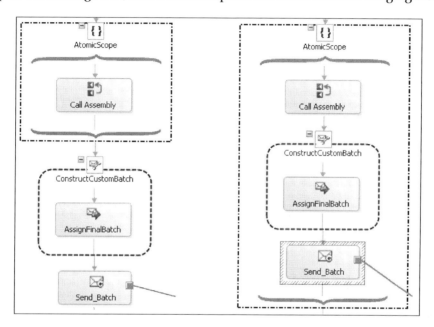

This call at least reuses one of the two persistence points to perform a send that was needed anyway. A better way to solve this problem is to create a `wrapper` class with a static method that instantiates the required objects, uses them, and returns the desired result. Keep in mind that the orchestration engine is smart enough to inspect any classes that you create to make sure they do not have `non-Serializable` members.

Don't use XmlDocument for a message type... ever

As we saw earlier, the orchestration engine will allow us to represent any message as an XmlDocument. Just because this feature is available does not mean that we should use it. XmlDocument within XLANGs (the orchestration engine) is actually a special class that wraps the XmlDocument; which oddly enough is not serializable. This class is dangerous for several reasons. First, it allows us to create messages and variables that will fail if any of their methods or properties are used; this is in the case of non-XML messages being represented by this message type. These errors will also only happen at runtime. This is a bigger problem because as new developers have to work with a solution, it will not be clear which messages they can modify and how. If you have edge cases using non-XML in an XmlDocument and your solution testing doesn't provide 100 percent coverage, you could end up with a fatal runtime error that you only find in production.

Worse still for messages that actually are XML, XmlDocument loads the contents into the DOM (Document Object Model) for processing. The first and most obviously dangerous side effect of this is that because the DOM allows random access to the document, it loads the entire document into memory. To make matters worse, in order to make this access fast, the memory requirement is often an order of magnitude greater than for the pure XML data. That means a 100K message will likely occupy 1MB of memory. If you have several of them and have moderate throughput, you will face memory pressure and the throughput of your solution will rapidly decline.

Another and more subtle issue often caused by using an XmlDocument is that the class allows for modification of the document through its members. Recall from the earlier pages that messages in BizTalk are immutable; that is they cannot be changed. This is at the center of the durability and distributed architecture of BizTalk. An XmlDocument will allow you to make local changes in a message that are not reflected in the message box. Under certain circumstances, such as when persistence points occur and orchestrations rehydrate on another server, your local changes may not appear anymore. This is precisely because messages truly are immutable. Troubleshooting issues such as this one are time consuming and difficult because it can be hard to reproduce.

If you need to pass non-XML messages through an orchestration, you should really use XLANGMessage to do this. This class makes the intention clear that the message is not XML and should not be treated as such. It also has a smaller memory footprint. Like XmlDocument, XLANGMessage can be assigned to any message—with the validation happening at runtime. This class can be found in the Microsoft.XLANGs.BaseTypes namespace of the Microsoft.XLANGs.BaseTypes.dll assembly.

Finally, if you must access the content of an XML message within an orchestration (normally done through a helper class) you should retrieve the body part as `XmlReader` rather than as `XmlDocument`. The `XmlReader` class is stream-based, like the rest of the BizTalk infrastructure; this preserves the flat memory footprint that is sought after in BizTalk.

Alternatively, you can also create .NET classes that match your schema using `xsd.exe`, which will generate classes conforming to the message schema. This technique will allow you to work with messages in .NET, which can be more useful in helper methods. Both of these techniques are accomplished using the `RetrieveAs` method of the `XLANGMessage` class, as shown in the following two methods:

```
public MyMessage SomethingInteresting(XLANGMessage message)
{
    MyMessage myMessage = message[0].RetrieveAs(typeof(MyMessage)) as
MyMessage;
    return myMessage;
}
public XmlReader SomethingElse(XLANGMessage message)
{
    XmlReader reader = message[0].RetrieveAs(typeof(XmlReader)) as
XmlReader;
    return reader;
}
```

Again, keep in mind that less is more. If you need to do extremely complex operations in many helper methods, you might want to reconsider your solution. All .NET data structures are memory resident, so using the `XmlSerializer`—which is what the previous example ultimately does—loads the entire message into memory. That said, it takes considerably less memory space than an `XmlDocument`.

Avoid loading messages into classes via the XmlSerializer

The `XmlSerializer` allows us to load messages into classes automatically. This class dates to the very first versions of the .NET Framework and is a great technique most developers are unaware of. Working in C# or Visual Basic .NET, it is much easier to work with classes and data structures than with the XML classes of the `System.Xml` namespace. This is the technique presented previously. This is a convenient feature and there certainly are some situations where it can be much easier to accomplish a given development task in .NET classes rather than in XML messages or maps. It is important to note, however, that the entire architecture of BizTalk Server is built around the concept of stream-based components. This means that message sizes, even for very large messages, will not adversely affect the operation of the platform. This gives BizTalk a very flat memory footprint and helps to make the product as scalable as it is. The `XmlSerializer` does not follow this same stream-based approach. On the contrary, classes serialized with the `XmlSerializer` are completely loaded into memory at one time and can have negative effects on the memory footprint of your solutions as a result. Generally speaking, if the messages are small, or the nodes that you send into a method for processing are small, then the impact may not be too severe. Keep in mind that even small messages, when there are a lot, can add up to large memory footprints.

Use direct bound ports and Content Based Routing

Many developers new to BizTalk don't grasp the power and flexibility of Content Based Routing (CBR) in BizTalk Server. CBR allows for the implementation of logical decisions that new developers often turn to orchestration to solve. In the following figure, we see an example of this. A decide shape is used to route a message based upon content within the message. This could be a total order amount, the status of the client, or anything else in the message. In this case, it is based on the vendor.

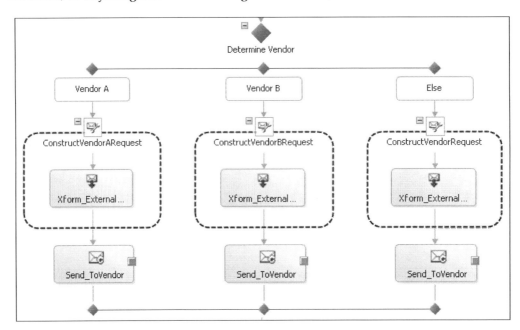

The previous orchestration clearly shows what routing decision is being made and is easy to understand, but it is not an optimal solution for many scenarios. For one, the solution is effectively hardwired. Changing any of the routing or adding new vendors will require recompiling and deploying the solution. A good alternative is to use CBR in BizTalk, which is often referred to as a **direct bound** port in an orchestration. To accomplish this, follow these three steps:

1. Create a property schema in the solution and promote the property you wish to use for routing. This can be done via the **Add New Item...** dialog in Visual Studio.

2. Configure the send port in the orchestration to use direct binding. This will cause BizTalk to submit the message directly to the message box; at which point it will be matched against any subscriptions and sent to all subscribers. This is shown in the following screenshot:

3. After deploying the new property schema, configure each send port you want to include with a filter (subscription) that matches the desired operation. Usually, this will be a message type, an operation, or receive port name, and a value for the promoted property. The following example shows a filter that makes this solution functionally equivalent to one of the branches in the orchestration in the previous figure.

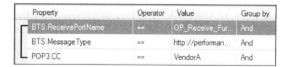

4. Although this may not be as graphically appealing as the orchestration approach, it does the same thing and is easier to change in the future. With this approach, new vendors can be added using only the Administration console. Many developers who become comfortable with CBR often forget that it can be used throughout BizTalk, not just on send ports.

Leverage filters in orchestrations

The most common way to receive messages in an orchestration is to use the
Specify Later option when configuring a port. This is then followed by binding the
orchestration to a receive port in the BizTalk Administration console. This pattern
does carry some significant benefits. It is very easy for administrators to understand
the flow of messages and also to know the impact of downtime or changes. The
drawback is that an orchestration is then coupled to a single port. Although this
port can have multiple locations, it is still just a single port. In simple scenarios, this
is not a bad approach but it makes reuse much more difficult as an orchestration
is effectively now coupled to a specific receive port, which must have external
messages flow into it. Because this results in a specific path of message flow, it also
tends to lead to large orchestrations. A simple way around this is to use a direct
bound receive port.

When configuring a receive port in the Port Configuration Wizard, simply change the
type to direct and use the default option of **Routing between ports will be defined
by filter expressions on incoming**. After configuring the port, you now use the Filter
property of the receive shape to define the expression that will match incoming
subscriptions. This filter functions just like the other filters that we have covered up
to this point. An example orchestration filter is shown in the following screenshot:

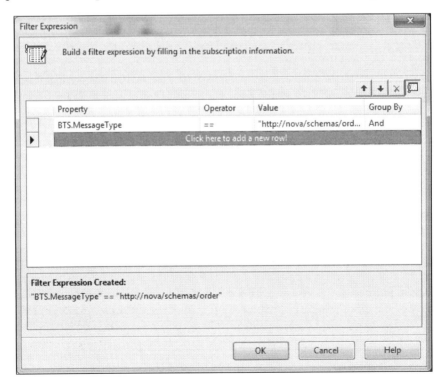

Importantly, inside of the orchestration's filter values (the right-hand side of the expressions) must be enclosed in quotes. The orchestration will not compile otherwise.

What this now allows us to do is chain orchestrations together, so that they can feed into each other in arbitrarily long or winding chains. This is a pretty advanced concept, so it may take a while to really leverage. This is an extreme approach to loose coupling and does not provide the crutch that a single large graphical representation, or even that Call Orchestration would offer us. One of the greatest advantages to this approach is that it actually decouples our orchestrations from each other, allowing them to change at different rates. Like all design decisions, simpler tends to be better, so don't go out of your way just to try to use this. Experiment with it and eventually you will find the right use for this technique.

There is another type of binding **Specify now** that we should never use as it performs the port creation from within the orchestration and results in very tight coupling that is not easily changed without recompiling.

Use distinguished fields instead of XPath

The X# language provides us with a few tools specifically designed to make working with messages easier. One of these is the xpath function, which can be used to set or retrieve values from an XML message. The syntax is as follows:

```
xpath(Message/Part, <<XPath expression string>>)
```

The XPath expression is a fully qualified expression including namespaces. The easiest way to get this expression is to navigate to the node you're trying to read or write in the schema editor and look in the properties window at the **Instance XPath**. Simply copy it from here. Other tools like XML NotePad and DanSharp XmlViewer also provide easy access to XPath expressions.

This can be really useful, but it carries a few side effects. First, it normally requires long function calls that can't easily be seen on the screen without scrolling, such as the following:

```
xpath(MyMessage, "/*[local-name()='MyMessage' and namespace-
uri()='http://nova/billing/schemas/internal/2011-05']/*[local-
name()='Number' and namespace-uri()='']") = "1234";
```

That's a pretty big assignment statement and this is only a simple example. A much easier way to do this is to use distinguished fields in your schema. Real-world examples will be much larger than this. A distinguished field is a schema annotation that is used by BizTalk to allow for XPath shorthand. In orchestration, this can make our statements much more simple.

To distinguish a field, simply right-click the node inside the schema editor and under the **Promote** option select **Show Promotions...**. This is shown in the following screenshot:

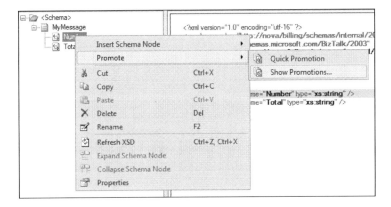

From here you have a list of all the nodes in the schema on the left (with the node you had right-clicked and already selected) and all the distinguished fields on the right. Simply click the **Add >>** button and then click **OK**. Be sure to save the schema, and if it is in a separate project to recompile, as shown in the following screenshot:

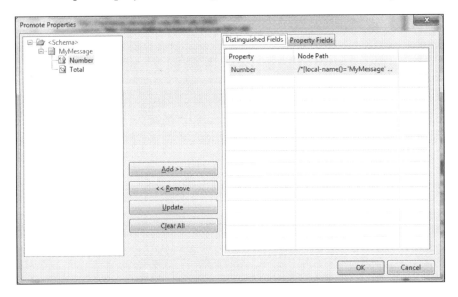

A visual queue is given to let us know that this node has been either distinguished or promoted. It is the little gold and blue icon now attached to the node. The resulting assignment statement is much easier to read and its intention is much more clear.

```
MyMessage.Number = "1234";
```

There is also another benefit that is not always apparent at first. The XPath statement before has the namespace in it and if we need to change our namespace, we must remember to go and change all these XPath strings in the orchestrations. Changing namespaces is common when versioning solutions (creating a 2.0 version, and so on) and the xpath function is evaluated only at runtime, so as long as the second parameter is a string, it will compile; even if it is the wrong string. Because the distinguished field is annotated in the schema with which we're working, it will be automatically updated when the schema's namespace is updated.

There is, however, one drawback to using distinguished fields; it is that they must exist in the message at runtime in order to avoid an error when evaluating them. If it's an important piece of data it should exist anyway, but you can also explicitly map in place holder or null values if needed. Zero would be a good example in a decimal field.

Avoid unnecessary looping on collections

I frequently see scenarios where developers receive a batch into an orchestration and then loop over the records to process them. I particularly see this from the SQL or WCF-SQL adapters; or for that matter from any database adapter. Often the result looks similar to the following figure:

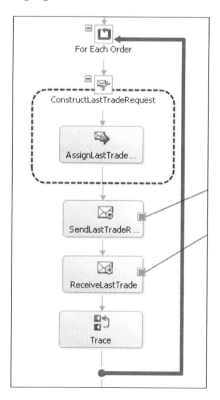

This is a bad use of orchestration for a variety of reasons. For one, although not clearly shown, it uses xpath and the DOM to create each individual message. We've already covered why that is not a good practice. Worse still, each submessage then does a send, which results in a persistence point. Larger messages will not work well in this sort of arrangement. If you needed to break apart a message in an orchestration, calling a pipeline with an XML disassembler from within the orchestration would be a much better approach to the xpath DOM assignment approach. Don't let that friendly loop lull you into a sense of familiarity. The previous loop is nothing like what you would write in a procedural or imperative language, it incurs a lot of overhead and there is no way to keep a single connection to the destination system open. The loop, like most orchestration shapes, is meant as a control structure, not a programming structure.

The problems actually only get worse from here. There is no transactional integrity between the individual requests. If one request fails, all the messages before it are already complete and are committed in the case of database transactions. It will also stop any subsequent messages in the batch from processing. You could add compensation or exception logic to address this, but it really just starts piling more bad approaches on an approach that is not elegant to begin with.

There are two better ways to approach this issue and the approach which you should use will depend on what you're doing. They are as follows:

- To debatch (disassemble) the message in the receive location, which also allows us better control over failures. The orchestration would then subscribe to the debatched message and the map on the receive port would map at this debatched level as well. This approach will result in many orchestrations running completely independently. The modeling path is simple and this works well in many cases. This will scale, even for very large messages, though you may end up with throttling due to large loads. BizTalk is designed to handle large loads.

- To simply map the multiple lines together in a single request. The classic SQL adapter even allows you to combine separate operations to different stored procedures or updategrams in a single request. The order of the nodes within the XML determines the order in which they execute. This can be a very useful technique as all operations complete in a single **Distributed Transaction Coordinator** (DTC) context. That is to say, they either all succeed or all rollback as one. There is much less deadlocking in the case of database connections because all the requests execute serially in this single DTC transaction.

This technique is very useful, but very large messages will strain the adapters. The SQL and WCF-SQL adapters tend to decline in performance above 50,000 transactions in a single message. That said, this amounts to a lot of transactions. Because we already discussed that ETL is normally better done with other tools like SSIS, that makes this approach even more useful in context.

Pipelines

This section introduces pipelines and some recommendations for their use in BizTalk solutions.

What are pipelines?

Pipelines are one of the least understood components of BizTalk server. They are a mechanism for processing message streams and are a realization of the **pipes and filters** design pattern. In this pattern, processing components are arranged in a chain and each link in the chain consumes the data from the link before it and feeds data to the link after it. This allows for different stages of processing to modify the stream that can make the data more useful. Two very important activities also occur in pipelines, namely, the conversion to or from native formats and XML and property promotion. An example of a pipeline with different stages would be the following:

1. Decrypt data.
2. Change from flat file to XML.
3. Authenticate the data or the sender.

The previous operations are dependent on order because it would not be useful to try to convert an encrypted flat file to XML. First, it must be decrypted, then later in the chain it can be converted to XML.

In BizTalk, these links in the chain are pipeline components and the chain they are a part of is a pipeline. For example, most of the artifacts in BizTalk pipelines, which have a `.btp` extension, are graphical representations. This helps us to see quickly which components are executed in what order and whether they are kept with the graphical concepts that drive BizTalk development.

Stages in a receive pipeline

The chain of components formed by a pipeline is segmented into different sections to help us organize and focus our efforts. These sections are called stages and each represents a specific opportunity to manipulate the message stream in a certain way. An empty receive pipeline is shown in the following figure, complete with its stages:

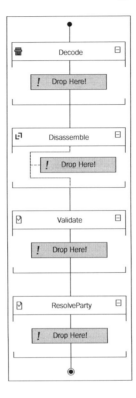

This image shows the four stages of a receive pipeline and how components are graphically laid out on them. As configured previously, this pipeline is equivalent to the **PassThruReceive** pipeline, which, as the name implies, simply lets a message pass through it unaltered.

Each stage can contain between zero and 255 components and in every stage except **Disassemble**, they are executed in the order in which they are laid out on the canvas. The descriptions of the stages are as follows:

- **Decode:** This stage is designed for decoding, which can include decryption. Generally, the components in this stage will be used to make the data more useful for later components. Decryption is a good example because, without it, no other stage can process the data in a meaningful way. S/MIME is also a format that requires decoding, which would be done in this first stage.

- **Disassemble:** This stage is responsible for determining which schema the data conforms to. This is done via a process called **message probing**, which inspects the message to determine the message type. In the case of XML messages, this is the namespace and root element node name. In the case of a flat file, this would be the layout of the raw flat file and would use the flat file schemas specified in the flat file disassemble pipeline component. This stage is also responsible for splitting messages apart. Both flat files and XML documents with envelopes can be used to break a batched message into individual submessages. This stage will produce one output message for each of the batched messages if batching or envelopes are used. Finally, this stage is also responsible for promoting properties that are often used for content-based routing in BizTalk. The first component in this stage that can identify the data will be used to process it and all the following components will be skipped.

- **Validate:** This stage is used to enforce schema constraints of the previously resolved schemas. The XML Validator is the most common component used in this stage and works for both flat file schemas as well as traditional XML schemas. If you use constraints in a schema such as types, lengths, or required fields, this is the stage that will enforce them; suspending messages that do not conform.

- **Resolve Party:** This stage is used to determine the sender of a message normally via the certificate thumbprint that was used to sign the message. Later components in BizTalk can use this information to determine how to process a message or where to send a response for a particular sender.

As we discussed type resolution in *Chapter 2, Introduction to BizTalk Development*, schemas in BizTalk are resolved by namespace and root element name in a global catalog. The XML Disassembler can be used to explicitly match a message to specific schema and thus resolve the name collision. To do this, you specify a **Document Spec** in the XML Disassembler component. The document spec name is the mechanism BizTalk uses to identify a schema in the DocumentSpec table of the management database. It is a fully qualified .NET name consisting of [type name], [assembly name], [version], [culture], and [public key]. An example would be as follows:

```
PRP.OrderProcessing.ExternalSchemas.PurchaseOrder, PRP.
OrderProcessing.ExternalSchemas, Version=1.0.0.0, Culture=neutral, Pub
licKeyToken=0e3c97569ac5667e
```

If that looks like a mouthful, you're right, it is, but this is how the GAC in .NET works and, as we covered in the last chapter, it does a specific job and works. You would need to do this if you had two different schemas with the same namespace and root element name in the same BizTalk group, which might happen if multiple applications use the same web services.

Stages in a send pipeline

The send pipeline works in almost the same way as the receive pipeline, but in reverse. This pipeline contains only three stages as there is no party resolution concept in a send pipeline. An example of a send pipeline is shown as follows:

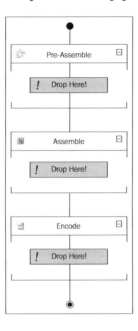

In this pipeline, the **Pre-Assemble** stage is designed to host any custom operations that should take place before the message is assembled (either as XML or flat format) and encoded. The **Assemble** and **Encode** stages work exactly like before, only this time they are undoing those equivalent operations from the receive pipeline. **Assemble** can combine multiple messages into a single message and can also convert from XML to flat file if needed. **Encode** is the last stage to process the message stream and can be used for encryption or other operations that happen immediately before the message is sent "on the wire".

Pipeline components

Pipeline components are .NET or COM components that are designed to work at a specific stage of a pipeline. They are either designed for send or receive pipelines and normally address a specific task such as decryption. Pipeline components are a good method for reusing custom messaging logic; once created, pipeline components can be added to the Visual Studio toolbox by right-clicking the toolbox and selecting Choose Items. Thankfully, the need to create custom pipeline components is fairly limited and you can go through many projects without them at all.

If you need to, however, the BizTalk Pipeline Component Wizard on codeplex (`http://btsplcw.codeplex.com`) is my favorite way to create pipeline components. It is an easy-to-use tool that walks you through the pipeline component creation process via a friendly wizard.

Metadata and message context

Pipelines are the place where message context and metadata are normally assigned. Every message in BizTalk has metadata associated with it. This metadata describes the message itself. In very simple cases, the metadata would include the name of the receive port. In the following, we can see an example of message metadata in a screenshot taken from the BizTalk Administration console:

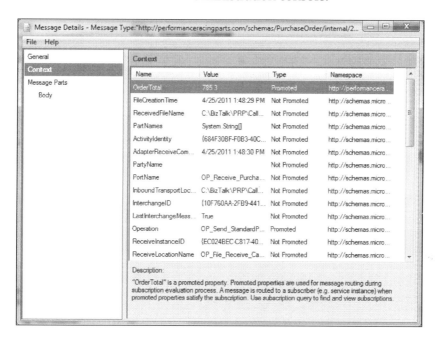

We can see a lot of information here and we can also see that some of it is marked as promoted. Promoted properties, as we covered before, can be used for content-based routing. Other properties, which are written, but not promoted, cannot. Understanding message context is an important aspect of working with BizTalk. In the process of promoting a property, the BizTalk runtime copies the data out of the message and into the Context. This makes the value quickly accessible for routing and other operations, which are the core purpose of property promotion, but it also adds to the size of the message context. It is a good practice to only promote those properties which you will need. Property promotion is covered in detail shortly. There are also size limits to the data that can be promoted.

Please note that this is different from the distinguished field concept we saw recently, which only provides a reference or pointer to the data within the message itself.

One of the places I have needed to use custom pipelines before was to promote message properties, especially those that exist in the message, but are not promoted. This is an easy operation once you have your pipeline component created and can be accomplished with this single line of code:

```
inmsg.Context.Promote("Property Name", "Property Namespace", "value");
```

Stream processing

Stream processing is at the core of BizTalk Server's scalability. Stream processing is nothing new, but is still a concept most developers are not terribly familiar with. I know wasn't until I worked with BizTalk that I really understood the power of stream processing. Fundamentally, stream processing is about breaking work into small enough pieces, so that they don't consume excessively large amounts of memory. Anyone who has ever written code to process flat files is familiar with the `ReadLine()` concept. `ReadLine()` saves a program from having to load an entire file into memory for processing. The line functions as a buffer and the program simply reads one line at a time. Most of the classes in `System.IO` namespace are stream-based and this is why they can work quickly and efficiently with large files.

BizTalk builds upon this concept and implements it throughout the product. Pipelines are stream-based; at runtime every component in a pipeline simply calls Read on the components before it and data is piped from one stream to the next for processing. This is why they are called pipelines and this is why they can process extremely large files without taking up the entire memory of the server or crashing any processes with the dreaded `OutOfMemory` Exception.

Stream processing is also used in mapping as well as in BAM and reading from and writing to the message box database. Generally, all that is needed to create your own streaming component (and you should always stream if you're writing custom code in BizTalk) is to implement a class derived from the abstract class `System.IO.Stream`. You then choose which methods to implement to provide the behavior you require.

Summary

In this chapter, we covered a large array of BizTalk development best practices including determining where to place logic in a solution, how to best use orchestration, and how pipelines work. All of these practices will be put to use in part II of this book.

4
Operating BizTalk

This chapter introduces BizTalk Server 2010 operations concepts that are critical for architects and administrators to understand in order to build and run BizTalk solutions. This chapter will provide an overview of operational architecture and will explain how to scale BizTalk installations. It will also introduce the deployment process for BizTalk solutions, and then introduce performance tuning and troubleshooting.

This chapter covers the following topics:

- Operational architecture
- Scalability
- High availability
- Disaster recovery
- Performance optimization
- Deployment process
- Troubleshooting BizTalk issues

Understanding BizTalk operational architecture

We have already explored the core conceptual architecture of BizTalk Server 2010, but now we will delve more deeply into how this architecture fits into the real world of Windows Servers and applications.

At its core, BizTalk is a .NET application built on top of SQL Server. This already tells us that we have two definite dependencies: SQL Server and Windows Server. We also have a core dependency on Active Directory to provide a service account and user access and control; that said, in smaller environments, BizTalk can use local groups, but this does not scale well. The core set of servers involved in a BizTalk environment are shown in the following diagram:

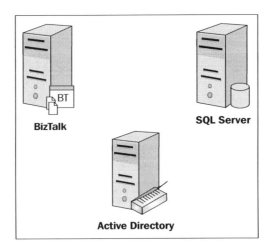

These three servers are the core moving parts in any BizTalk environment. SQL Server hosts the message box and all the other databases. BizTalk provides most of the processing and Active Directory provides authentication. This book does not cover Active Directory, as that is already expected to be running in your enterprise, but the other two will be explored in detail.

Administering BizTalk Server

Most administration and operation tasks for BizTalk Server are performed in the BizTalk Administration console; an MMC Snap-In designed to provide access to all the settings in a BizTalk group through a single interface. MMC provides a common user interface approach for Windows administration tasks and the use of an MMC Snap-In makes BizTalk very familiar to most administrators. Like most MMC Snap-Ins (IIS, Active Directory, and so on), there are three panes in the BizTalk Administration console Snap-In from left to right: navigation, information, and actions.

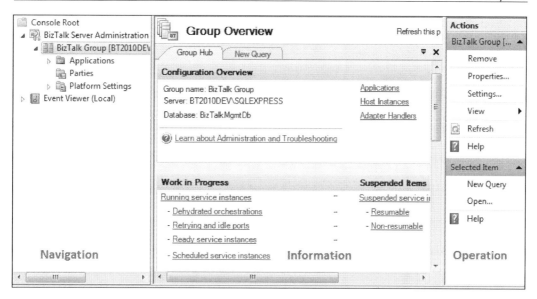

As you click on different nodes in the left navigation pane, a different context comes up in the center and right panes. The right **Actions** pane changes further when different objects are selected in the center information pane. This context allows us to change specific settings more easily depending on where we have set our focus in the console.

The root node in the navigation pane displays a **Console Root** folder with the **BizTalk Server Administration** and **Event Viewer (Local)** nodes beneath it. By default, the first node will have the BizTalk group of the local machine listed within it, but by right-clicking the **BizTalk Server Administration** node, we can connect to other BizTalk groups. This allows us to remotely administer multiple BizTalk groups from a single workstation. It also allows us to perform most administration tasks without logging into the BizTalk Servers directly. When connecting to a BizTalk group, we actually provide the connection information for the management database, which is the brain of BizTalk.

Within the BizTalk group, there are three primary areas of the console that we use to manage our solutions; each is represented by a node. They are introduced as follows and can be seen in the previous screenshot:

- **Applications**: This node houses all the applications deployed to a BizTalk Server group. It is from here that we can configure and control specific applications in BizTalk. An application in BizTalk is the logical grouping for a set of related artifacts that normally form a solution. Within each application, the artifacts are categorized in the nodes, as shown in the following screenshot:

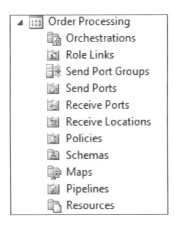

These nodes largely correspond to concepts that we covered in the previous chapters. When our BizTalk application deploys locally from Visual Studio, all the assemblies should deploy to the same application, and thus be part of the same "solution". This view will list all artifacts from any assembly deployed to this application. **Policies** are BRE rule sets; this is their formal name. **Send Port Groups** are simple grouping mechanisms for the **Send Ports**. **Role Links** tie parties to ports and orchestrations.

- **Parties**: These are mechanisms for working with trade partners and are particularly suited to solutions that require the same general processing for messages, but may need to send the results, or intermediary requests, to different endpoints. Parties are heavily utilized in B2B scenarios to create easily extensible solutions. A party can represent a trade partner or another system or division within the enterprise and is a key factor to EDI.

- **Platform Settings**: This is the place where the settings for a BizTalk group and all its subordinate objects reside. Hosts, host instances, servers, message boxes, and adapters are all configured here. As the name implies, this is where we work with settings that affect the core BizTalk platform.

Scalability in BizTalk Server

According to Wikipedia, "*scalability is the ability of a system, network, or process to handle growing amounts of work in a graceful manner, or its ability to be enlarged to accommodate that growth*". There are generally two types of scalabilities in the computer world: scale up, which means moving to a larger and more powerful server, and scaling out; which means adding more servers. For most software, scaling up is the simpler or even the only path. BizTalk is fundamentally designed to scale out with no changes needing to be made for the software running a solution. As we move further into the era of multicore processors, we are actually blurring this distinction and shifting more to the scale out model, even when we choose to scale up. Only software and platforms that are made to be parallel can take full advantage of the multicore architectures now prominent in the industry.

Scaling SQL Server

There are two specific areas where BizTalk can scale out. The first and generally most important is the SQL Server area. SQL Server is frequently a bottleneck for BizTalk solutions. Often, this confuses administrators, even ones who know SQL Server, because they see low utilization on BizTalk Servers and don't see high utilization on SQL Servers. Most often, this is because SQL Server tends to be a disk bound application, meaning that the real bottlenecks tend to be the disk queues of SQL operations waiting to take place.

BizTalk Server has been carefully designed to fully exploit SQL Server in an extremely optimized manner, and subsequently exploit the BizTalk databases, specifically the message box, which should not be on a shared SQL instance used by other applications. In fact, the message box should have its own instance separated even from the other BizTalk databases.

While we're on the subject, now is probably a good time to raise a very important caveat about the message box. During configuration of BizTalk, the Maximum Degree of Parallelism (Max DOP) setting on your SQL Server will be changed to one (1). This is because the message box is a highly tuned database that works very differently from most other databases. The job of most databases is to hold data that will be returned as record sets. The Max DOP setting controls how SQL Server will try to run queries in parallel to each other to speed up their results. It is an instance-wide setting in SQL Server and defaults to zero (0), which allows SQL Server to use all available processors. For nearly all databases, the default Max DOP setting allows SQL Server to perform the query and return the data faster by breaking the query up amongst the processors on the server. This is a divide and conquer approach if you will. This optimization in SQL Server will actually harm the performance of the message box database. The message box is structured in such a way that setting the Max DOP to any value other than one will cause the message box operations to slow down. This is because the operations performed on the message box are generally single record (and small record at that) operations. The overhead to parallelize them turns out to be more than beneficial from executing them in parallel. This will cause BizTalk to slow down if the SQL instance hosting the message box has the Max DOP set to any value besides one.

Having said all this, the other databases that make up BizTalk actually benefit from not setting the Max DOP to one. This is a great demonstration of why you may want to consider multiple SQL Servers or at least multiple instances for your BizTalk installation. Generally, SQL Server should be configured into two instances: one for the message box and one for all other databases. These can all be on the same physical server, but they should be separated from other databases and from each other. Newer versions of SQL Server do allow tighter resource control over databases, but this is still good advice for SQL 2008 R2. Within these databases, it is also a good idea to separate indexes from data storage to improve performance.

Adding more SQL Servers, or even just instances, to your BizTalk installation is a way to scale out the SQL Tier of your environment, but BizTalk also provides another way to scale out SQL Server by creating multiple message boxes. The idea is that one message box functions as the master message box, managing subscriptions, and the others function as runtime message boxes for delivering matched subscriptions (that is, starting orchestrations and send ports). This allows the master message box to focus only on subscription matching and thus it performs even better. It is suggested that if you create separate message boxes, so that you have at least three in total, then one should master and the other two should be publishing, due to the extra overhead involved in using multiple message boxes. The intention is that these message boxes can each exist on different servers or at least on different SQL instances.

This is a very sophisticated technique and approach to addressing scalability, but like many tasks in BizTalk, this turns out to be surprisingly easy to accomplish. Simply right-click the **Message Boxes** node in the BizTalk Administration console (under **Platform Settings**), select **New**, and then select **Message Box...**.

This will bring up a configuration dialog allowing you to specify the server and database name for this new message box. After you have created your new message boxes, you can go back to the master message box and disable new message publication, which will instruct the master message box to only perform routing and subscription matching. This entire operation can be performed while the platform is running.

If you ever need to remove a message box, you simply disable new message publication and let it continue running, then delete that message box.

 Please note that you cannot delete the master message box without designating a new one.

Scaling BizTalk Server

After sorting out any SQL Server issues and scaling challenges, the next place to consider is the BizTalk tier. There are two ways to scale out the BizTalk tier: one is to add more hosts and host instances to the group, and the other is to add more servers. Both turn out to be quite easy in BizTalk.

Adding more hosts and host instances

To add more hosts, you simply right-click the **Hosts** node in **Platform Settings** and select **New | Host...** from the context menu. The dialog that will appear is shown in the following screenshot:

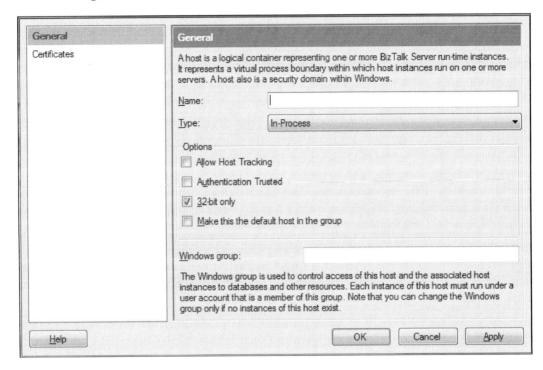

In this dialog, you can specify the name and the Windows group that the host users will need to be a part of. You can also choose to mark a host as 32 bit in case you're working with components that do not support 64 bit runtime. Allowing different Windows groups for hosts enables us to strictly control security permissions. If we have a location that receives (or sends) messages to a non-secure endpoint, we can isolate the execution of that port or location by using a less privileged account; this will help enforce security within our application. Once you create the host, you perform a similar operation to create a new host instance for that host. If you now left-click the **Host instances** node, you will notice that the **Actions** pane, on the far right, provides an alternative to right-clicking for a context menu.

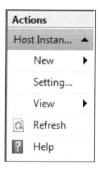

Clicking **New** here is the same as right-clicking and selecting **New | Host Instance** from the context menu. Again, this is common in all MMC Snap-Ins. From this dialog we configure the settings for a specific host instance shown as follows:

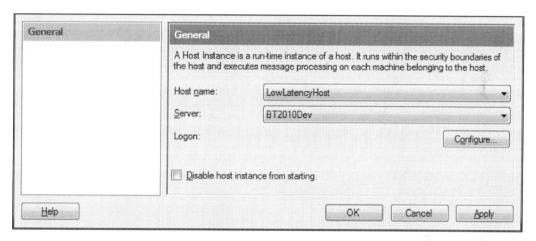

These settings consist of **Host name:**, which would be the host we created before, and the server within the group on which to configure this host instance. We must also provide **Logon:** credentials for the Windows service that will be automatically created on this server for us. We can optionally decide to make sure this host instance is not capable of starting. This can be useful if we're setting up new hosts and instances on many servers, but are not yet ready to start them. We will see this presented more thoroughly later in this chapter, in the section, *Presenting the best practices for BizTalk configuration*.

Adding more servers to the group

This step is a little more complicated, but only a little. All you have to do is install BizTalk on the new server and then run the **BizTalk Server Configuration** tool on the new server. When the wizard opens, click on **Advanced Configuration** and under **Enterprise SSO**, select **Join an Existing SSO System**, and under **Group**, select **Join an existing BizTalk Group**. Once this is done, the last task is to create host instances on the new server for all existing hosts; the same process we just did. As soon as we start the new host instances through the BizTalk Administration console, the new server will immediately begin processing the transactions. Adding new servers to the BizTalk group turns out to be very simple and enables us to quickly stand up with more capacity as needed.

As more servers are added to the group, they simply continue to pull work items off the queues independently. The more servers in the group, the more work it is able to perform. There is no practical limit to the number of servers that can be added to a BizTalk enterprise installation.

Exploring high availability in BizTalk

High Availability (HA) is the ability of an environment to deal with failures or outages without causing service or processing interruptions. For example, failures would be the loss of servers or services within the environment. BizTalk gives us a good degree of high availability inherent in the group concept, but the same is not true for SQL Server, or some of the other services involved in our BizTalk installation. The following are some examples of how to make your BizTalk installation highly available. There is an excellent poster available from Microsoft that details scaling out BizTalk Server that is located at `http://www.microsoft.com/download/en/details.aspx?id=15223`.

High availability in SQL Server

SQL Server can be made highly available with Windows clustering, now known as **Failover Clustering**. Failover clustering has been around in the Windows platform since NT 4 and has been improved with each release. This technology is meant to provide failover for services in Windows environments. The basic idea is that the cluster is a logical construct consisting of two or more nodes (nodes being Windows Servers); clients connect to this logical resource rather than a specific server. Only one node is active at any given time with the others being passive, but they are all capable of being active in the event of an active node failure. This switch over happens automatically and is the core feature of the Failover Cluster. Failover Cluster allows us to run services in the cluster and ensures that an instance of the service will be running on one of the nodes in the cluster. It is really a way to treat multiple servers as a single computing resource that has much higher uptime due to the ability to transfer the service to a passive node. This is exactly how SQL Server is clustered. Because SQL Server ultimately stores data on disk, this storage must be a shareable resource, normally on a SAN. The active node logs transactions and works the same way as SQL Server normally does. When the active node fails, one of the passive nodes becomes active, takes control of the storage resource and starts the SQL service. This failover process is demonstrated in the following screenshot:

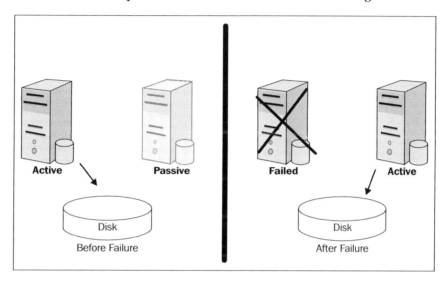

After the failover, clients continue to use the same resource to connect to the new server because the resource is a logical resource that exists in the cluster. In BizTalk Server, this failover is automatic. Running host instances will lose connectivity to the message box database at the time of SQL failure and will automatically attempt to reconnect repeatedly. As the passive node becomes active, these connections will succeed, and BizTalk will continue processing as if nothing had happened. More configurations are covered in the section, *Examining Sample Installation Topologies*, later in this chapter.

Clustering centers around making storage, networks, and the application's cluster resources. All this is done through an MMC Snap-In that is part of the Windows Server Manager and is a feature that can be installed in Windows Server. MSDN contains a great amount of information about configuring failover clustering and specifically clustering SQL Server located at `http://msdn.microsoft.com/en-us/library/ms189134.aspx`. To configure a cluster, this documentation will be the most up-to-date and best resource for you to use. Although it provides extremely advanced features, Failover Cluster is a fairly simple technology to work with and I strongly encourage you to experiment with it. It is critical for getting high availability out of Windows Server solutions.

High availability with clustered BizTalk hosts

The BizTalk runtime can also be clustered much like SQL Server. There is limited applicability for when to do this because the group concept in BizTalk provides a large degree of high availability automatically. This is precisely why persistence and durability are so critical to BizTalk's scalability. Adapters use a transaction to deliver a message to the message box. Once it is there, it is marked for processing in a transaction and eventually marked as "processed" in another transaction. Every part of BizTalk functions in this transactional manner; including orchestration. If an orchestration were running on a server that simply went dark (power failure perhaps), the BizTalk runtime would detect that this orchestration was no longer running and would load it to another server from its last persistence point. This is a pretty sophisticated capability and, like most of BizTalk, is something we just get for free as part of the infrastructure.

There certainly are instances where clustering BizTalk hosts is a good idea. A good example is for adapters that are not safe for parallel operations, such as the FTP and MSMQ adapters when used for the receive operations. Because the FTP protocol does not provide a way to lock a file, there is no way to know that the file is being read by another host instance. If our environment had two BizTalk Servers, each running a host instance with an FTP receive, we could very well have the same file read into BizTalk twice. This would not be a desirable situation.

The solution to this is to allow only one host instance to run these adapters. This is easy to specify in the BizTalk Administration console. To do this, we simply create a new BizTalk host and then assign the adapter **handlers** that we want to run in this host. The handler is the binding between an adapter and a host. Adapters can have many handlers for different hosts and have different ones for send and receive operations. This allows us to have a fine-grained level of control over the partitioning of our solutions in our environment. Creating a host was covered previously and assigning the handlers is fairly easy. In the BizTalk Administration console, expand the **Platform Settings** node and click on **Adapters**. The list of configured adapters is displayed. If you click on a specific adapter, in our case the **FTP** adapter, you are shown which handlers are set up for both send and receive operations. If we double-click **Receive**, or click the **Properties** option in the actions pane, we can change the assigned handler; that is, which host this operation is bound to. In the following screenshot, we can see that the **Receive** handler has been assigned to a host named **SingleInstanceHost**:

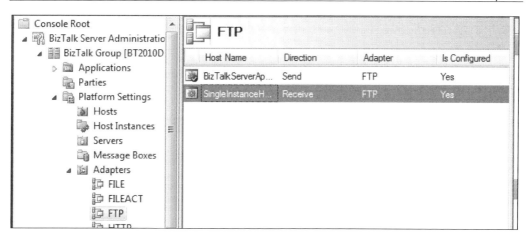

We can also use the **New** operation to create new handlers, so that certain applications use one host for an adapter and others can use another host. In the previous scenario, we could easily create a poor man's cluster by marking the host instance as disabled on all servers except one. This would ensure that the host instance only ran on one server. Unfortunately, however, it would not provide automatic failover. Failover would require an administrator enabling, and then starting, one of the other host instances.

To accomplish real clustering of the host instance, we need to create a cluster resource like before. Clustering a host instance is similar to clustering SQL Server, though it does not require shared storage for data files. This is shown as follows:

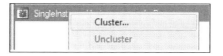

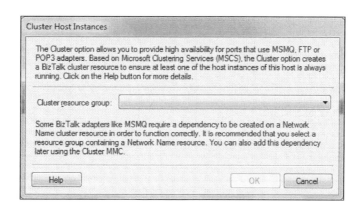

Understanding disaster recovery

Disaster recovery is generally one of the least understood parts of BizTalk Server. This could be because the product does so much for us that we don't give serious thought into how it works, until there is a disaster. The vast majority of BizTalk installations are not set up properly for disaster recovery. This section will outline how disaster recovery works in BizTalk and how to make sure it is working correctly in your environment.

Unlike high availability or scalability, disaster recovery is what we turn to after a true disaster, such as fire, flood, or earthquake. These are the sorts of disasters that wipe out entire data centers. These types of disasters can be extinction-level events for many enterprises. IT has a long history of planning to cope with these sorts of disasters.

BizTalk has several specific aspects that require more planning and discipline for disaster recovery than most applications. Unlike many applications, you cannot use the raw data and transaction log files in BizTalk to perform disaster recovery. In fact, you can't even use the normal SQL disaster recovery plans that most enterprises have already established. Generally, most enterprises create a backup job that simply backs up all the databases on a server. This will not work with BizTalk. This is because BizTalk involves many databases that interact with each other often through DTC. The use of multiple databases is why BizTalk can be so well distributed and can scale so well, but it requires the databases to stay in sync with each other. This is also why mirroring cannot be used in SQL Server, because mirroring cannot ensure transactional integrity between multiple databases. BizTalk is backed up through the concept of **log shipping**.

In SQL Server, a database is represented by two (or more) physical files; a **Master Data File (MDF)** and a **Log Database File (LDF)**. The MDF stores all the data for a database and the LDF is where transactions are actually written before being committed. This allows SQL Server to defer some processing and to hold intermediate results (or on-going transactions) without changing the current state of the database until a transaction is complete. This is critical for providing rollback capability and also for making SQL Server able to handle read operations while simultaneously processing write or update operations. Unless the database is brought offline gracefully, which normally means processing the transactions into the MDF, the state of the database will be unreliable without the LDF. Log shipping involves moving differential snapshots of the transaction log to a new file that can be used to restore the database without taking it offline.

The BizTalk backup job

Backup for the databases in BizTalk is accomplished with transaction log marking and is performed by the only supported method for backing up BizTalk databases: an included SQL job designed specifically for this purpose. This job, Backup BizTalk Server, marks all the databases in a BizTalk group with the same log mark at the same time. It then copies the differential transaction logs as files to a new location. This multi-database synchronized marking and shipping is shown in the following figure:

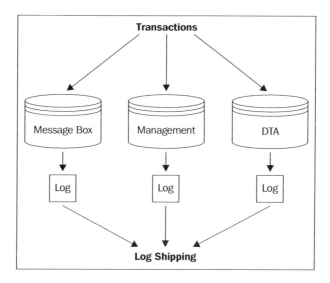

The job runs by default every fifteen minutes; once per day, it creates a full backup of all the databases, the other times it creates only the transaction logs. Unfortunately, for many BizTalk environments, this job is not configured to run by default because it requires a location to move the files to. This location should be a network share or on a SAN. As soon as you set a location in the backup job configuration, you can and should enable this job.

Ultimately, this is also only half the process, the other half is configuring a destination for these transaction logs to be imported into. The destination SQL Server for a restore will use the backup files and the differential logs to recreate the state of the original databases on the new server. This does mean, however, that we could lose some transactional history if we perform a true disaster recovery. The maximum amount of data lost is the time window that the BizTalk backup is scheduled to run in, which defaults to the previously mentioned 15 minutes. This value can be lowered or increased depending on your requirements.

Standing the new BizTalk environment up

The destination SQL Server has several jobs that run on it to help it track and process the backed up files. When time comes to stand this server up as the replacement, you disable the jobs that import log files and run a restore job (these jobs are created for you with scripts that ship with BizTalk). You then run other scripts on the individual BizTalk Servers in your new environment to configure them to point to this new database. If these are completely new servers, you can simply configure them to join an existing group as if you were adding new servers to a group. The scripts are really designed for transferring existing servers to point to the new databases. This is common if you're using backups to restore the BizTalk Servers.

All of this is well documented in the BizTalk documentation and on MSDN, but it is presented here for clarity. There is, however, one final option to provide disaster recovery and that is the stretch-cluster or geo-cluster. In this scenario, a node in the SQL Failover Cluster runs in a geographically remote location. This allows auto-failover without log shipping, but it requires immense bandwidth and is currently not feasible for most organizations. Also, due to the laws of physics, which dictate how fast information can travel over a network, it is not appropriate for very long distances. It also requires SAN technology that supports mirroring, which at this point tends to be proprietary and expensive. If you have this bandwidth available, you could also have nodes of your BizTalk group configured in the redundant location and disaster failover would be almost completely automated. Finally, it is important to keep in mind that there is no job that cleans up the files after the log shipping; they need to be deleted periodically to keep the shared storage location from becoming full.

Examining sample installation topologies

In this section, we will examine several example topologies for BizTalk installations. These are provided only for reference and should be used as a guide for designing your own specific topology.

A single application with a single database

In this configuration, there is a single BizTalk Server and a single SQL Server. This is the most basic configuration BizTalk with which should ever go into production. The BizTalk and SQL Servers should always be separate machines for scalability reasons; although, with the growing capability of Intel-based servers, this is becoming less of an issue. The backup job is configured, but only for moving the files to a fileserver for safe keeping.

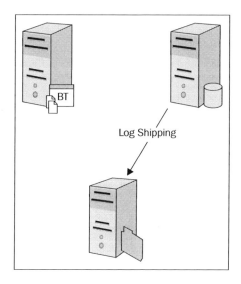

This base configuration will work well for small environments and it is quick to stand up, but it lacks high availability and the disaster recovery is weak, though it is sufficient. Recovering from a disaster will require a lot more effort as no previous preparation has been made. This configuration is suitable for BizTalk Standard Edition.

Dual application with dual database (active/passive)

This common topology leverages two application servers for BizTalk and a Failover Cluster for SQL Server. The passive node provides the ability to seamlessly recover in the event of a server failure on the SQL Tier. It also does not require extra SQL licenses as the secondary node is passive. Log shipping is used again, but not completely implemented, as the standby recovery servers are not actively processing the shipped log files.

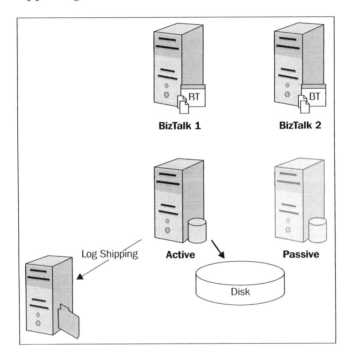

This configuration enables us to afford good high availability. Loss of either BizTalk Server, or a node in the SQL cluster, will have little impact and processing will continue automatically. The primary limitation is that due to the passive nature of the second SQL node, it sits there idle, not processing anything. Combined with the fact that the Max DOP settings are slowing down our primary SQL instance for some operations, this is not an ideal configuration. We are also susceptible to overload on the BizTalk Servers if only one is active, but generally this is acceptable. It is normally better to run at reduced capacity in a failure than not to run at all.

Dual application with dual database (active/active)

This configuration builds on Dual application with dual database (active/passive) by making the second SQL node active. This is done by creating two clustered instances of SQL Servers and designating one to be active on each of the servers. The first instance runs the message box and the second runs all other databases required by BizTalk. In addition to the good high availability we had before, we now gain better throughput and processing as both SQL Servers are processing transactions and the Max DOP setting only affects the message box instance.

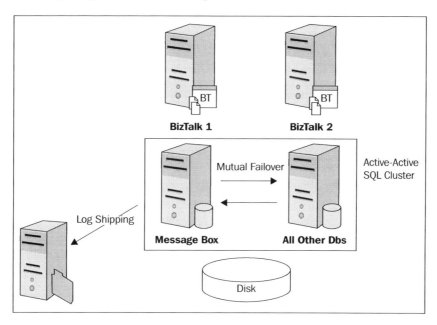

In the event of a SQL node failure, one server simply runs both instances. This is not as bad as it sounds, though it will probably reduce our throughput. There is still little real disaster recovery built into this option as the log shipping of the backup job is not being read into a live failover database.

Sample Enterprise topology

This topology has a passive node added to the active/active SQL cluster and allows high availability failover without performance degradation. There are enough BizTalk Servers to more than handle the load and Enterprise SSO, and a single instance host has been clustered as well. The weak point is clearly the shared disk, but most SANs have some sort of failover capability built into them. In the event of two SQL nodes being lost, both instances would revert to a single node and would likely be affected throughout, but would still continue to process. The topology is shown in the following figure:

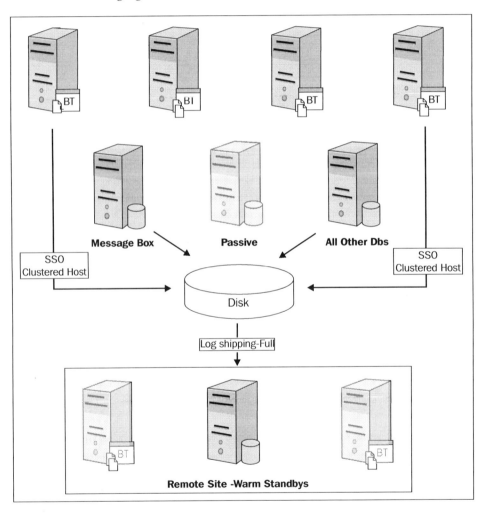

Importantly, this is the first example of a configured disaster recovery capability. Not only will this installation run even with the loss of several servers, it is set up to quickly be failed over to a new remote environment. If practiced well, this can be done in a short amount of time. The log shipping destination SQL Server is continually reading the logs as they arrive, so that the databases are up-to-date in case a failover is needed.

To save costs, the remote sites can simply be warm standbys rather than fully running machines. This is an area where virtualization technology can really help us. In my experience, virtualization does not work as well for BizTalk as for other servers. This is because the BizTalk group concept already encapsulates many similar features. It is also because BizTalk will use many resources, including ports, which can harm some virtualization approaches, most commonly through post exhaustion in high volume scenarios. Also, BizTalk Servers tend not to be greatly underutilized like the typical low utilization target of virtualization. Importantly, having all your servers virtualized on one large physical server is not buying you anything other than a false sense of security. The major risk to most of these components is hardware failure and if you over-virtualize, you may be opening yourself up to much more risk than you realize. The benefit to virtualization with disaster recovery is that we can reduce the costs of keeping a ready and capable disaster recovery environment. It is generally understood that such an environment will not perform as well as our primary environment (unless we are prepared to pay twice the cost), but it is better to have a functioning, but slower, environment for disaster recovery than none at all.

Walking through the BizTalk deployment process

As discussed before, BizTalk applications are built using Visual Studio on a developer's workstation, but when the time comes to deploy to server environments, we move away from Visual Studio towards more capable approaches. One of the most critical requirements of software deployment is knowing that the solution being deployed is exactly what was tested, approved, and intended for deployment. BizTalk provides us with an MSI installer capability for deploying BizTalk applications that helps us meet this requirement. The basic steps in BizTalk application deployment are the following:

1. Compile and deploy solution.
2. Export MSI of application.
3. Import MSI onto target group.
4. Install MSI onto target servers.

The first step simply deploys the application on our workstation or build server. From here we want to export an MSI from BizTalk that can be used for installing the application elsewhere; normally the progression of test, UAT, and production. This MSI package consists of all the assemblies that contain the artifacts and can also contain the bindings that tie these artifacts together, as well as any custom assemblies or pipeline components that our solution requires; even BAM and BRE.

There are two primary ways to export an MSI from a BizTalk Server. One is through the BizTalk Administration console. Simply right-click the application and select **Export | MSI file...**, as shown in the following screenshot:

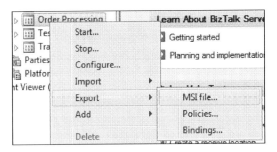

This brings up a wizard that walks us through selecting which artifacts, dependencies, and resources will be included in the MSI. We can even bring in global party information and IIS virtual directories. The other way to accomplish this is with the BTSTASK.exe command line utility. It is useful to walk through the graphical wizard to understand how it works, but in automated builds, we will use BTSTASK. This is covered in detail in *Chapter 11*, in the section *Building and deploying*.

The next step is to import the application to the group. This step will create records in the management database for all the artifacts in the package and thus make BizTalk aware of them so it can use the loading process we discussed in *Chapter 2, Introduction to BizTalk Development*. Just as with export, there is a graphical wizard for importing MSI packages as well. This wizard is very simple and easy to use; it allows us to pick an installation path and also allows us to specify the target bindings. This last part is critical as it allows a single MSI to contain bindings for all the environments we will deploy it to. The only difference in the installation between test, UAT, and production is specifying which target bindings to use.

The final step is to install the MSI, which can also be done in the final step of the import MSI wizard. Unlike the import, which happens once per BizTalk group, the installation must happen for every BizTalk Server in the group. The installation is the step that will physically install the assemblies on the server, create an application in the server's Windows applications list, and register the assemblies in the GAC.

The core concept behind the MSI package installation is that we can use the exact same binary package to install the application on all of our environments. We simply create different bindings (which are added as resources) for each environment. This gives us certainty that a package has not changed between environments and that the core artifacts are the exact same. This can make promotion very controlled and very auditable. Better still, MSI automatically knows if two packages are the same by using metadata in the package, so there is less confusion over file names. If you try to install a package a second time, it will present you with the options to remove or repair the application.

Presenting the best practices for BizTalk configuration

As we have seen, BizTalk is a capable, scalable, and a powerful platform for running messaging and middleware solutions. However, more often than not, it is not configured in a way that maximizes its potential. The default configuration for BizTalk creates only one host and one host instance; this means, by default only one .NET thread pool will be used to run all the processing performed by BizTalk, including receiving, sending, orchestration, tracking, and BAM. Under these circumstances, it is very easy for a BizTalk Server to underperform. Typical signs will include low throughput combined with low CPU utilization. Often, the root cause is thread starvation as different parts of BizTalk are queued, awaiting processing threads.

Separating BizTalk hosts

The basic recommendation for a BizTalk configuration is to create four hosts and host instances for each host on every server. These are generally as follows:

- Receive host
- Send host
- Orchestration host
- Tracking host

You then assign the receive handlers for all adapters to use the receive host and the send handlers to use the send host. All orchestrations should be bound to the orchestration host, which you can mark as the default host. I often name this host, `BizTalkServerApplication`, which is the host BizTalk creates for you by default. The tracking host is now left only to perform tracking (an option in the host configuration), and in this way, tracking will not interfere with processing. Under high loads, BizTalk will defer tracking in favor of transaction processing. This allows the platform to continue servicing requests in overload scenarios as it can catch up on tracking when the overload subsides.

Host-specific settings

These simple changes will vastly increase the processing capability of any BizTalk platform and should be performed on any environment. You may want to expand this host list to include low latency hosts, which are then configured with a lower and more aggressive polling interval that will allow them to process messages faster. The host settings in the BizTalk Administration console control the majority of the throttling and performance settings for BizTalk. Again, these are well covered in the documentation located at `http://msdn.microsoft.com/en-us/library/aa561042(v=BTS.70).aspx` and the default values will work for most scenarios. If you do start to change these settings, it is important you have set up repeatable stress testing that allows you to measure the effects of the change. It is also important that you only change one setting at a time, so as to know what the true effect of the change is.

BizTalk Settings Dashboard, shown in the following screenshot, is the unified settings interface for all BizTalk performance-related settings. Here we can see that on the left there is a section to highlight the settings we want to see: **Group**, **Hosts**, or **Host Instances**. On the right are the settings for the selected entry on the left. As you change selections, the options available also change. The **Hosts** and **Host Instances** settings also contain different tabs for different sets of settings. The settings for **Group** are shown in the following screenshot:

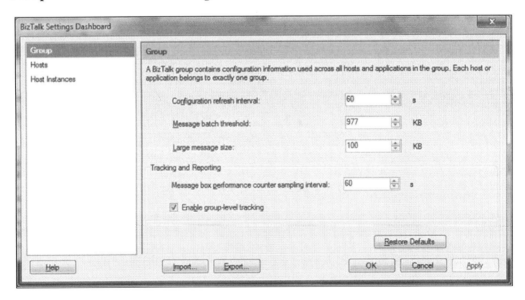

HTTP performance optimization settings

In addition to the platform settings in the BizTalk Administration console, there are a few other critical settings that should be adjusted in BizTalk environments. The most important is the maximum connections allowed for HTTP based send adapters, including SOAP, HTTP, and HTTP-based WCF adapters. These settings are configured in the `BTSNTSvc.exe.config` or `BTSNTSvc64.exe.config` file. This is the .NET configuration file for the BizTalk Server process (the BizTalk runtime). Because .NET respects the HTTP 1.1 specification, this value defaults to two concurrent connections to the same server for a given process. This is appropriate for workstations, but not for servers, and certainly not for BizTalk Servers that are sending HTTP based requests. Without changing this value, the default limit of two will greatly reduce the throughput of any BizTalk solution making use of HTTP based send ports. The configuration change required is shown as follows and all you must do is add this to your existing configuration file:

```
<configuration>
  <system.net>
    <connectionManagement>
      <add address="*" maxconnection="10" />
      <add address="www.novaenterprisesystems.com" maxconnection="25"
/>
    </connectionManagement>
  </system.net>
</configuration>
```

As we can see from this configuration element, we can specify DNS names and specific connection settings for them. We can also use IP addresses for this purpose or the asterisk (*) as a wildcard.

A thorough covering of these and more performance settings is available on MSDN at `http://msdn.microsoft.com/en-us/library/ff629772(v=BTS.70).aspx`.

Troubleshooting BizTalk issues

In addition to letting us configure and administer BizTalk applications, the Administration console also acts as our window into a running solution and environment. When you click on the group node in the navigation pane, the page shown in the information pane is the **Group Hub** page. This page gives us an overview of the current state of the applications in that BizTalk group. The **Group Hub** page contains the following sections:

- **Configuration Over**: This section lists the name of the group, the location of the management database, and also the state of applications, host instance, and adapter handlers, depicted with green, blue, and red icons, respectively. In a production server, all nodes should generally be green. This makes it much easier for everyone to quickly tell that everything is running.

- **Work in Progress / Suspended Items**: This section lists running service instances on the left and suspended service instances on the right. Service instances can be send ports or orchestrations (anything that subscribes to messages). This dashboard allows us to quickly see how many service instances are running or, more importantly, suspended in our group. Well-designed BizTalk solutions should not produce suspended messages. Suspended messages mean something is wrong and needs to be corrected. This aspect of BizTalk is critical, as it is not designed to hold too much information for too long, but to pass the information on and move it out of the message box.

- **Grouped Suspended Service Instances**: This section displays similar information to the previous section, but the results are grouped together by application, error code, service name, or URI.

- **Tracked Service Instances / Tracked Message Events**: This section displays links to queries that will show us any messages or service instances for which tracking has been enabled.

- **EDI Status Reports**: This section displays transaction reports for B2B solutions.

- **EDIINT Status Reports**: This section displays status reports for the transport normally used by B2B solutions.

Clicking any of the links in the previous sections will bring up details about that subject; for all sections other than configuration overview, the details will be new tabs in the information pane displaying a query. The query tool in the Administration console is the same for all this information, but allows us different context depending on what we're examining. An example, **Suspended Service Instances**, is shown as follows:

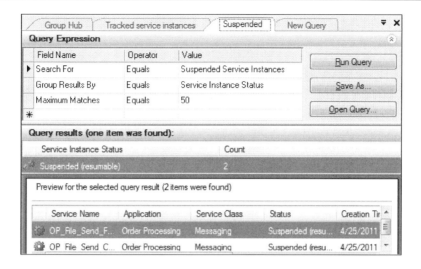

In this screenshot, we can see the query expression that was used to build this specific view. The query tool itself consistently follows the same pattern that allows us to select: **Search For**, **Operator**, and **Value**. Depending on what we select in **Search For**, the options for **Operator** and **Value** change. Mostly, the option for **Operator** is **Equals**, but for time based values like suspension time, greater than and less than operators are available for using with a date and time based value. Other **Search For** options will list specific sets of values to choose from; some allowing free text entry. This tool is used to help us create queries that display views we may specifically be interested in. We can save queries for later use to help in troubleshooting specific issues.

If we right-click on one of the results of the query, a context menu appears; this menu also changes depending upon the context of the selected item. For messages, the menu appears as follows:

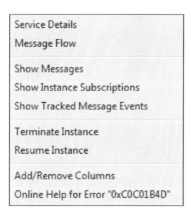

Here we can see details about the message, including its content and context, as well as having the option to resume or terminate the message. For orchestrations in this results pane, an option **Orchestration Debugger** is present that allows us to graphically trace through an orchestration to see which shapes were executed and when. This can be a very useful tool for debugging issues with orchestrations, but should be used sparingly.

This same query tool allows us to view tracked service instances and message events. This capability, formerly done through the Health and Activity Tracking tool (HAT), which has since been largely retired, allows us a window into the past processing activities that have taken place in a BizTalk group. As we discussed previously, BizTalk, by default, internally tracks a great deal of information on what processing has taken place in the DTA database. On any port or orchestration, we can specify what level of detail we want to track down to complete a message- or property-level detail before and after pipeline processing. This can be turned on or off by an administrator in the BizTalk Administration console through the Tracking tab of the configuration for a specific port or orchestration. This capability greatly aids us when we start experiencing issues and can be performed in any environment, including production. That said, there is a cost to overusing tracking information. The DTA (tracking) database will grow extremely large if we track too much detail for too many service instances. This will also impact the throughput of our environment by causing more database writes and general IO operations. As useful as this tracking information is, it should be used sparingly. If we want visibility into processes, Business Activity Monitoring (BAM) is a much better approach than tracking information.

Summary

In this chapter we have learned how BizTalk runs on servers in our environment and the different roles and servers required for building scalable and reliable BizTalk installations. We learned about scalability and high availability, as well as disaster recovery. We also examined sample topologies and their benefits and requirements. We ended with some configuration best practices and a brief introduction to troubleshooting issues in BizTalk Server. This concludes Part I of the book.

Part 2

Part 2

The rest of the book will cover the story of Performance Racing Parts (PRP); a company just beginning to use BizTalk Server. PRP is a distributor of car and motorcycle aftermarket components. The company has been around for thirty years and has experienced rapid growth in the last ten. PRP sells parts via its own call center application and a public facing website. PRP also receives sales through a mail order catalog that is outsourced for processing. PRP recently purchased an inventory management system and is currently assessing how to integrate it into their enterprise which contains a CRM system. Eventually all purchase orders must be sent to the new inventory management system for processing. As a stop gap, orders today are entered a second time manually. The company assessed integration and middleware products and has decided to try out BizTalk Server. You have been tasked with implementing their solutions.

5
Basic Messaging Solution

This chapter will walk through the first BizTalk solutions for Performance Racing Parts (PRP). These solutions will be messaging only, but leverage useful and expressive designs.

Pass thru messaging scenario

The IT Director at PRP decides that a quick and simple project with low risk is the best path forward with BizTalk. You review the project backlogs and find a request by the finance department to consolidate reports from the different ordering systems in the enterprise to a single file share. Currently, this is a manual job that often loses reports and takes time from IT staff to copy files; aspects that make it disliked by IT as well as finance. Initially, the idea was to write scheduled task scripts to copy the files, but you decide that BizTalk can do this as well. Further, this process can change and may use SharePoint or FTP in the future, so the company would prefer a configuration approach over a code-based approach.

You must create a simple BizTalk solution that will receive binary files from two directories and copy them to a single destination. One directory is for call center order reports; the other is for website order reports. As this project is a pass thru messaging solution it will only involve using the BizTalk Administration Console:

1. Open the BizTalk Server Administration Console (**Start** | **Programs** | **Microsoft BizTalk Server 2010** | **BizTalk Server Administration Console**).

2. Expand the **BizTalk Group** node.

3.   Right-click the **Applications** node and select **New | Application...**.

4.   Name the application **Order Processing**.

5.   Expand the new **Order Processing** application, right-click the **Receive Ports** node, and select **New | One-way Receive Port...**. Name this new port **OP_Receive_Reports** and click **OK** when done. The naming convention follows the basic pattern [Application]_[Direction]_[Noun]. This will help us organize the artifacts in this solution over time. More information is provided in the appendix under *Naming Conventions*.

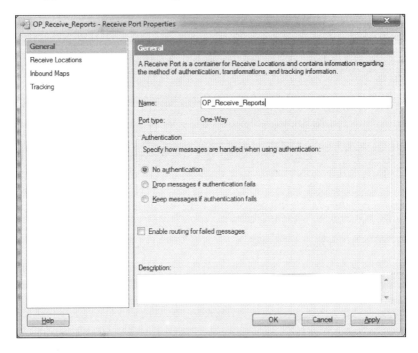

6.   Click the **Receive Locations** item on the left side of the **Receive Port Properties** dialog that you just created and click **New...** on the right side. Name this receive port **OP_File_Receive_Reports_CallCenter** and select **File** as the transport type.

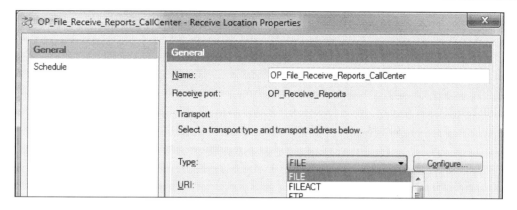

7. Be sure not to change the **Receive Pipeline**. It should remain the default **PassThruReceive**.

8. Click on the **Configure** button and set this new location to point to the pickup folder C:\BizTalk\PRP\CallCenterReportDrop with a File mask of *.* as shown in the following screenshot:

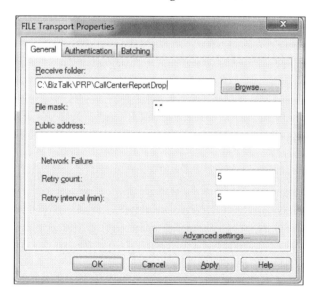

9. Click **OK** to close each of the dialogs.

We now need to create a send port that will send the files to our destination location, which is very similar to the receive location we just set up.

1. Right-click **Send Ports** in the Administration Console and select **New | Static One-way Send Port**.

2. Name this send port **OP_File_Send_Reports** and select **FILE** as the **Type**. Click on the **Configure** button and set the transport properties so that the destination folder is `C:\BizTalk\PRP\SendReports` and the file name is `%SourceFileName%;` the port should resemble the following screenshot:

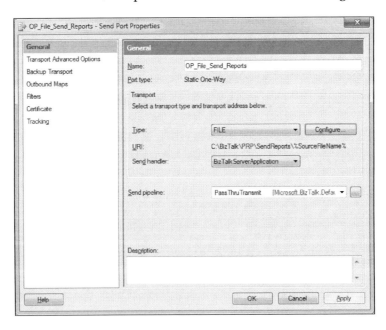

3. Now we must connect our **Receive Port** to our **Send Port**. This is done via **Subscription** and the simplest form of subscription is the **Send Port Filter**. This type of filter, as the name suggests, is configured on the send port itself.

On the left side of the **Send Port Properties** dialog click on the **Filters** node. Then click on the **Property** column to select a property to filter by. You |will notice there are many properties, but we are only interested in the **BTS.ReceivePortName** property. Keep the default operator of == and type in the **Value** of **OP_Receive_Reports**. This is the name of the receive port we created before and will be used to connect the two ports together.

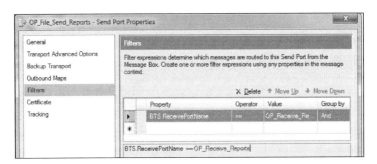

4. Click **OK** to close the send port configuration dialog.

5. Finally, we need to start these ports in order for messages to flow through. The easiest way to do this is to right-click the **Order Processing** application in the Administration Console and select **Start**.

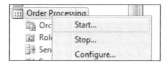

6. Accept the default properties in the next dialog and click **Start**.

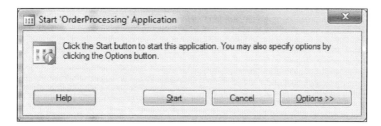

You should now be able to drop any file in the receive location (`C:\BizTalk\PRP\CallCenterReportDrop`) and it will be routed to the send location (`C:\BizTalk\PRP\SendReports`).

If this does not immediately work, the most likely cause is that the user account under which the BizTalk host instance is running does not have permission to either receive or send paths. If you have not already done so, grant this user **Full Control** to `C:\BizTalk\PRP`.

The File Receive adapter will need a specific permission that is part of the **Modify** set of rights, but is not granted by default; this is the **Delete Sub Folders and Files** option, which can be granted in the **Advanced** tab of Windows Explorer. It is simply often easier to grant **Full Control**.

The second most common cause will be if the subscription is not entered correctly. This is where typos can cause some headaches in BizTalk. To see if the message has suspended you can refer to *Chapter 4, Operating BizTalk*.

Examining the solution

Let's review exactly what's happening at this point in this solution. This is explored in detail in *Chapter 2, Introduction to BizTalk Development*, but we'll summarize here for convenience:

1. Message (File) is received as raw binary by file adapter.
2. Message is submitted to message box.
3. A subscription matched for send port **OP_File_Send_Reports** on messages from received port named **OP_Receive_Reports**.
4. The subscription is filled (that is, work item queued) for send port **OP_Receive_Reports** which retrieves the work item and uses the file adapter to write out to the file system as raw binary.

At first glance, this may seem like it was a lot of steps, but we didn't write any code or have to do any extra work to get reliability, locking (concurrency), persistence, high availability/scalability, and tracking. These are all features that come as part of the BizTalk platform and did not require custom code.

Now let's see how much more work it is to add another receive location to handle the web sales reports.

Adding a second receive location

Right-click **Receive Locations** in the BizTalk Administration Console (under the **OrderProcessing** application) and select **New | One-way Receive Location.**

1. You will be presented with a list of **Receive Ports** to attach this receive location to (this is required, as there can be no orphan receive locations). Select the only Port in the list **OP_Receive_Reports** and click **OK**.

2. In the **Location Details** dialog that pops up, enter the name **OP_File_Receive_WebSiteReports**. Configure the receive location transport type to **FILE** to read files from `C:\BizTalk\PRP\WebSiteReportDrop` much like we did before. Use the same mask, ***.***, as before and be sure to leave the **PassThruReceive** pipeline.

3. When you click **OK** you will see the list of receive locations in the Administration Console. You will notice that the new location is *disabled* so you must *enable* it (which can be done by right-clicking the location and selecting **Enable**).

You should now be able to drop files in either location and they will be moved to the destination folder.

You may be asking yourself 'Why all this just to move some files, why not use a script'? at this point. That's a good question, so let's address some of the motivations. Suppose you wanted to change from file shares to FTP sites. All you would do is change the transport type in your send port or receive locations. Perhaps you want the reports to be sent to a SharePoint document library or maybe an iSeries server. This is also not a problem; these are just other adapters (equating to transport types). Not even routing (that is, filtering) changes pose a problem and are in fact activities that can be performed by operations staff if need be. This decouples the creator of the application from the operator of that application.

Transport properties

At this point, it is worth exploring some of the other advantages we have over scripting or other common solutions to this trivial example. First let's look at some of the `Send Port Properties`; do this by right-clicking (or double-clicking) the send port **OP_File_Send_Reports**. There is a screenshot of these properties after the next paragraph.

We can see under the **Transport Advanced Options** that we can set the **Retry Count**, **Interval**, and other settings. Importantly, we also see a setting for a **Service Window**. This is a setting that will control when BizTalk will send messages on this port. Outside of the service window, messages will simply queue up in the message box to be delivered when the service window is reached. This allows us to address another aspect of coupling: time. Time is perhaps one of the most insidious forms of coupling. It is usually not a thought in our solution development. Our test environments and workstations are always running when we are using them. Normally this sort of dependency rears its head in production or late in testing. Even in this trivial example we are able to resolve this without changing our solution or writing any code.

Sending applications drops the files in the receive locations, and they do not care that the destination is down. They do not need to care because they are decoupled from the process.

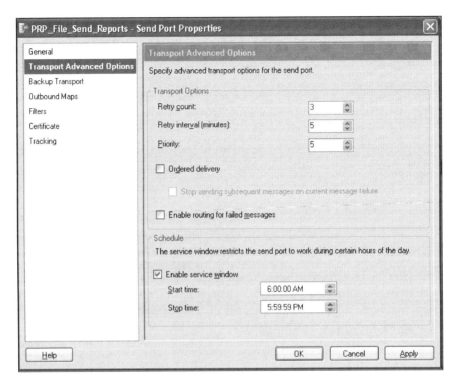

We can also specify a backup transport to use in the event of failure of the primary transport. This backup transport will become active after the primary transport fails (that is, its retry count has been exceeded) and it has its own retry count and service window settings. We are completely free to use a different transport type altogether such as FTP. This feature can be used to provide automatic failover or even instant failover by setting the retry count on the primary transport to zero.

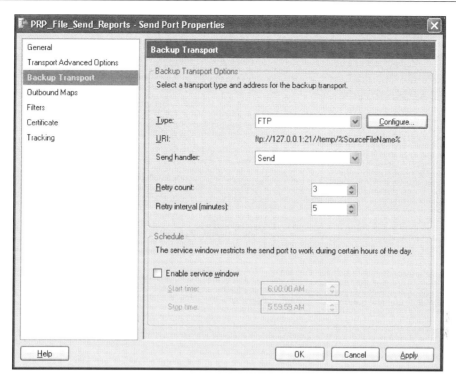

The receive location has similar settings that can be used to provide service windows as well. In the receive context, a service window simply stops the receive location from trying to pick up messages. Providing these capabilities in a script would be much more difficult. You would quickly exceed the amount of time we spent creating this solution and it would still not be as robust.

Although this lesson is intentionally trivial it should be pretty clear how flexible BizTalk can make even a simple solution. Flexibility, after all, is one of the primary motivations for using BizTalk. Now let's take a quick look at exactly how this solution works in detail.

Basic subscriptions

Click the **BizTalk Group** node in the Administration Console (above **Applications**). You will see a **Group Hub** tab that gives you an overview of the group and a tab called **New Query**. Click on the **New Query** tab. This allows us to query the BizTalk server for a variety of information; in this case we will select **Subscriptions**.

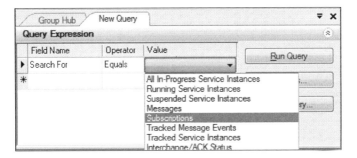

We can then further refine our search by using the **Subscription Type** field and selecting the value **Activation Subscription**. **Activation subscriptions** are subscriptions that are used to initiate a service. Services can be either orchestrations or send ports. This is an important distinction because it shows that there is a marked difference between receiving and doing (read sending) in BizTalk. The other subscription type option, **Instance Subscription**, is for service instances that are already active and awaiting another message.

By clicking the **Run Query** button, we can see the list of results returned. At the top of this list will be our most recently added subscriptions: the send port **OP_File_Send_Reports** is the one we are interested in. From returned list itself we can see some summary information about the subscriptions.

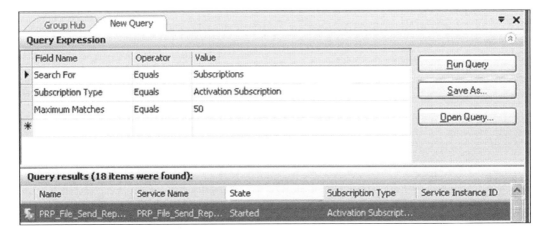

Right-clicking anywhere in the results allows us to see our command options: **Subscription Details** (the default double-click handler) and **Add/Remove Columns**, which is self-explanatory. This behavior is typical of the BizTalk Administration Console query tool and the columns to be added are unique to the specific view of the query (driven by the **Search For** criteria).

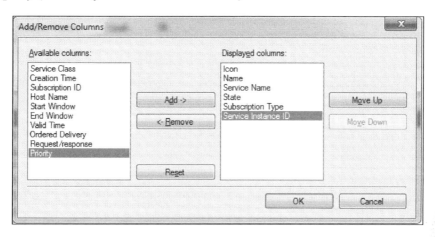

This allows operators, administrators, and developers to create unique views into BizTalk applications to facilitate their respective roles. These queries can then be saved as `.btq` files by right-clicking the tab at the top of the query and sorted by clicking any column header. More about the query tool in the BizTalk Administration console was covered in *Troubleshooting BizTalk issues* in *Chapter 4, Operating BizTalk*. Double-clicking the **OP_File_Send_Reports** entry will allow us to see its details.

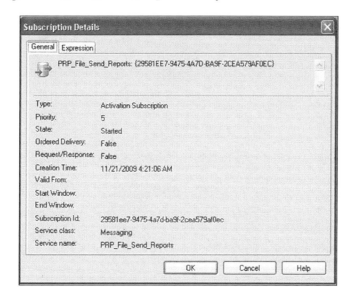

The **Expression** tab shows us the details of the subscription itself and here we can see the subscription that we entered earlier (plus some bits that BizTalk has put in for us).

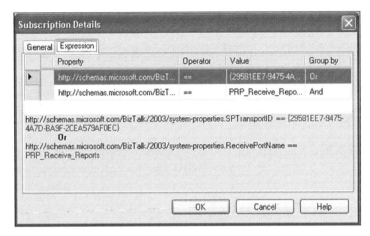

You will notice that these subscription details are read only, but this is a very useful place to find why messages aren't routing the way you expect. You would be surprised how easy it is to type a subscription incorrectly.

If we were to go back to our send port OP_File_Send_Reports and stop it, then run the subscriptions query again, we would see its state listed as **Stopped** under the **General** tab that we looked at in the previous screenshot. If we were to go unenlist that send port, the subscription would disappear from the **Activation Subscriptions** query altogether. This should help to drive home the point that BizTalk operates on a publish-subscribe model that is highly expressive. Subscriptions are only present when they are enlisted and only active when started. If you have a send port, but it is not enlisted, the messaging engine doesn't actually know it exists. When ports are stopped (or enlisted, but not started) the messaging engine will see them and will queue messages for them. This is similar to the service window concept we saw before in the port configurations.

Simple XML messaging with maps

After the success of the report collecting solution, the team decides it's time to develop a real solution with BizTalk. The call center application team have already developed an XML export for purchase orders that occurs in real time. They decided to write out an XML file containing the purchase order when it is saved to their database. These files need to get to the fulfillment system, which came with a purchase order import capability that uses XML files. The two file formats do not, however, match.

The immediate goal of this project is to receive purchase orders from the call center application, transform them to the format required by the fulfillment system, and then deliver them to the fulfillment system. Recall from the section on *Solution structure* in *Chapter 2, Introduction to BizTalk Development*, that we will need two external formats and one canonical format to accomplish this. The canonical format is used to decouple the solution we are building. Our intention is to build this as the base for what will be an order messaging bus for the enterprise. This is clearly going to be only the first of several integrations connecting purchase orders to the fulfillment system, so the team decides to add an additional element to the canonical schema: `SalesChannel`—to identify which line of business the purchase order came from.

After reading about *Visual Studio Solution Structure* in *Chapter 2, Introduction to BizTalk Development*, you decide to download a blank solution template to use for the new project. You are also given the XSD format that the fulfillment system requires for import. Importantly in following best practices and solution structures described earlier you already know the development tasks are as follows:

1. Create a Visual Studio solution (download from `http://biztalk2010patterns.com/documents/order-processing/purchaseorder.zip`).

2. Import the fulfillment schema (`http://biztalk2010patterns.com/documents/order-processing/Schemas/SalesOrder.xsd`) into the external schemas project.

3. Generate an external schema for the call center application format (`http://biztalk2010patterns.com/documents/order-processing/messages/PoPurchaseOrderExport.xml`).

4. Create a canonical schema for a purchase order.

5. Create maps from call center to canonical and canonical to fulfillment formats.

6. Create ports and locations to tie the integration together.

Creating schemas

Once the solution is open use the Solution Explorer to navigate to the **External Schemas** project and right-click the project icon selecting **Add | Existing Item**.

Next, navigate to the `SalesOrder.xsd` that you downloaded and saved. Click **Add** and the schema will now be part of the **ExternalSchemas** project.

When talking to the lead of the call center development team, you learn that they are writing out their XML using a class serializer and do not actually have a schema, but can provide sample XML documents. Fortunately, BizTalk provides a facility to generate XSD Schemas from well-formed XML documents. You receive one of these sample XML documents (`PoPurchaseOrderExport.xml`) and save it to the `UnitTests\TestData\External` folder for future reference. We want this artifact to exist in the solution for later use both in testing and sharing the artifact with other developers:

1. To add it to your solution right-click the **External** data folder and **Add | Existing Item** (being sure to change the file type mask to **All Files (*.*)** in the lower right side.

2. In Visual Studio Solution Explorer again right-click the **External Schemas** project and select **Add**, but this time select **Generated Items**. From the dialog (as shown in the following screenshot) select **Generate Schemas** and click **Add**.

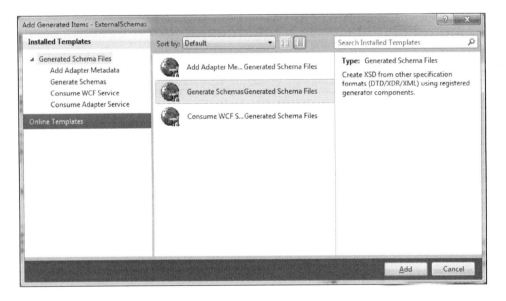

The next dialog that appears allows you to select an input document type and instance. For our project, we will use **Well-Formed XML** and navigate to the PoPurchaseOrderExport.xml that we were provided with by the call center development team (this should be in UnitTests\TestData\External).

 The first time you run the **Well-Formed XML** option of the **Add Generated Items** wizard, you will be shown a message stating that the component has not been installed. This message shows you the path to a visual basic script (.vbs) file that you must execute before this wizard will work.

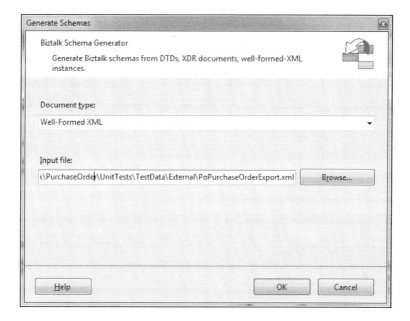

You now have the schemas that you will receive purchase orders in and translate them to. There are two primary options facing you as you move forward: directly map from the call center format to the fulfillment format or create a canonical schema that will form the basis for all purchase order integrations at PRP. Despite the fact that the upfront cost is marginally higher to create the canonical format you decide that it is a better approach to follow. Create the canonical schema as follows:

1. In Visual Studio Explorer right-click **Internal Schemas** and select **Add | New Item**. In the dialog that follows select **Schema** and enter the name **PurchaseOrder.xsd**.

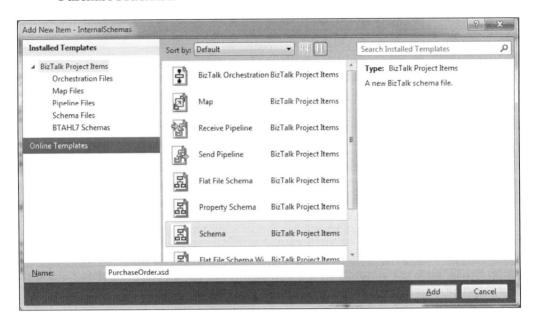

This schema will be the stable internal representation of the concept of a **Purchase Order** in our BizTalk solution. Like many of the wizards and tools in BizTalk, you have already been helped along considerably, but there are some settings that are a good idea to change. For instance, the **Target Namespace** in the schema has been set as **http://PRP.PurchaseOrder.InternalSchemas.PurchaseOrder**. Now there is nothing inherently wrong with this namespace, but in following popular convention we should rename it to **http://performanceracingparts.com/schemas/PurchaseOrder/internal/2011-050** so it will be more useful.

The first part of the name is the company's name; even if this is not a URL we own, it is still their name. The schemas part defines that this is a message contract rather than an interface contract (which would be used for defining web services and operations). **Purchase Order** is the functional area of the enterprise that this schema will serve. Were we building the invoice integrations they would use invoice instead. The next part defines that this is an internal schema that is not meant to be used by anyone or anything outside of BizTalk. This is important because even if another system in the enterprise wants a schema to use they should always use an external schema and map at the port level. This really is a best practice in BizTalk and saves a lot of pain over the lifetime of an integration solution. The last part is also significant. The schema is given a date to make versioning easier. As explained in *Chapter 2, Introduction to BizTalk Development*, a versioning strategy is critical to the long term success of any integration or service orientation initiative. You may also choose to use a version number.

With our schema's framework in place we complete the schema by performing the following steps:

1. Rename the root element from **Root** to **PurchaseOrder**.
2. Right-click the **PurchaseOrder** record and add a child field element called **Number**.
3. Add a child element named **Date** and set its **Data Type** (under **General** in the **Properties** window) to **xs:date** as shown in the following screenshot. This will restrict the valid values of this element to the **xs:date** data type, which also checks for validity of the date itself rather than just the format.

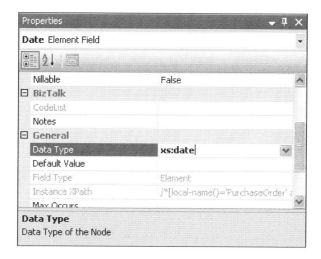

4. Create a **Total** node and set its **Derived By** property to **Restriction** and **Base Data Type** to **xs:decimal**. This will allow us to further restrict this type into meeting our business requirements, namely that a purchase order cannot be for a negative amount. We set the **MinFacet Value** to **0** (zero) and keep the default **MinFacet Type** as **Inclusive**.

5. Create a **SalesChannel** element and set **Derived By** to **Restriction**. This time go to the **Enumeration** section of the **Restriction** group of the properties and enter the values: **Call Center, Website, Mail Order, Field Sale, Third Party**.

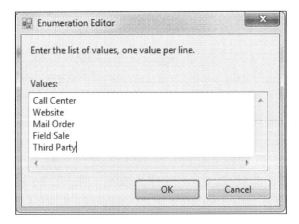

6. Create child records for **ShipTo** and **BillTo**, but leave them empty for now.

7. **BillTo** and **ShipTo** will contain the same data and rather than defining them twice (as is quite common) we will define a common type to be used in both.

This contact type will define a name, phone number, and address. Note that when you add child nodes in a schema there are a variety of options and they are context sensitive. For now, we are concerned only with **Elements** and **Records**. Right-click the Schema folder icon above **PurchaseOrder** and select **Insert Schema Node | Child Record**. Rename the **Record** to **Address** and add to it **Street**, **City**, **State**, and **PostalCode** child elements.

8. Click on the **Address** node and set the **Data Structure Type** property to **AddressType**. This effectively makes the data structure we just defined a reusable type that we can use throughout our schema. This is shown in the following screenshot:

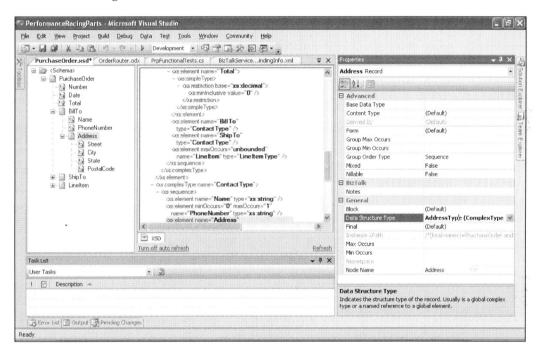

9. Delete the **Address** record. Don't worry, the **AddressType** we defined will still be in the schema.

10. Right-click the **Schema** folder icon above **PurchaseOrder** and select **Insert Schema Node | Child Record**. Rename the **Record** to **Contact** and add to it **Name** and **PhoneNumber** child elements.

11. Add a child record to **Contact** called **Address** and set its **Data Structure Type** to **AddressType (Complex Type)**. Instantly you will see that it contains the fields and types we defined earlier.

12. Change the **Data Structure Type** of the **Contact** record to **ContactType**.

13. Delete the **Contact** record.

14. Set the **Data Structure Type** of **BillTo** and **ShipTo** to **ContactType**.

15. Create a child record of **PurchaseOrder** and call it **LineItem** (be sure to set its **Max Occurs** property to **unbounded** (*) so that more than one **LineItem** is allowed).

16. Add to **LineItem**: **CatalogNumber**, **Quantity**, **UnitCost**, and **Description** elements.

17. Change **Quantity** to be **Data Type** to **xs:positiveInteger** (this is not **Base Data Type**).

18. Change **UnitCost** to be a restriction of **xs:decimal** with **0** as the **MinFacet Value** (like we did for **Total**).

This schema looks pretty complete and everyone is pleased that you have defined the canonical format of what a Purchase Order is to Performance Racing Parts.

Creating maps

The solution now requires two final artifacts: a map from **PoPurchaseOrderExport** to the canonical **PurchaseOrder** and one from **PurchaseOrder** to **SalesOrder**. BizTalk provides a robust tool for translating formats via a graphical interface in the BizTalk mapper. The mapper has three main panes that are used to create a map: a source on the left that is the input format, a destination on the right that is the output format, and a canvas in the middle used to connect the two and perform translations. More information about the mapper can be found at: `http://msdn.microsoft.com/en-us/library/aa547076(BTS.70).aspx`.

Following best practices and conventions, these maps will be called **Ext_ PoPurchaseOrderExport_To_PurchaseOrder** and **Int_PurchaseOrder_ To_SalesOrder**. The pattern of this name is [Int/Ext]_[SourceSchema]_To _[DestinationSchema]. This naming makes it easy to quickly see what this map is meant to accomplish.

Creating a map from external PoPurchaseOrder to PurchaseOrder

Right-click the **Maps** project in Solution Explorer to add the first of these maps (via **Add | New Item**) and name the map **Ext_PoPurchaseOrderExport_To_ PurchaseOrder.btm**.

After clicking **Add** you will see a blank mapping canvas that allows you to select the source schemas (on the left) and destination schemas (on the right) for the map. The center grid is the mapping canvas itself.

Clicking the link on the left brings up the Schema browser. Expand the **Maps** project and the **References** node, then expand **External Schemas** and the **Schemas** node. Select the **PRP.OrderProcessing.ExternalSchemas.PoPurchaseOrderExport** schema.

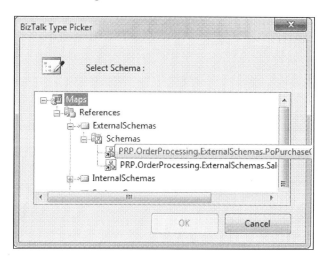

For the destination schema, select **PRP.OrderProcessing.InternalSchemas. PurchaseOrder**.

By clicking on the root node of either schema, we can select **Expand Tree Node** and easily see our entire schema.

Click the node **PurchaseOrderNumber** on the left-hand side, under **PoPurchaseOrder** and drag it to the **Number** node under **PurchaseOrder** on the right. Now drag **PurchaseOrderDate** on the right to **Date** on the left.

If you click and drag the **Item** record from the left to the **LineItem** record on the right, a context menu appears asking how you would like to link the records and their children. Click **Link by Name** and the records will automatically link by name match. The other option, **Link by Structure**, is simply by order of the nodes (**Direct** is a normal link and **Mass Copy** simply drops a Functoid of the same name between the nodes). Now map **ItemNumber** to **CatalogNumber** and **Amount** to **UnitCost** for the line item.

Your map will look something similar to the following screenshot:

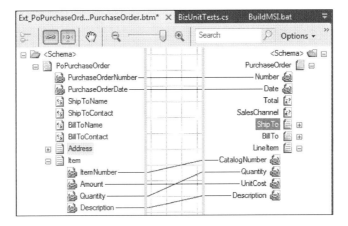

You notice that there is no order total on the input schema **PoPurchaseOrder**. It has already been decided that order total is a meaningful piece of information so it must be added. We will use two Functoids to provide this information:

1. Open the **Mathematical Functoids** section of the tool box and drag a **[X] Multiplication Functoid** onto the map canvas between **Item** and **LineItem**.

2. Connect the **Amount** and **Quantity** elements from the **PoPurchaseOrder** (on the left) to the **Multiplication Functoid**. This will give us an item total.

3. Expand the **Cumulative Functoids** part of the tool box and drag a **[∑] Cumulative Sum Functoid** onto the map to the right of the multiplication one.

4. Click and hold on the **Multiplication Functoid** and drag to the **Cumulative Sum Functoid**, this tells the map to create a sum of the input value.

5. Click and hold on the **Cumulative Sum** and drag to the **Total** element of the **PurchaseOrder** (right-hand side) schema.

Click around the elements you have already mapped and notice how the mapper highlights complete paths through the map for any node. Clicking **Amount** on the left highlights which elements this node maps to on the right, in this case there are two. Clicking **Total** on the right highlights the source nodes and Functoids used to calculate this value. These are some of the improvements in BizTalk 2010 that make mapping more expressive and easier to work with on large or complex maps.

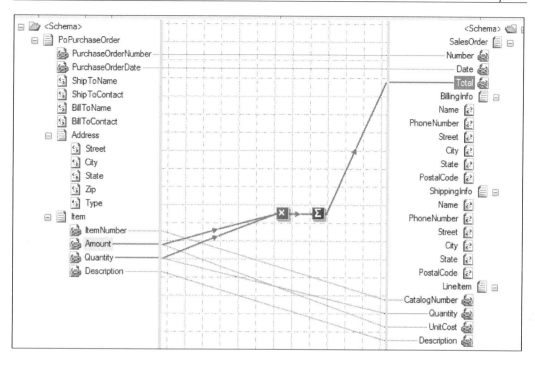

We are yet to map the address elements and this presents a problem for us because if we look at the example XML message we can see that the address type (**Billing** or **Shipping**) is expressed in the **Address** element itself.

```
<BillToContact >Some Contact</BillToContact>
<Address >
  <Street>123 Fake St</Street>
  <City>Whatever City</City>
  <State>MD</State>
  <Zip>60606</Zip>
  <Type>Billing</Type>
</Address>
<Address >
  <Street>401 N Michigan Ave</Street>
  <City>Chicago</City>
  <State>IL</State>
  <Zip>60611</Zip>
  <Type>Shipping</Type>
</Address>
```

To get around this, we will use some logical Functiods, but to keep our map clean and easy to understand we will do this on a new page. Right-click the ribbon at the bottom of the map (on or near the **Page 1** tab) and click **Add Page**.

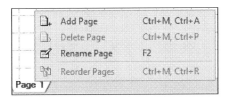

After the page is added, right-click it again and click **Rename Page** and change it to **Shipping**. Naming pages helps us keep the intent of that part of the map clear.

Map the **ShipToName**, **ShipToContact**, **Street**, **City**, **State**, and **Zip** nodes from the left schema to the appropriate children of the **ShipTo** node on the right. Then drag an **[=] Equal Functoid** from the **Logical Functoids** group onto the upper center of the canvas.

This will be used to control node output. The output of any **Logical Functiod** can be connected to a node on the destination schema to control if that node will be output or not. Conditions that evaluate to true output the node, while those that are false suppress output generation for that node.

Drag the **Type** node under **Address** on the left to the **[=] Equal Functiod** then double-click the Functoid to bring up the properties window. The second row of the configuration warns us that it is incomplete, but allows us to create a new constant value input simply by clicking the **Value** cell and typing in a value; use the value **Shipping**. We can see in the right of this dialog that the Functoid input types are a schema element and a constant value; mouse over either of these icons to see more information. This dialog is also where we can add labels and comments to help document our maps better.

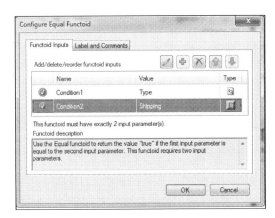

Now connect the output of the **[=] Equal Functoid** to the **ShipTo** node on the right. Your map will now look similar to the following screenshot:

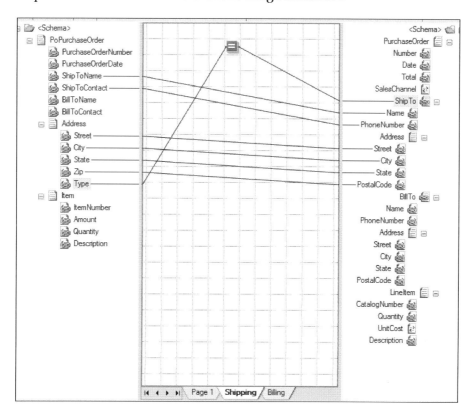

Add a new page named **Billing** and repeat the process you carried out for **Shipping**, using the value **Billing** in the **Equals Functoid**.

Finally, you are left with only **SalesChannel** which is not filled in. For this, we will simply force a value of **Call Center** because we only receive purchase orders in this external format from the call center application. To do this, we'll use the **String Concatenate Functoid** with a single constant input value of **Call Center**. To add this constant value, simply double-click the **String Concatenate Functoid** then type in the value in the **Value** cell. The **String Concatenate Functoid** works even with only one input and is a good way to insert constant values (you can also use the **Value Mapping Functoid** and set the first parameter to **true** and the second to **Call Center**.

When working this way in maps, it is useful to see details about the schema you are mapping to; fortunately the mapper also facilitates this. If you click the **SalesChannel** node on the right (in the **PurchaseOrder** schema) you can see the details of the node as we defined it earlier. All the details are read-only, which makes sense. You can also click **Enumeration** under the **Restriction** properties to view the list of possible values and even copy the values out if they are more complex or, like me, you don't trust yourself to retype something exactly.

Testing the map

Visual Studio will also make it easier for us to test maps. If you right-click the map in Solution Explorer, you will see a command to do this. Since we have not defined an input instance, Visual Studio will simply generate one, but we already have one we'd like to use, so let's do that. Click the map in the Solution Explorer and look at the **Properties** at the bottom (by default). In the properties window you can specify a **TestMap Input Instance**; select the sample XML file we generated our external schema from (`PoPurchaseOrderExport.xl`).

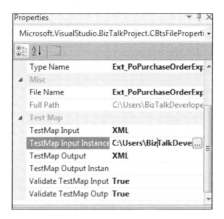

We will need to build the solution in order to test the map, you will receive an error otherwise, stating that the artifacts have not been built. Now right-click the map again and click **Test Map**.

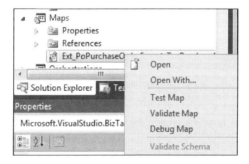

The output window in Visual Studio will show the results of the map test and allow us to see the output:

```
Invoking component...
TestMap used the following file: <file:///C:\Users\BizTalkDeverloper\
Documents\Visual Studio 2010\Projects\BizTalkPatterns\PurchaseOrder\
UnitTests\TestData\External\PoPurchaseOrderExport.xml> as input to the
map.
Test Map success for map file C:\Users\BizTalkDeverloper\Documents\
Visual Studio 2010\Projects\BizTalkPatterns\PurchaseOrder\Maps\Ext_
PoPurchaseOrderExport_To_PurchaseOrder.btm. The output is stored in
the following file: <file:///C:\Users\BizTalkDeverloper\AppData\Local\
Temp\_MapData\Maps\Ext_PoPurchaseOrderExport_To_PurchaseOrder_output.
xml>
Component invocation succeeded.
```

By holding the *Ctrl* key and left clicking the link on the bottom right of the output window, we can see the results of the mapping and ensure that everything looks the way we had planned. We view this XML in an Internet Explorer window, but if we right-click anywhere in that window we can select **View Source** to get to the raw XML. It is useful at this time to save this output to our **UnitTests** project under the `TestData\Internal` folder as `PurchaseOrder.xml`. Be sure to right-click that `Internal` data folder and **Add** | **Existing Item** and change the file type mask to **All Files (*.*)** to ensure the artifact is packaged with the code and does not just exist on your machine. This will be useful when we need to test other maps that use this format and also to compare expected results with actual files when we get to automated testing later on.

Creating a map from canonical PurchaseOrder to SalesOrder

1. Right-click the **Maps** project in Solution Explorer to add the first of these maps (via **Add** | **New Item**) and name the map **Int_PurchaseOrder_To_ SalesOrder.btm**.

2. On the **Source Schema** (left) navigate to **References** | **InternalSchemas** | **Schemas** | **PRP.PurchaseOrder.InternalSchemas.PurchaseOrder**.

3. On the right side click the **Open Destination Schema** and navigate to **References** | **ExternalSchemas** | **Schemas** | **PRP.PurchaseOrder. ExternalSchemas.SalesOrder**.

The names in these schemas very closely match, so map each of the nodes and the schemas. Note that they are both content complete so we don't need any Functoids this time. If you right-click the **Number** node on the left and click **Indicate Matches** you will see that the mapper suggests a mapping, that in this case is correct. Microsoft incorporated some of the search technology from Bing into the mapper to assist this and it can be helpful in complex schemas.

Your map should look similar to the following screenshot:

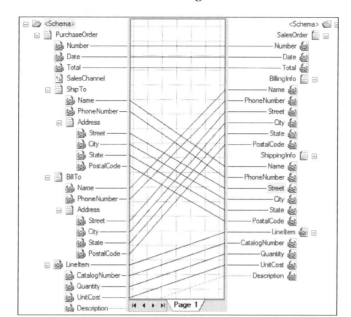

To test this map we can use the `PurchaseOrder.xml` file we saved to our `UnitTests\TestData\Internal` folder earlier. Testing maps this way is a very convenient and simple way to make sure nothing has been missed. This sort of testing leverages the rules of XSD to validate both the input and output documents. If you are not leveraging these tools (and not leveraging XSD schema validation) then you are not using BizTalk to its full potential.

The artifacts for our solution are now created. We can build and deploy the solution from the build menu. It is important to note here that one should always use the **Deploy Solution** menu option, not the individual project's **Deploy** option. Visual Studio is managing dependencies for us and already knows the appropriate build order. It is best to trust it to do its work.

Wiring up the solution

After deploying the solution from Visual Studio, open the BizTalk Administration Console and go to the **Order Processing** application. The project template is set to restart the BizTalk host instances after deployment of the **Maps** project (which is last in the Visual Studio build order), so there is no need to do this manually. Forgetting to do this will make your new changes appear not to be deployed at runtime (there will be an assembly load failure, as discussed in *Chapter 2, Introduction to BizTalk Development*).

If you still have the console open from before, you will have to refresh it to see the new artifacts that were deployed. This can be done by right-clicking anywhere in the navigation pane and selecting **Refresh**. Here we can see how the Administration Console organizes the artifacts in an application in an easy to manage structure. Importantly it doesn't matter which projects, read which assemblies, these artifacts are in, they all deploy to this application for this solution. As explained in the section on solution structure, we are gaining a lot of flexibility from this architecture.

We now have to create ports for our new solution; this will be done from within the BizTalk Administration Console.

Creating the receive port

Create a one-way receive port called **OP_Receive_PurchaseOrders** with a receive location called **OP_File_Receive_CallCenter_PurchaseOrders**. These names are meant to link the one-to-many relationship of **Ports** to **Locations**. We want to see which application, action, and noun are in a port and see which port, adapter, and system are in a location.

For the receive location, select the **FILE** transport and set the receive path to `C:\BizTalk\PRP\CallCenterOrders`. Also, be sure to set the pipeline to **XMLReceive**. Not doing this will result in a failed message because BizTalk never inspects the message to determine its message type.

On the receive port, be sure to select the map **Ext_PurchaseOrderExport_To_ PurchaseOrder**. This will tell BizTalk how to translate the received message on its way to the message box. The message will enter the message box as a canonical **PurchaseOrder** allowing us to build a solution around our stable canonical format that we own and control specifically for BizTalk.

Creating the send port

Create a static one-way send port called **OP_File_Send_Fulfillment_SalesOrder** and select the **FILE** transport. Configure the transport to send to `C:\BizTalk\PRP\ SendInventoryPurchaseOrder` and keep the default `%MessageID%.xml` filename. This will name the file with the BizTalk Message ID, a GUID, that guarantees global uniqueness.

On the **Outbound Maps** section of the send port configuration, select the map **Int_PurchaseOrder_To_SalesOrder**.

The last step is to wire up a filter to route these messages. Though you could use **BTS.ReceivePortName** like we did before, it is really quite a weak subscription and could result in invalid XML (or whatever arbitrary file) being sent to our send port. You instead could use **BTS.MessageType** with a value of **http://performanceracingparts.com/schemas/PurchaseOrder/internal/2011-05#PurchaseOrder** as the message type value.

Testing the solution

If you now start the BizTalk application by right-clicking it and selecting **Start**, the new ports will be enabled and started. You should now be able to copy `PoPurchaseOrderExport.xml` to the receive file location `C:\BizTalk\PRP\CallCenterOrders` and see **SalesOrders** output to the location `C:\BizTalk\PRP\SendInventoryPurchaseOrder`.

This solution is still very basic, but we are now using some more features of BizTalk to accomplish our goals and, importantly, we have laid the framework for what will be a larger and more feature rich application as we continue.

Content-based routing and promoted properties

The solution goes to production and is working well, but like all software business users, they decide they would like to build upon it further. This is a good thing no matter what the reason is, even if it was a missed requirement. The business would like to route orders above a certain amount to a different location than standard orders. This will allow them to be input into the fulfillment system more quickly and allow the users of that system to process them more quickly. The decision is made to make this priority limit $1000 and greater (inclusive). Orders below this limit will continue to function as they currently do.

Property promotion

The easiest way to do this is with **promoted properties** in BizTalk. To do this we must add a **Property Schema** to our **InternalSchemas** project. This is done with the **Add | New Item...** wizard from the Solution Explorer. Name this new schema **OrderProcessingProperties.xsd** and be sure to use the **Property Schema** template.

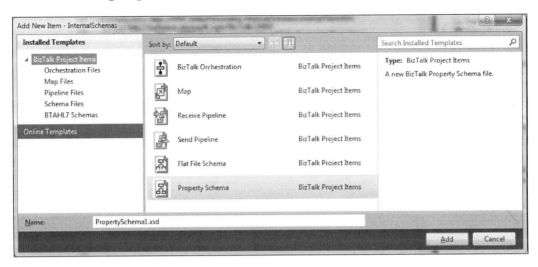

The first thing to do is to change the namespace of this new property schema to **http://performanceracingparts.com/schemas/PurchaseOrder/internal/properties/2011-05**.

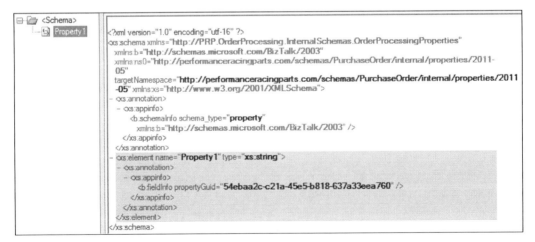

Then rename **Property1** to **OrderTotal** and change its type to **xs:decimal**. Save the schema before you proceed to save yourself a headache later.

Double click the **PurchaseOrder** schema in the Solution Explorer and expand to root element so you can see the **Total** node. Right-click the **Total** node and click **Promote | Show Promotions…** (I never use **Quick Promotion**; it never does what I want, honestly). Property promotion was introduced in *Chapter 3, BizTalk Development Guidelines*.

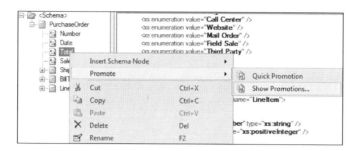

Click the **Property Fields** tab on the right of the dialog to switch from **Distinguished Fields** to **Property Fields**.

Click the folder icon on the upper left and navigate to your new property schema **OrderProcessingProperties.xsd**. Total should still be highlighted on the left and once you specify the property schema the **Add >>** button should become enabled. Click it to add **Total** as a property. Since we only have one property it will be assigned to it on the right. The dialog will look like the one shown in the following screenshot:

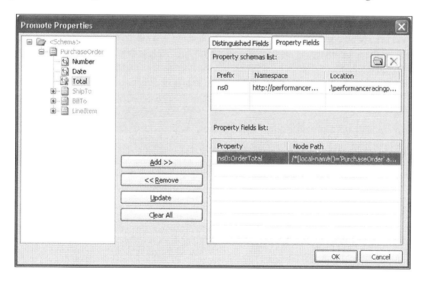

Click **OK**. You have successfully promoted the **PurchaseOrder.Total** element. It can now be used for routing. Save all open documents in Visual Studio and deploy the solution.

Updating the solution routing

Go back to the BizTalk Administration Console and right-click the **Order Processing** application and click **Refresh**. This will refresh all the artifacts in the administration console. Double-click the existing send port **OP_File_Send_Fulfillment_SalesOrder** and click the **Filters** section on the left. Click the blank column below **BTS. MessageType** and look for the property **PRP.OrderProcessing.InternalSchemas. OrderTotal** (the properties are alphabetized, but you can also type in **PRP** to scroll to it). Change the **Operator** to **<** (less than) and set the **Value** to **1000**. We have now successfully enabled routing for standard orders. Here is another example of how naming conventions can have a big impact on BizTalk solutions. By following naming conventions, all the properties in a solution will be grouped together and will be easier to find in all of the BizTalk tools: Visual Studio, Administration Console, Tracking Profile Editor, and so on.

Now we must create the new send port for priority orders. This will be called **OP_File_Send_Fulfillment_PrioritySalesOrder**. It will still use **FILE** transport and send to **C:\BizTalk\PRP\SendInventoryPriorityPurchaseOrder**. Be sure to set the **Outbound Map** to **Int_PurchaseOrder_To_SalesOrder** and set the filter as we did before. This time our filter expression will look like this:

```
BTS.MessageType == http://performanceracingparts.com/schemas/
PurchaseOrder/internal/2009-10#PurchaseOrder
```

and

```
PRP. OrderProcessing.InternalSchemas.OrderTotal >= 1000
```

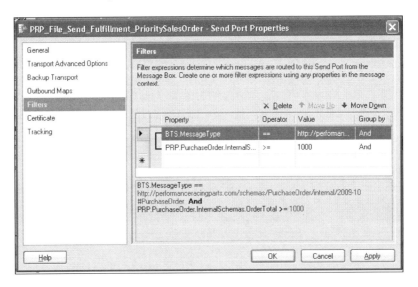

Click **OK** to close the **Send Port Properties** dialog. Right-click this new send port and click **Start**.

We can now drop our sample `PoPurchaseOrderExport.xml` and see where it routes. In order to make sure this is working the way we expect we should add a new XML document to `UnitTest\TestData\External` called `PoPurchaseOrderStandard.xml`.

Paste in the contents of `PoPurchaseOrderExport.xml` and delete the second line item. You should now be able to drop both the test XML files `PoPurchaseOrderExport.xml` and `PoPurchaseOrderStandard.xml` and see them route to the normal and priority locations.

The most common problems you will have creating solutions like this have to do with mismatched subscriptions. It happened to me twice when writing this lesson and the subscription viewer we covered earlier is how you go about resolving such issues. Any typos or misspellings in the Filters will cause the subscription not to work; resulting in failed messages. Importantly, filters entered this way do not have quotes around them and the type of the promoted property will affect routing; that is, it will have an impact on the type of comparison performed: string or numeric.

Multicasting messages

PRP's CRM system can be fed with purchase orders to build and maintain profiles on customers. We need to send every order received by the fulfillment system to the CRM system. The CRM team had been planning to create some sort of integration with the inventory system so they can already receive the same XML format as the fulfillment system.

There are a variety of ways we could do this, but the simplest is through a send port with a Filter subscription. This solution has no impact on the current implementation and can be achieved completely through the administration console. This is a good example of how operators and administrators can add to BizTalk solutions without the need to go back to the development team or how the development team can easily add to an existing solution.

Adding the new send port

To accomplish this you must create a new send port and the subscription for it that routes all orders in its direction.

The new send port will be called **OP_File_Send_CRM_SalesOrder** and will be configured to use the **FILE** adapter on the location **C:\BizTalk\PRP\CRM**.

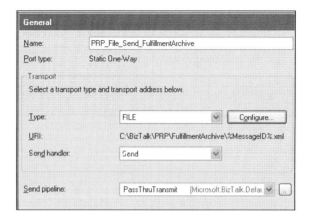

We want to use the same outbound map that we used on the other ports because the CRM application is already expecting the format used by the fulfillment system to which we currently send messages.

Additionally this port will need a filter to direct messages to the destination. The filter will consist of the receive port name and the message type as follows:

    BTS.ReceivePortName == OP_Receive_PurchaseOrders

And

    BTS.MessageType == http://performanceracingparts.com/schemas/
    PurchaseOrder/internal/2009-10#PurchaseOrder

We are purposely using the receive port name because we only want newly received orders. At this point in the solution it is not necessary, but this distinction will be more significant as our solution grows.

After making these changes be sure to start the new send port and then test the solution as you have before, by dropping XML files. The sales orders should go to the appropriate fulfillment directories as well as the CRM folder C:\BizTalk\PRP\CRM.

How this works behind the scenes is that we have two overlapping subscriptions. They are both matched for the order that arrives. They each get a copy of the message, technically a reference to a single immutable message instance. Each service then completes its work, updating the reference to mark it as complete. When the message has no more references it is purged from the message box. Ultimately when people think about a messaging bus, this is an artifact at the very core of BizTalk: publish-subscribe.

Summary

This chapter introduced messaging-only scenarios such as simple pass thru, basic XML with mapping, content-based routing, and message multicasting. We also learned about routing messages based on metadata or context, as well as content. These tools alone are enough to create many BizTalk solutions, but they will also be the basis for the next chapters.

6
Unit Tests and BAM

This chapter introduces Unit Testing and Business Activity Monitoring (BAM). These will be added to the current solution to make it more stable and maintainable, as well as to provide visibility. Unit Testing and BAM are critical components to any BizTalk solution because they both provide understanding and monitoring. Unit Tests allow developers to understand how a solution is meant to work and to run it for themselves. BAM provides visibility that can be tailored to the technical or business aspects of a solution.

What are unit tests?

We can already see that dropping the test files manually and inspecting the results is tedious and error prone. It also requires intimate knowledge about the expected behavior of the solution that can be lost over time through turnover or forgetfulness. Fortunately, there is a simple way to automate our tests and allow us to make them repeatable and reliable. This will let us know if we break anything in the solution over the course of its lifetime. It is common to start with writing the tests before we build the solution and I encourage it strongly; but because I want the focus of this book to be BizTalk and not Test Driven Development, I will simply add them to the solution we have now. Ideally, you will tie the tests themselves to specific solution requirements and thus create a good deal of documentation before development begins in earnest, or at least before it completes.

There are many ways you can create unit tests for BizTalk, but by far the most widely used is the **BizUnit** framework (`http://bizunit.codeplex.com`). BizUnit is an automation framework to create tests for distributed systems. It is open source and freely available. Anyone with experience of NUnit or JUnit will be at home fairly quickly with BizUnit. The framework, however, does not use NUnit and can be harnessed from either JUnit or Visual Studio Unit Testing.

Importantly, BizUnit does not use code, such as C#, to create tests. BizUnit tests are XML files that lay out the steps of the test to be executed. This allows for their rapid construction. As we will see shortly, tests for the solution we just built are extremely quick to build and require only a little editing of XML.

Tenets of a good test

Before we dive into BizUnit, it is probably logical to discuss what exactly makes a test good in the first place. Good tests are self-encapsulated and completely independent; that is, they run in isolation and are repeatable. They should also test a specific aspect of functionality. Rather than being one big test that covers the entire solution, a test should target a specific scenario. This will allow the test to clearly reveal its intention and form the basis of living documentation for an integration or service solution. Later, developers can refer to these tests to know what the expected behavior is and can convey this information to business users. Good unit tests are as follows:

- Self-encapsulated
- Repeatable
- Target a specific functional aspect

This means that all the unit tests for a solution will be completely independent of each other. This makes it easier to diagnose specific issues and also to address changing or developing a specific aspect of the solution.

Importantly, unit tests should treat the solution as a black box. This makes BizUnit tests different from many other code-based unit tests, most of which test specific methods, which in BizTalk would be most analogous to a map or policy. BizUnit tests are designed to test the solution the way the real world will. This is a good match for BizTalk as most middleware/service solutions are responsible for receiving input and producing output in a very discreet manner and in discreet locations. This fits well in the BizTalk model of endpoint isolation. There are other built-in testing tools for finer grained testing of maps and schemas that will be covered as the concepts are introduced.

Composition of a test

Like any xUnit-based testing framework, there are three stages to a BizUnit test, which are as follows:

- Setup
- Execution
- Cleanup

These three stages help us achieve our goals of good testing. The setup and cleanup stages prepare and then reset the environment respectively. This is critical to making tests repeatable and also not interfering with other tests or the order in which tests are run. Often the setup and cleanup stages will be nearly identical. This is because you want to have a clean slate on which to run your tests.

The execution stage is where the real work happens. This is where actions that cause events in BizTalk, as well as validations, will take place. A good example would be creating a file in a specific location or sending a message via SOAP or MSMQ, then verifying that the message was received and processed correctly by checking the downstream system for results. Normally, this would be a file, database, or queue. In this way, BizUnit tests are by nature black box tests. The BizTalk solution is the box and you cause an event on one side of the box and verify the results on the other side of the box.

Additionally, good tests and test suites not only verify expected behavior—positive result tests—they also verify negative behavior. That is, they check to ensure that only the expected results take place. This can be a challenge in BizTalk because many subscribers may receive a single message. It is critical if you have any sort of branching logic to make sure that only one branch is, in fact, executed. This is all the more important with routing and filters.

In the case of test suites collection of tests, we must also ensure that failure situations are handled appropriately because, despite our best efforts, there will always be failures, and designing tests to handle them gracefully from the beginning is critical to a successful solution.

Test steps

Each stage of a test consists of zero or more test steps. These steps are the building blocks that we use to create tests and each fills a specific common need in integration or service projects. BizUnit includes dozens of test steps including steps to work with files, queues, databases, HTTP, SOAP, and many others; being open source it is also easy to add whatever steps you may need.

The steps themselves follow a common structure as well. This structure includes the name of the .NET class that implements the test and parameters for the step. Some steps will have nested parameters or other structures, commonly for validation, or for more complex tasks like database queries.

We'll start pretty simply with BizUnit, but make no mistake as this is a powerful framework that allows us to create amazingly powerful and expressive tests. We can also develop our own test steps if we need to, and the fact that it is open source makes this fairly easy as you can examine the implementation of any test step that you've worked with. There are even test steps for working with LoadGen—a load generation tool provided by Microsoft for use in stress and performance testing.

Tests for the current solution

Our solution at this point is quite simple. Because BizUnit tests are black boxes, we should really think of the business purpose for which we will create a test, rather than the technical purpose. If we were to consider what test we should have, there would be two distinct tests so far, which are as follows:

- Priority Order Routing
- Normal Order Routing

Let's start by making these two tests to cover the solution as it stands by following the following steps:

1. The first task is to add a reference to **BizUnit.dll** to the **UnitTests** project. I like to place this assembly in the **3rdPartyAssemblies** directory of the solution, so that it always travels with the solution and makes source control easier. BizUnit will still need to be installed on any machine that runs these tests. We covered more about solution structure back in *Chapter 2 Introduction to BizTalk Development*.

2. Like all the guidance in this text, it is intended to make your solution portable and easy to build between developer environments. To add this reference, simply right-click the **References** folder beneath the **UnitTests** project and click **Add Reference**. You will be presented with a file explorer window and you should navigate to the **BizUnit.dll** assembly and select it.

3. If you really want to make sure you are creating a portable solution, you can change the **UnitTests.csproj** file in the **UnitTests** directory to use a relative path for this assembly (which it should do by default). In this file, there is an **ItemGroup** node for the reference to BizUnit.

4. We can see in the following XML code, which is an excerpt from **UnitTest.csproj**, that Visual Studio has used a relative path location for the assembly hint used to load this reference. This helps the solution compile under different directories or development machines:

```
<ItemGroup>
  <Reference Include="BizUnit">
```

```
        <HintPath>..\3rdPartyAssemblies\BizUnit.dll</HintPath>
    </Reference>
  </ItemGroup>
```

For the sake of brevity, the first two tests are provided for you in the solution template downloaded for this book and all we need to do is add them. We can add them to the **UnitTest** project by using the **Add | Existing Item wizard** for the following files:

- `CanRoutePriorityPurchaseOrder.xml`

- `CanRouteStandardPurchaseOrder.xml`

- `TestEntities.dtd`

They should be added to the **BizUnitTests** folder in the **UnitTests** project.

If we examine **TestEntities.dtd**, we can see entries for input and output directories used by the solution as follows:

```
<!ENTITY CRMDirectory "C:\BizTalk\PRP\CRM">
<!ENTITY NormalSendDirectory "C:\BizTalk\PRP\
SendInventoryPurchaseOrder">
```

Again the motivation here is for portability and modularity. Some of these paths must be hardcoded due to the way either BizUnit or BizTalk work (BizTalk needs a real location for receiving the file), but by using entity definitions this way, we can simply change our DTD file if we need different environments. Document Type Definition (DTD) is a predecessor to XML schema (XSD), but was designed to provide a different set of capabilities. In this section, we are exploiting entity definitions to create shortcuts, or stand-ins, to commonly used values that we can control in a single location. Commonly, there would be different DTDs for different environments—developer and build would be the two best examples.

Changing test locations

If you are not using the `C:\BizTalk\PRP` folder structure that this course uses, you can simply change this DTD and all the tests will now use whatever locations you have chosen.

Standard Purchase Order test

This test verifies that a `PoPurchaseOrderExport` XML file, with a total order amount less than 1000 created in our receive location, will be picked up and sent to the normal send directory as well as the CRM directory. This matches with the business requirements of the solution up to this point.

The following is the structure for our Standard Purchase Order test:

The steps to be followed for setup are as follows:

1. Delete files from the `standard order output` folder
2. Delete files from the CRM folder

The steps to be followed for execute are as follows:

1. Create an XML file in the receive call center orders location
2. Verify that one file has been created at the `standard order output` folder
3. Validate that the file created at the `standard order output` folder meets the following requirements:
   - Conforms to the `SalesOrder.xsd` schema
   - Has a specific namespace
   - Has the expected Order Number and Total

The steps to be followed for cleanup are as follows:

1. Delete files from the `standard order output` folder
2. Delete files from the CRM folder

If we examine `CanRouteStandardPurchaseOrder.xml`, we can see that it has the three sections that we talked about before. We can also see an XML DOCTYPE declaration that instructs the parser to use our `TestEntities.dtd` as follows:

```
<!DOCTYPE TestCase SYSTEM "TestEntities.dtd">
```

Test setup and cleanup

The first BizUnit test step in the test setup is shown as follows:

```
<TestStep assemblyPath="" typeName="BizUnit.FileDeleteMultipleStep">
  <Directory>&NormalSendDirectory;</Directory>
  <SearchPattern>*.xml</SearchPattern>
</TestStep>
```

We can see that this step specifies that a `FileDeleteMultipleStep` is to be executed and provides the directory and search pattern to perform this operation. The `FileDeleteMultipleStep`, as its name implies, will delete multiple files from the directory matching the search pattern. Simple test steps all work this way. More complicated steps have more parameters and sometimes nested structures that allow for expressive testing.

In this test, both setup and cleanup simply delete files from the expected output directories—in this case the standard send and CRM directories.

The test execution stage

This is where the vast majority of testing is done, even for this simple test. The first step creates a file in the directory that our solution looks in for orders; again using the DTD entity to abstract the physical location out of the test as much as possible, which is shown as follows:

```
<TestStep assemblyPath="" typeName="BizUnit.FileCreateStep">
  <SourcePath>External\PoPurchaseOrderStandard.xml</SourcePath>
<CreationPath>&OrderReceiveDirectory;\PoPurchaseOrderStandard.xml</
CreationPath>
</TestStep>
```

As we can see, this test step is also very simple. The next step, again as its name implies, checks for the existence of a file in a specific location, matching a specific mask, and an expected number of results as follows:

```
<TestStep assemblyPath="" typeName="BizUnit.FilesExistStep">
  <Timeout>10000</Timeout>
  <DirectoryPath>&NormalSendDirectory;</DirectoryPath>
  <SearchPattern>*.xml</SearchPattern>
  <ExpectedNoOfFiles>1</ExpectedNoOfFiles>
</TestStep>
```

This helps us to be more precise about what output we produce.

The next step, the `FileValidateStep`, is the most compelling step as it shows how BizUnit can help us ensure that our output message meets our expectations, shown as follows:

```
<TestStep assemblyPath="" typeName="BizUnit.FileValidateStep">
 <Timeout>10000</Timeout>
 <Directory>&NormalSendDirectory;\</Directory>
 <SearchPattern>*.xml</SearchPattern>
 <DeleteFile>false</DeleteFile>
 <ValidationStep assemblyPath="" typeName="BizUnit.XmlValidationStep">
<XmlSchemaPath>..\..\..\ExternalSchemas\SalesOrder.xsd</XmlSchemaPath>
 <XmlSchemaNameSpace>http://inv...2009-10</XmlSchemaNameSpace>
  <XPathList>
   <XPathValidation query="/Number">1929132</XPathValidation>
   <XPathValidation query="/Total">785.3</XPathValidation>
  </XPathList>
 </ValidationStep>
```

```
  </TestStep>
  <TestStep assemblyPath="" typeName="BizUnit.FilesExistStep">
   <Timeout>3000</Timeout>
   <DirectoryPath>&CRMDirectory;</DirectoryPath>
   <SearchPattern>*.xml</SearchPattern>
   <ExpectedNoOfFiles>1</ExpectedNoOfFiles>
  </TestStep>
```

This step has had some values truncated for brevity, but we see an example of a much more expressive test step. It allows us to specify a maximum timeout period, to delete the file when we're done validating it, which schema to validate it against, and even which parts of the message we would like to validate for specific values.

The test for priority orders is very similar, but checks a different output location and validates different values. At this point, the tests themselves are complete and we simply need to run them.

Harnessing a test

To harness the BizUnit tests we use Microsoft Unit Test for simplicity. NUnit could also be used with very few changes. In C#, we can harness a BizUnit test with two lines of code which are as follows:

```
[TestMethod]
public void CanRoutePriorityOrder()
{
  BizUnit.BizUnit test = new BizUnit.BizUnit(
    "CanRoutePriorityPurchaseOrder.xml");
  test.RunTest();
}
```

This is fairly simple code and very straightforward: instantiate a BizUnit object loaded via the constructor with the BizUnit test case and an XML file, and run the test. The important aspect to note is the use of relative path locations. We'll see this in our test cases themselves and it is important to consider and keep in mind.

To run these tests the UnitTests project already contains a `BizUnitTests.cs` file that contains the two test harness methods. Simply uncomment them and you can use the Test menu in Visual Studio to run them. *Ctrl+R, Ctrl+T* will run all tests in the current context. This means if your cursor is in the test method `CanRoutePriorityOrder` (between the braces) then only this test will run. If your cursor is outside of that method, but inside the `BizUnitTests` class, all the tests in the class will run. *Ctrl+R, Ctrl+T* will run the tests in debug mode and allow you to step into them, including stepping into BizUnit test steps.

Visual Studio Project Settings for tests

Because MSTest is designed to work in server environments as well, we need to take some steps to make our test cases run correctly. We'll need to edit the **Test settings** for everything to work here. In Visual Studio, click the **Test** menu and expand **Edit Test Settings**, selecting the **Local** settings. Under the **Deployment** section, you will need to check the box **Enable deployment** and in the **Additional files and directories to deploy**, you will need to add two directories: **\UnitTests\ BizUnitTests** and **\UnitTests\TestData**. This can be done via the **Add Directory...** button on the right. These settings will tell MSTest to copy the relevant test files to the local directory used by MSTest. This is required so MSTest will find the BizUnit test xml files and the input messages for the tests.

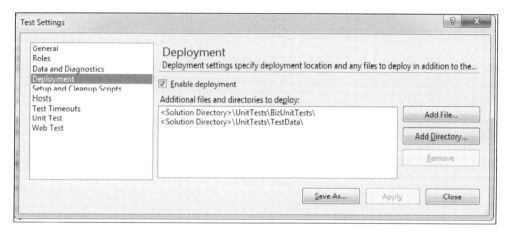

Finally, run the tests and see that they produce the expected output. They should both pass. If they don't, the errors in the test results should be able to point you in the right direction. You can also check your **Group Hub** page for suspended messages to see where they might be. *Chapter 4, Operating BizTalk*, provides more information about tracking down issues in BizTalk.

Creating BAM for a solution

Business Activity Monitoring (BAM) is quite possibly the most important aspect of BizTalk and it is also the most overlooked. There are so many flashy parts of the platform that are immediately eye catching, like maps and orchestrations, that many developers simply overlook the use of BAM. Until recently, it was also not well understood. As discussed in *Chapter 2, Introduction to BizTalk Development*, BAM is an amazingly powerful toolset that allows us to create rich interactive reporting based on our BizTalk solutions. BAM does not require custom code and produces so much value that it is amazing to see solutions that don't leverage it.

Creating a basic BAM profile

Our solution has been running for some time, but it is clear that our CRM is not an easy way to see which orders are going through our integration. You decide to create a BAM profile for the current solution to provide visibility into the process.

You are asked to create a basic tracking profile for the following information:

- Order Total
- Order Date
- Billing State
- Shipping State
- Sales Channel
- Order Received

As discussed in *Chapter 2, Introduction to BizTalk Development*, some of these are business data and others are milestones. Milestones are points in time when events happen, such as when messages are received or sent. Business data is normally content from the message itself, but can also be context or metadata. In the previous list, only Order Received and Order Sent are milestones.

Creating an Activity

Creating BAM activities is done via an Excel plugin. Open Excel and go to the **Add-Ins** tab. Click the **BAM** Add-In and click **BAM Activity…** as shown in the following screenshot:

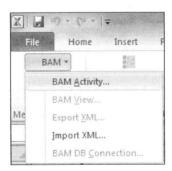

Enable Excel Add-In for BAM

Be sure to enable the Excel plugin by going to **File | Options** navigating to **Add-Ins** and clicking the **Go** button at the bottom of the dialog near **Manage: Excel Add-ins**. From here you will see the **Business Activity Monitoring** add-in. Be sure to check the box to enable it.

The window will be empty when it opens, as shown in the following screenshot:

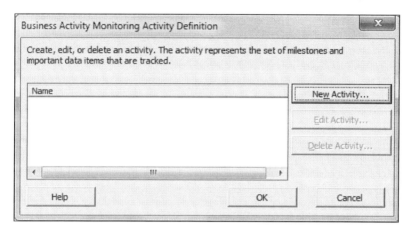

Click **New Activity...** on the right to create a new BAM activity. Name the new activity **Purchase Orders** and the **New Activity** dialog shown in the following screenshot will appear:

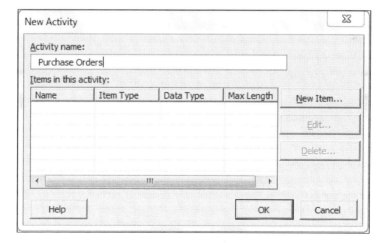

Click the **New Item...** button and add the following items selecting the appropriate **Item Type** for each:

- Order Total: Decimal
- Order Date: Text
- Billing State: Text
- Shipping State: Text
- Sales Channel: Text
- Order Received: Business Milestone

Click **OK** when you're done and then click **OK** again on the **Business Activity Monitoring Activity Definition** dialog. Doing so will launch the **View Creation** wizard. This is where we will define which data we want in a specific view. Recall that a view is a presentation of one or more activities. Click **Next >** to begin this process.

Creating a View

All of the view-related user interfaces resemble the activity from the previous section and you now see the **View Creation** wizard on your screen. At this point, your only choice will be **Create a new view**, click **Next >** to continue. Name the new view **Received Orders** and select **Purchase Orders** as the activity to drive the view. Click **Next >**.

Select all the items as the **View Items** and click **Next >**. Click **Next >** when back at the **View Creation** wizard. We are next provided with the opportunity to create dimensions and measures. We will not do that at this point, so click **Next >** again. Click **Next >** again at the summary page of the wizard. A dialog telling you that **You have successfully created a new view** will appear, click **Finish** to close the wizard. Save the Excel file as **OrderProcessing.xlsx**.

Now you must deploy the view. The tool used to do this is BM.exe, a command line utility that controls BAM. This tool is located in: `Install Directory\Microsoft BizTalk Server 2010\Tracking`. It can be useful to add this path to your environment in Windows.

The following are the steps to deploy the tracking activity:

1. Open a command line (which can be done by clicking the **Windows** button and typing **cmd** into the **Search programs and files** box).

2. **CD** into the directory containing **OrderProcessing.xlsx**.

3. Type the following command:

```
bm deploy-all -definitionFile:OrderProcessing.xlsx
```

The format of the command is: bm [operation] [parameters].

At this point, navigating to `http://localhost/bam` will bring up the BAM portal. We can see the view, **Received Orders**, and activity, **Purchase Orders**, that we created, but we still have to create a tracking profile to bind the activity to the solution. Without this step, nothing will appear in the BAM data.

Creating the Tracking Profile

Start the **Tracking Profile Editor** (TPE) by clicking **Start | All Programs | Microsoft BizTalk Server 2010 | Tracking Profile Editor**. When the **Tracking Profile Editor** starts, it is an empty window consisting of two panes. The one on the left is where we view our activity definition and the one on the right is where we view our event source.

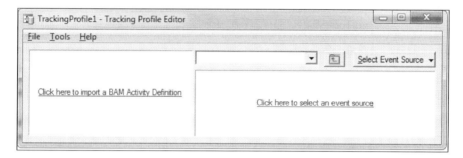

1. Click on the **Click here to import a BAM Activity Definition** link in the left pane.

2. Select the **Purchase Orders** activity in the list that displays all activity definitions.

3. Click the **Select Event Source** dropdown in the upper right corner of the TPE and click **Select Messaging Payload**. This will allow us to browse for a specific event source that is a messaging payload. In the **Select Event Source Parent Assembly** dialog, we can see all the BizTalk assemblies on the server. Now, perform the following steps:

    ° Double-click **PRP.OrderProcessing.InternalSchemas**

    ° Select the **PRP.OrderProcessing.InternalSchemas.PurchaseOrder**, which is the specific schema we want to track

    ° Expand the **<Schema>** and **PurchaseOrder** nodes in the right pane to see the schema elements

4. Drag all the following matching elements from the schema on the right to the profile on the left:

   ° **Total**

   ° **Date**

   ° **Sales Channel**

   ° **ShipTo.Address.State**

   ° **BillTo.Address.State**

5. You now need to set the port mappings for each of these elements. All the elements should be bound to the receive port: **OP_Receive_PurchaseOrders**. To do this, perform the following steps:

   ° Right-click each element on the left starting with **Total** and click **Set Port Mappings**. A dialog opens to allow you to see all the ports.

   ° Type in **OP_Receive_PurchaseOrders** (or a substring) or simply scroll to this port name in the list.

   ° Click the **>** button or double-click the port name to assign the port to this tracking profile element.

   ° Repeat the process for the **Date**, **Sales Channel**, and both **State** elements.

We can see here how the naming convention we're using for port names is significant, in that it makes working with the tracking part of a solution infinitely easier. As your BizTalk environment grows, these conventions become even more important.

We have two elements remaining that haven't been mapped yet: **Order Received** and **Order Sent**. We get a visual cue that these are milestones because of the clock icon by which they are represented. To map these, perform the following steps:

1. Click **Select Event Source** on the right and click **Select Messaging Property** from the list. Expand the **<Schema>** and **MessageProperties** nodes on the right.

2. Drag **Port Start Time** on the right to the **Order Received** milestone on the left.

3. Bind **Order Received** to **OP_Receive_PurchaseOrders** like we did for the other elements.

4. Save the profile as **PurchaseOrderTracking.btt** in the **Tracking** folder of the solution.

5. Click **Tools | Apply Tracking Profile**.

At this point, your tracking definition is now bound to your solution via the profile we just applied. You can now run any of your Unit Tests and watch the results appear in the BAM portal. To do this, navigate to `http://localhost/bam`. On the left-hand side, you will see **Views** that you have access to. Expand the **Activity Search** node under **Received Orders** and you can now see our **Purchase Orders** activity. Clicking **Purchase Orders** will bring up the BAM query window. If you highlight all the columns in the left of the **Column Chooser** section and click the **>>** button to assign them to the right, you will be able to select the items you want to see in your result set, as shown in the following screenshot:

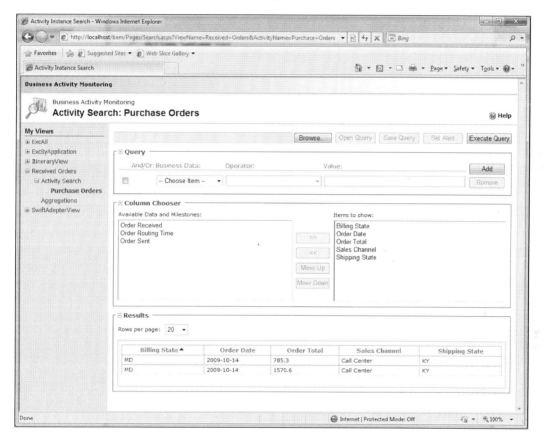

Clicking **Execute Query** at the top right will return the records from BAM. If you click on one of the records, you can see details for that specific instance. Every time you run your unit tests, you should see two more entries appear in the BAM Portal.

We can already see how just this basic tracking sets up visibility into our solution that can be very valuable for either technical or business users, particularly in the operations space. The query section of the window allows us to create queries that can search on either data or milestones. The operator for a query changes depending upon the type in the activity. The types and operators are described in the following table:

Data Type	Operator
Text	Is Exactly
	Contains
	Does not contain
	Is empty
	Is not empty
Milestone	At
	On or before
	On or after
	Before
	After
	In the last
	Before the last
	Is empty
	Is not empty
Integer and Decimal	Equals
	Greater than
	Greater than or equal
	Less than
	Less than or equal
	Not equal
	Is empty
	Is not empty

With just this set of tools, we are already able to create expressive queries that will enable us to find specific sets of transactions as they pass through our solution. We can also save the queries as XML documents to load them later on. Each column in the results is also sortable by clicking the heading.

Clicking on any of the rows in the results pane will bring us to the details of this activity instance. The activity status or details page, displays exactly what we saw in our activity definition: milestones and data.

Many developers I teach BAM to, are put off at first by the use of an Excel plugin and the lack of 'code' behind the solution. In reality, however, this is one of the greatest strengths of BAM. We have not written a single line of code, but we have extremely reliable tracking now integrated with our solution, that is infinitely better than any of us could do in anywhere near similar time on our own. To see how advanced this is, we will now examine the BAM infrastructure a little. There is a great deal of documentation on BAM available at `http://msdn.microsoft.com/en-us/library/aa561326(v=BTS.70).aspx` and there is an excellent book that I highly recommend, *Pro Business Activity Monitoring in BizTalk 2009, Geoff Snowman and Jeff Sanders, Apress.*

Examining the BAM database infrastructure

As impressive as all of this is so far (and recall that we're only scratching the surface), the real amazing part of it is the infrastructure which is automatically created and deployed for us.

BAM tables

If we open SQL Server Management Studio and look in the `BAMPrimaryImport` database, we can see that the following tables were created for our tracking solution:

- `bam_Purchase Orders_Active`
- `bam_Purchase Orders_ActiveRelationships`

- bam_Purchase Orders_Completed

- bam_Purchase Orders_CompletedRelationships

- bam_Purchase Orders_Continuations

These tables hold the raw BAM data that is moved here by the BizTalk engine as it cleans out the message box and DTA databases. This also means that if a BizTalk environment is overloaded, it will slow down BAM processing to increase transaction processing, then process the BAM information when the transaction load declines. In a production solution, this is a profound and important feature. Many home-built tracking and instrumentation frameworks slow down the run time through synchronous calls. BAM does not.

BAM views

Browsing around in our BAMPrimaryImport database, we can also see there are several views created for both the activity and the view.

 What we see in the BAM portal is actually directly driven from these views, not the tables. If you plan to query BAM directly either through SharePoint or Reporting Services, it is critical that you query the views and not the tables. As we will see shortly, these views are recreated periodically so it is important to only query them and not the underlying tables.

The views created for activity are as follows:

- bam_Purchase Orders_ActiveInstances

- bam_Purchase Orders_AllInstances

- bam_Purchase Orders_AllRelationships

- bam_Purchase Orders_CompletedInstances

- bam_Purchase Orders_InstancesForArchive

- bam_Purchase Orders_RelationshipsForArchive

The views created for view are as follows:

- bam_Received Orders_ViewPurchase Orders_ActiveAliasView

- bam_Received Orders_ViewPurchase Orders_ActiveView

- bam_Received Orders_ViewPurchase Orders_CompletedAliasView

- bam_Received Orders_ViewPurchase Orders_CompletedView

- bam_Received Orders_ViewPurchase Orders_View

BAM maintenance

In addition to these views, there are also two SSIS packages created for each activity that are as follows:

- bam_DM_Purchase Orders
- bam_AN_Purchase Orders

Data maintenance

The data maintenance package is denoted by the DM in its name and must be configured on the schedule you choose to run. The package uses the concepts of windows and partitions. Each time the package is run, it creates a new set of the base tables for completed instances and completed relationships named bam_Purchase Orders_[GUID] and bam_Purchase Orders_[GUID]_Relationships. These new tables have a GUID in their name so there are no name conflicts. The package then recreates the views, so that the new tables are included in them. This keeps the tables from getting too big and slowing down the SQL server. This package also marks the partitions with a date. Any partition whose date is outside the time window will be either archived or deleted. The default time window is six months and the default action is to archive to the BAMArchive database.

This means that if you set this package to run every month it will create a partition each month with the completed tracking data for that month. After six months, the first partition will be archived off into BAMArchive and then deleted from BAMPrimaryImport. The data will no longer show up in the BAM Portal, but you will have it if you need it in BAMArchive, which is not an operational store and therefore can grow very large without causing trouble. The benefit here is that BAMPrimaryImport, and consequently the BAM Portal, will be kept clean and thus perform better. This is an ideal way to address business users who like to hoard data with the common request 'we need everything saved forever' paired with the common requirement 'but nothing can slow down over time'.

The options covering the time window are month, day, hour, and minute; which enable us to control exactly how we want BAM to partition and archive, or purge. This enables BAM to serve the same purpose for high volume or long duration solutions. The archive option controls the cleanup. It can be used to move the records to the BAMArchive database, the default behavior, or to simply delete the records.

Analysis

The analysis services package, denoted by the AN in its name, was not created at this time, as there are no cubes for our tracking solution. We will cover this shortly and it is one of the most compelling aspects of BAM. As with the data maintenance package, you must create the job to run the analysis services package on a schedule that you choose, which is very simple as the package has no parameters or extra configuration. Both of these packages are ready to run out of the box, but must have a SQL job set up to actually execute them. Depending upon your specific volume and data retention needs, you should determine the schedule on which to run these packages.

At this point, it should be clear that BAM is bringing a lot to the table and that working with an Excel plugin is not as bad as you may have at first thought. As we explore more advanced BAM features, such as dimensions and aggregations, the choice of excel becomes far more obvious and the results more impressive.

Receiving a new Legacy Order format

The current solution is working well and all the stakeholders are pleased. It comes to your attention that a business analyst has created an InfoPath form to fill orders that has become quite popular with some of the travelling sales teams.

Microsoft InfoPath

This is a part of the Office suite specifically designed for working with electronic forms, specifically as XML. InfoPath is commonly used as a presentation layer for XML documents and provides rich features that make working with forms easy and still provide separation between the data in the form and the presentation of that data. For more information see the following: `http://office.microsoft.com/en-us/infopath/`.

Until now the sales people would just save this form or print it. Subsequently, either sales or call center staff would rekey the order into the call center application or web portal. The duplicate work, crossing two operating centers, is causing friction. Because the InfoPath form is built on an XML template anyway, you decide they should just submit the form to the File Share that BizTalk receives call center purchase orders from.

The sales team give you their format schema and InfoPath template; now you must incorporate it into your solution. To do so you will need to perform the following steps:

1. Add the schema that the sales team have provided you with, **InfoPathPurchaseOrder.xsd,** to External Schemas. This schema and a sample message are available at `http://biztalk2010patterns.com//documents/ order-processing`.

2. Create a new map **Ext_InfoPathPurchaseOrder_To_PurchaseOrder.btm.**

3. Select **InfoPathPurchaseOrder** from External Schemas as the left-hand source.

4. Select **PurchaseOrder** from Internal Schemas as the right-hand destination.

5. Map the **Sales Channel** as **Field Sale** using a **String Concatenate** Function.

6. Map the **Customer** items to both the **ShipTo** and **BillTo** nodes mapping:
   ° **Name** to Name
   ° **PhoneNumber** to PhoneNumber
   ° **Address1** to Address/Street
   ° **City** to Address/City
   ° **State** to Address/State
   ° **ZipCode** to Address/PostalCode

7. Map the **OrderItem** attributes to **LineItem** as follows:
   ° **ItemNumber** to CatalogNumber
   ° **Quantity** to Quantity
   ° **Price** to UnitCost
   ° **Description** to Description

8. Select the file **UnitTest\TestData\External\ InfoPathPurchaseOrder.xml** as the **Test Map Input Instance**.

9. Build the solution then test the map.

10. Deploy the solution.

11. Refresh the Administration Console.

12. Add the map **Ext_InfoPathPurchaseOrder_To_PurchaseOrder** to the receive Port **OP_ Receive_ PurchaseOrders**.

13. Copy the file **InfoPathPurchaseOrder.xml** to the receive location **C:\BizTalk\PRP\CallCenterOrders** to verify whether the solution works. The file should end up in **C:\BizTalk\PRP\SendInventoryPurchaseOrder** in the SalesOrder format.

Because we receive these in the same location as our existing call center purchase orders, we do not need a new receive location, yet BizTalk is smart enough to identify the incoming message type and decide which map to use. This is done in the XMLReceive pipeline in our receive location through the process of message inspection. You will recall that a message type in messaging solutions is identified by XML namespace and root element name. BizTalk identifies the received message type then looks for a map that matches the message type.

Creating a BizUnit test

Although we have seen that this solution is working, we should also create an automated test so that we can verify it continues working and also to document expected behavior of the solution:

1. Right-click the **BizUnitTests** folder in the **UnitTests** solutions and select **Add | New Item** to add a new XML file named **CanRouteNormalInfoPathOrder.xml**.

2. Copy the contents of **CanRouteStandardPurchaseOrder.xml** and paste them into this new file.

3. Change the **testName** attribute of the **TestCase** root element to **CanRouteStandardPurchaseOrder**.

4. Change the **FileCreateStep** to use the **InfoPathPurchaseOrder.xml**.

5. Change the **XmlValidationStep** so that the **XPathValidations** use the values 57463 for Number and 505.43 for Total.

6. Create a new test method in **BizUnitTests.cs** to run the test. You can copy one of the existing test methods and change the method name to **CanRouteNormalInfoPathOrder**. Be sure to change the name of the XML file in the constructor to **CanRouteNormalInfoPathOrder.xml**.

All of your tests should pass for the solution at this point. As we can see, in just a few steps we were able to receive a completely new format and have it flow all the way through our solution by only adding a map. This is the goal of the internal schemas concept. Changes to the periphery of our solution should not impact the solution itself. As proof of how effective this was, we can now actually see our new **Field Sale Orders** listed in the BAM Portal.

Summary

In this chapter, we were introduced to BizUnit tests and created tests for our current solution. We also created monitoring with BAM and ended by adding support for a new message format. All of these add value to our solution and their importance should not be overlooked. Automated unit testing is critical to solution success and monitoring is so powerful that BAM alone is worth the cost of BizTalk. The BAM infrastructure can actually be used from .NET and WCF applications that aren't even part of BizTalk. The flexibility of the solution structure that we chose was also evident as we made changes with ease.

7
Leveraging Orchestration

Messaging only solutions can be made very powerful and complex, but some actions are best done with a more robust and feature-rich toolset. This is what orchestration was designed to address. This chapter introduces orchestration in BizTalk and refactors our current solution to incorporate orchestration. We will then see how to use orchestration for service composition including error and fault handling.

Introducing orchestration

Orchestration is the workflow engine of BizTalk. It allows developers to create sequential workflows similar to flowcharts commonly used by business analysts. The orchestration engine predates Workflow Foundation (WF), but was created by the same team and many of the concepts are similar. Orchestration is specifically focused on messaging or system to system choreography, whereas WF is targeted more at human workflow. We have intentionally not started with orchestration earlier because it is overused in situations where it is not necessary. To demonstrate this point, we will now modify our existing solution to use an orchestration instead of promoted properties. These were covered in *Chapter 3, BizTalk Development Guidelines* and *Chapter 5, Basic Messaging Solution*.

Orchestration basics

The graphical representation of this flowchart such as the construct that we work with when creating orchestrations is called the canvas. Like a real canvas, at first it is empty. In the following screenshot, we can see what a new (empty) orchestration canvas looks like:

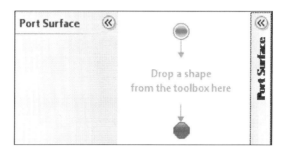

The green and red dots represent where the orchestration starts and where it finishes. These are simple visual cues; these don't actually do anything. On the sides of the canvas, we can see two **Port Surface** areas. These are where we would place logical ports that are used to bind an orchestration to the outside world.

 Please note how the concepts of *binding* and *port* are reused within orchestration; they also fundamentally mean the same thing as in the context we saw them before. Nearly all of BizTalk uses a common lexicon that describes its core concepts.

On the left side of your screen (by default) is the **Toolbox**. Orchestration, like much of BizTalk, uses a customized toolbox in Visual Studio that is specific to it. This **Toolbox** contains only 22 shapes, but they are enough to implement very rich logic designs and patterns. Shown in the following screenshot is the complete orchestration toolbox. I've broken the image out side by side for better presentation:

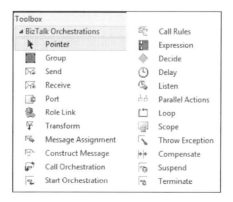

Although they look simple so far (and have cute little icons), these shapes really are enough to meet the vast majority of service composition needs. Our solution will only use a handful of them. Again like most of Visual Studio, when we drop a shape from the toolbox onto the orchestration canvas, there will be a properties window specifically for that shape (or any shape that we highlight). What properties are in this window will depend on what shape is highlighted.

There is also an **Orchestration View** window that appears when we work with orchestration. This window is on the upper right of Visual Studio by default, grouped with the solution explorer that we've worked with up to this point. This window is shown as follows:

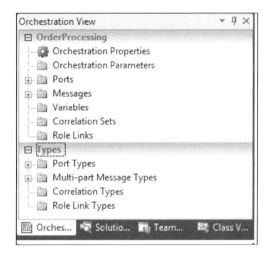

As we can see in the **Orchestration View**, there are two distinct parts: the top one is labeled with the name of the orchestration, in this case **OrderProcessing**, and the bottom one is called **Types**. The top section contains artifacts specific to this orchestration, and this could be thought of as members in a .NET class. The bottom section contains orchestration types that are in all the orchestrations in the current Visual Studio project. We discussed this in more detail in *Chapter 3, BizTalk Development Guidelines*.

Creating the orchestration outline

We will now modify our current solution to use an orchestration. To do this, we must create a new orchestration and start adding shapes to the canvas. The steps for this are as follows:

1. Add a new orchestration to the project **Orchestrations** called **OrderProcessing.odx** via the **Add | New Item wizard**.

2. Add the following orchestration shapes for the solution:

   ° A Receive shape named **Rcv_PurchaseOrder** and set the **Activate** property to `true`

   ° A Decide shape following the receive shape named **Decide_Priority** and rename **Rule_1** on the left to **If_Priority**

   ° A Send shape named **Snd_PriorityPurchaseOrder** in the left branch of the decision

   ° A Send shape named **Snd_StandardPurchaseOrder** in the right branch of the decision

At this point, we have the basic skeleton for our orchestration and it is immediately clear why many developers are more comfortable with this approach than the messaging solution we have used up to this point. It is an imperative model that is all in one place and the intent is explicitly clear as shown in the following figure:

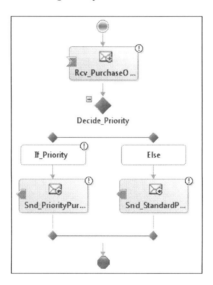

We can also see that there are clear visual cues as to what elements of our solution are incomplete. Clicking any of the red exclamations will display the error and provide a simple way to resolve the issue. A simple way we should generally not use due to the increased coupling that can result. Visual Studio is trying to be our friend and it is telling us what the problems are, but its solutions to the problems aren't always the best in terms of design, so resist the urge to use them.

Creating the PurchaseOrder message

First, we will need to create a message for this solution to be processing. As covered in *Chapter 3, BizTalk Development Guidelines*, we should always use multipart messages in orchestrations. They are far more flexible and allow us to change the orchestration easily in the future, should we need to. We will now add a multipart message for our purchase order schema to the solution:

1. In the **Orchestration View** of Visual Studio:
   - Expand the **Types** section.
   - Right-click **Multipart Message Types** and click **New Multipart Message Type**.
   - Rename the message **MultipartType_1** to **PurchaseOrderType**.
   - Rename the part **MessagePart_1**, following **PurchaseOrderType**, to **Body**.
   - Click **Body** and then in the properties window click the **Type** dropdown and expand **Schemas** selecting **<Select from a referenced assembly…>**.
   - Select the **PurchaseOrder** schema from **Internal Schemas**.
   - Right-click **Messages** in the top part of the **Orchestration View** and click **New Message**. This will create the message instance in our orchestration itself.
   - Rename **Message_1** to **PurchaseOrder**.
   - Click **Message Type** of this new **PurchaseOrder** message and expand **Multipart Message Types**, selecting our **PurchaseOrderType** that we created previously.

2. Click each send and receive shape and change the **Message** to our new **PurchaseOrder** message.

You'll notice that despite the fact that we corrected the listed issues for each of the send and receive shapes, the warnings did not go away. We have corrected the first issue to uncover the second, namely, that we need to provide ports to connect these shapes to.

Adding ports to the canvas

The solution now needs ports connected to the receive and send shapes. This will provide channels to which we can send and receive messages from the rest of BizTalk:

1. Expand the **Toolbox** and drag a **Port** onto the **Port Surface** area to the upper right side of your canvas. A wizard will appear to walk you through the process of creating a new port on the canvas as follows:

   ○ Click **Next**.

   ○ Enter the value **ProcessessPurchaseOrderPort**, as shown in the following screenshot and click **Next**:

   ○ Create a new **Port Type** with **Port Type Name**: **ProcessessPurchaseOrderPortType**. Keep the default values for **Communication Pattern** and **Access Restrictions**, as shown in the following screenshot, and click **Next**:

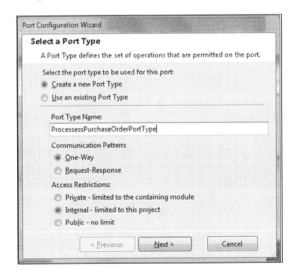

- Keep the default values for **Port direction of communication** and **Port binding** and click **Next** again, as shown in the following screenshot:

- Click **Finish**. After the wizard closes, the new port will be in the right hand port surface and we can see a single operation on it called **Operation_1**. Rename **Operation_1** to **OP_Receive_PurchaseOrder**.

2. Click and drag the **Rcv_PurchaseOrder** to the **OP_Receive_PurchaseOrder** to connect the shape to the operation. This will create a line connecting the receive shape and the port and also assigns the message type property for the operation to our multipart message.

3. Repeat the process in the previous step to create the **Send Ports** and **Types**. These will both use the communication direction **I'll always be sending messages on this port** as follows:

   - Use the names **StandardPurchaseOrderPort**, **StandardPurchaseOrderPortType**

   - **PriorityPurchaseOrderPort**, **PriorityPurchaseOrderPortType**

   - Rename the operations to **OP_Send_PriorityPurchaseOrder** and **OP_Send_StandardPurchaseOrder** respectively

   - Connect the send shapes to their corresponding ports/operations

If you want to make your orchestration neater, you can move the **PriorityPurchaseOrderPort** to the left side of the canvas, even after it is connected.

Implementing the logical comparison

We now have a nearly complete solution. The only piece missing is the `If_Priority` conditional check, which still contains a red exclamation mark. Double-click that shape and an expression editor window will appear. This window, which is used by several shapes, is intentionally limited in capabilities because the creators did not want entire programs being written here. Pressing *Ctrl + Space Bar* will bring up a context list and here we can see our **PurchaseOrder** message. If you *Tab* or click the message it will auto complete. Now entering a left parenthesis will bring up the list of promoted properties available for this message. We're looking for our property that we mentioned earlier.

Enter the following expression: **PurchaseOrder(PRP.OrderProcessing. InternalSchemas.OrderTotal) >= 1000** and click **OK**.

The expression editor is shown in the following screenshot. Note the three icons in the upper left. These allow you to display an object member list, parameter info, and word completion based on the current context.

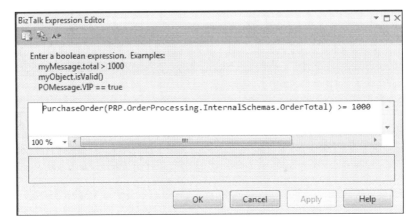

Our orchestration is now complete. We did have other options available for the conditional, namely, using a distinguished field or even an XPath query, which should generally be avoided for reasons explained in *Chapter 3, BizTalk Development Guidelines*. As a brief reminder, the primary reasons were due to versioning and changes that will only surface at runtime, but also for readability reasons.

Once we deploy, our solution must wire it up or configure its bindings in the BizTalk Administration console as follows:

1. Refresh the Administration console and navigate to the **Order Processing** application.

2. Click on the **Orchestrations** node.

3. Double-click the **OrderProcessing** orchestration (the only one).

4. Set the bindings as follows:

   ° Host: **BizTalkServerApplication**

   ° Set the Inbound Logical Ports such as

   ProcessPurchaseOrderPort to **OP_Receive_PurchaseOrders**

   ° Set the Outbound Logical Ports such as

   PriorityPurchaseOrderPort to **OP_File_Send_Fulfillment_Priority-SalesOrder** and **StandardPurchaseOrderPort** to **OP_File_Send_FulfillmentSalesOrder**

   ° Click **OK**

5. Right-click the orchestration and select **Start**.

We are now ready to run. The solution template is setup to restart host instances after deployment of the Maps project—the last one in the build order. If you're not using the downloaded template, be sure to restart your host instances in order for the changes to take effect. If we now run our test **CanRoutePriorityOrder**, we will see that it fails with the following error:

```
BizUnit.TestStepExecutionException: BizUnit encountered an error
executing a test step ---> System.ApplicationException: Directory does
not contain the correct number of files!
 Found: 2 files matching the pattern *.xml.
```

So what's going on? Why did this happen? If you comment out the cleanup state of the test, you can actually inspect the files and see that we have two of the exact same transactions. Indeed this is part of the reason we have unit tests because it is not that messages aren't going through, but that we're getting too many of them; duplicates of the same message. The cause for this is simple and can be seen if we go to the activation subscription query that we looked at earlier in *Chapter 5, Basic Messaging Solution*. Recall that we got to that query by navigating to the **Group Hub** page in the BizTalk Administration console and creating a new query with **Search For** set to **Subscriptions** and **Subscription Type** set to **Activation Subscriptions**. We have a new subscription matching on receive port and message type as follows:

```
http://schemas.microsoft.com/BizTalk/2003/system-properties.
ReceivePortID == {1215B90E-AD4F-4AB6-BCBD-A92BFD4717A8}  And http://
schemas.microsoft.com/BizTalk/2003/system-properties.MessageType
== http://performanceracingparts.com/schemas/PurchaseOrder/
internal/20011-05#PurchaseOrder
```

This is because our orchestration is already expecting a typed message and we bound it to that receive port. To resolve this, all we have to do is go and remove the filters from our send ports. Be sure that the tests have passed before proceeding. Amazingly, our BAM still works even though we've completely re-engineered the solution internally. Behold the glory of BAM.

Checkpoint

So, we have our first orchestration and it required quite a few steps to make it do what our messaging only solution was already doing. This is an example of a terrible orchestration that should not be created. Let's list some of the pros and cons of this solution as follows:

Pros	Cons
Simple to follow code path: we can easily see what this solution does.	Twice the number of trips to the message box: this will make the solution take longer to run.
	Requires recompiling and deploying to change the routing threshold value: this makes maintenance more difficult.
	Took more time to create: there were many more steps here.
	Has more bindings: the simplicity is deceiving, there are actually more parts to manage here.

The list of pros is not very long. Despite that, we will keep the solution as it is and grow it into a better solution. Many of the tasks that are normally accomplished via orchestration can also be done via messaging. All the orchestration engine does anyway is orchestrate messages; it really does run on top of the messaging framework in BizTalk. We will now expand our solution to be more useful than simple routing.

Consuming the order discount service

The company's CRM system, which we already send orders to, allows for a discounting feature that calculates a discount amount based on the customer's purchase history and standing. This feature is accessible via a web service. We need to call this service on priority purchase orders to apply a discount as specified by the CRM. Orchestration is by far the easiest, but not the only way to consume services and create more complex service compositions. Recall that this service, despite being hosted in our enterprise, is in fact an external schema. When we look at the service, we can see that it uses the same message structure for the request as for the response—a simple message that contains an order number, customer name, and order total.

Adding the service artifacts to the solution

The steps for adding the service artifacts to the solution are as follows:

1. Right-click **ExternalSchemas** and select **Add Generated Items**.

2. Double-click **Consume WCF Service**.

3. Type in the following URL for the discount service:
   `http://localhost/DiscountService/DiscountService.svc?wsdl`.

4. Click **Get**, then **Next**.

5. Keep the existing namespace and click **Import**.

6. Click **Finish**.

If you look at the artifacts created, there are three schemas (xsd), an orchestration, and two binding files (xml). The orchestration is the IDE trying to help us, but it is not really being our friend here. It breaks our separation model. We don't want to use it. The only useful things in it are multipart message types and ports for the service request and response, which we already know how to create and we will do so later on. Now we will delete this orchestration and move the bindings to a more appropriate location as follows:

1. Delete the orchestration that was created: `DiscountService.odx`.

2. Move the `*.BindingInfo.xml` files that were created to the `Bindings` folder or just exclude them from the project. We will use `DiscountService.BindingInfo.xml`, but once we have imported it we will not need it again.

Creating the maps

We must now create maps to consume the service. We want to simply send our purchase order out of the orchestration and get back a response. The order processing orchestration should be as unaware of this discount service as possible and thus be as decoupled as possible. The request and response schemas for the discount service are located in `DiscountService_tempuri_org.xsd`.

1. Create a map in the Maps project named **Int_PurchaseOrder_To_DiscountServiceRequest.btm**.

2. Select the schema **PurchaseOrder** from **InternalSchemas** for the left side of the map and **GetCustomerDiscount** from **ExternalSchemas** for the destination on the right.

3. Map **BillTo.Name** to **CustomerName**.

4. Map **Number** to **OrderNumber**.

5. Map **Total** to **Total**.

This is where saving our previous internal purchase order format can prove to be useful. If we like, we can now use this file as the input to test our map with:

1. Create a map named **Ext_DiscountServiceResponse_To_PurchaseOrder. btm**.

2. Select **GetCustomerDiscountResponse** as the source schema and **PurchaseOrder** as the destination.

3. Map **Discount** to **Total**.

Now we simply need to modify our existing orchestration to call the discount service from within the priority branch as follows:

1. Add a send shape named **Snd_DiscountRequest_PurchaseOrder** in the **Is_Priority** branch before the **Snd_PriorityPurchaseOrder** shape.

2. Assign the **PurchaseOrder** message to this shape.

3. Add a receive shape for the discount service named **Rcv_DiscountResponse_ PurchseOrder**.

4. Create a new message **OrderDiscount** to hold the response in and make its type the multipart type **PurchaseOrderType**. Assign this new message to **Rcv_DiscountResponse_PurchseOrder** via the properties window.

5. Create a port to call the service by dragging a port shape onto the **Port Surface** and perform the following steps:

    ○ Name the port **DiscountServicePort**

    ○ Name the port type **DiscountServicePortType**

    ○ Select Request-Response as the communication pattern

    ○ Select **I'll be sending…** as the direction and keep the **specify later** option

    ○ Rename **Operation_1** to **OP_Send_DiscountRequest**

6. Connect the **Snd_DiscountResponse_PurchseOrder** and **Rcv_ DiscountResponse_PurchseOrder** shapes to the **OP_Send_DiscountRequest** operation (on the Request and Response connectors).

7. Create a new message **DiscountedPurchaseOrder** of multi-part type **PurchaseOrderType** to hold the final order.

8. Drag a **Message Assignment** shape following the **Rcv_DiscountResponse_ PurchaseOrder** shape and perform the following steps:

    ○ Rename **ConstructMessage_1** to **Construct_ DiscountedPurchaseOrder**

>   ° Assign **DiscountedPurchaseOrder** as the **Messages Constructed** property of **Construct_DiscountedPurchaseOrder**
>
>   ° Rename **MessageAssignment_1** to **Assign_ DiscountedPurchaseOrder**

At this point, we need to assign the discount to the original purchase order payload and we have three options on how to do this. We can:

- Use an XPath expression
- Use the existing promoted property
- Use a distinguished field to work with this value

Distinguished fields

Although we can use our existing promoted property to perform the value assignment for the purchase order, we can also use a distinguished field for the same purpose. As discussed in *Chapter 3, BizTalk Development Guidelines*, distinguished fields provide an XPath short hand for use in orchestrations. The benefits of distinguished fields over promoted properties are twofold: one, they use a compact and familiar notation and two, they are not loaded into the message context. To create the distinguished field follow the steps as follows:

1. Open the **PurchaseOrder** schema in the **InternalSchemas** project.
2. Navigate to the **Total** node and right-click on it.
3. Click **Promote | Show Promotions**.
4. Click on the **Distinguished Fields** tab in the upper right.
5. Click on the **Add >>** button to mark the field as distinguished.
6. Click **OK**.
7. Build the solution.

Go back to the **OrderProcessing** orchestration, as we're now ready to use our new distinguished field. If we double-click the **Assign_DiscountedPurchaseOrder**, we again see the expression window. Enter the following two lines of code into the expression window:

```
DiscountedPurchaseOrder.Body = PurchaseOrder.Body;
DiscountedPurchaseOrder.Body.Total = OrderDiscount.Body.Total;
```

The first line assigns the **PurchaseOrder** we received to the **DiscountedPurchaseOrder**. The second line assigns the discounted order total that we get back from the web service call.

Finally, click the shape **Snd_PriorityPurchaseOrder** and change the **Message** property to **DiscountedPurchaseOrder**. Failing to do this would cause the old message to be sent out of the orchestration, negating all our previous work. Deploy the solution and refresh the BizTalk Administration console.

Creating a new send port

We now need to create a new send port to consume this web service. The steps for creating a new send port are as follows:

1. Right-click **Send Ports** and click **New | Static Solicit-Response Send Port....**

2. Name this port **OP_Wcf_Send_OrderDiscount**.

3. Select **WCF-BasicHttp** as the **Type**.

4. Select **XMLReceive** as the **Receive** pipeline.

5. Click **Configure** to configure the port type.

6. Enter http://localhost/DiscountService/DiscountService.svc as the **Address (URI)**.

7. Enter http://tempuri.org/IDiscountService/GetCustomerDiscount as the **Action**.

>
>
> **SOAP Action**
>
> Although the previous Action may look like a URL, it is not. SOAP Actions are much like XML namespaces in that they are qualifiers that simply provide uniqueness. They do not need to correspond to an actual URL, and generally do not.

8. On the **Messages** tab, be sure to uncheck **Propagate Fault Message**.

9. Click **OK**.

10. Assign the outbound map **Int_PurchaseOrder_To_DiscountServiceRequest** and the inbound map **Ext_DiscountServiceResponse_To_PurchaseOrder**.

11. Click **OK**.

12. Double-click the orchestration **OrderProcessing** and assign **OP_Wcf_Send_OrderDiscount** to **DiscountServicePort**.

13. Click **OK**.

14. Start the application.

We have now connected the order discount service into our solution. We should be able to run our unit tests and see the results come out. The unit test **CanRoutePriorityPurchaseOrder** will fail, however, after the test fails, we will see a failed test row in the **Test Results** window in Visual Studio. Double-clicking on the failure will bring up a detailed error page for that specific test failure. Near the top of the test results, we will see the reason for the failure, which is shown as follows:

```
Test method UnitTests.BizUnitTests.CanRoutePriorityOrder threw
exception:
BizUnit.ValidationStepExecutionException: BizUnit encountered an
error executing a validation step ---> System.ApplicationException:
XmlValidationStep failed, compare 1492.07 != 1492.070, xpath query
used: /*[local-name()='SalesOrder' and namespace-uri()='http://
inventorymanagement/schemas/purchaseorder/external/2009-10']/*[local-
name()='Total' and namespace-uri()='']
```

The failure is because our output amount is not the expected value. Again our unit tests are providing a safety net for us. They are, in fact, telling us something isn't right and needs to be addressed. Because this is a trivial example, we can simply replace the expected total amount with the value that is left in the order now, which is 1492.070 (a 5 percent discount).

Handling SOAP Faults

So far, we have a working solution, but this is not necessarily the sort of solution you would want to go to production with. The solution is far more fragile than it at first appears. Although it will retry if a service is down, it will not be able to be resumed in the case of a SOAP or other service-side fault. This can cause us a lot of pain.

Using scopes and exceptions

Expecting the unexpected is generally a good rule and orchestration is no different in this regard. We are provided with a few different tools to help us handle the unexpected within an orchestration; one of them is the **scope** shape. A scope is a container or context block in which we can place other shapes almost to function as a unit of work. Scopes help us logically organize our orchestrations. Scopes can contain their own messages, variables, and correlation sets that are local to them and their children. This helps us avoid having too many orchestration global artifacts complicating our solutions.

Scopes also allow us the use of **transactions**. Every scope has a transaction type, as does an overall orchestration. The transaction types are listed as follows:

- **None**: This transaction type means that no special transactionality is added to the shapes within the scope.

- **Atomic**: This transaction type is fully ACID compliant and will commit all changes together or rollback as a group. This type of scope has special limitations, such as not being able to have send and receive shapes in it. This makes sense because the message box is a decoupling mechanism and we cannot hold a long lasting lock on it. Atomic scopes also allow for working with services components (DTC/Enterprise Services).

- **Long Running**: This allows us to specify that a group of shapes is considered to be a connected group and transacted together, but is not fully ACID compliant. Because they are designed to run for a long time, they can be neither atomic nor isolated, but they are durable and consistent. Long running scopes also allow us to nest other scopes.

Finally, scopes also allow for exception handlers; much like a try/catch block in .NET. Exception handlers allow us to specify different expected exceptions in order of most (first) to least specific and bring the same benefit we get from them in traditional code; namely, that we know something has gone wrong and have an opportunity to resolve it.

Along these lines, orchestration also allows **compensation blocks**; which are used to undo completed transactions. Importantly, compensation blocks are only available in long running transactions; they are in fact the key to the consistency and durability that we discussed previously. Compensation blocks can be executed even after a scope is complete from either an exception handler or another (parent) scope or compensation block.

Encountering a SOAP Fault

We will now force a fault in our service; we can do this in the computer management console (or IIS Manager) by stopping the web service application. Click **Start**, right-click **Computer** and select **Manage**. Expand **Service and Applications** at the bottom of the left side. Click on **Internet Information Services (IIS) Manager**. Expand the root node of the local server and expand **Sites**; then expand **Default Web Site**. Click the **DiscountService** website and select **Stop Application** from the **Actions** pane on the right-hand side.

If we run our priority test again, we can see that it fails (eventually). We can also see in the BizTalk Administration console that we now have a dehydrated instance of our send port. We have triggered the retry mechanism in the send port, but eventually the port will exceed the retry and suspend. This actually isn't as bad as it first appears. We can simply resume these service instances from the BizTalk Administration console after restarting the service. The real problem comes when something else happens, something unexpected. If we navigate to `C:\inetpub\wwwroot\DiscountService` and edit the `web.config` file, we can see the following setting near the bottom:

```
<CrmDiscountService.Properties.Settings>
 <setting name="ThrowFault" serializeAs="String">
  <value>False</value>
 </setting>
</CrmDiscountService.Properties.Settings>
```

This setting exists solely for the purpose of our experiments, but as the name implies, it is telling this service if it should throw a fault. This fault is not explicitly listed in the service contract exposed by this service, but this doesn't mean that the service developer won't throw it. If we change this value to **True**, our priority test will now fail.

If we look in the BizTalk Administration console, we can see that the orchestration itself is suspended this time. Double-clicking the suspended orchestration will allow us to see the details of this service instance, which is shown as follows:

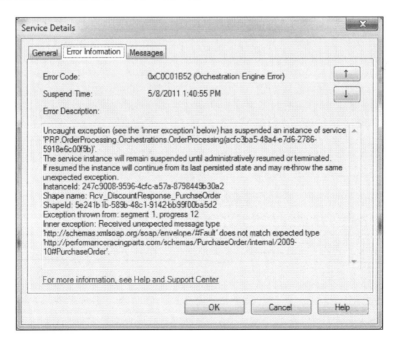

If we click on the **Error Information** tab, we can see the exact error text. Importantly, we can see the name of the shape that threw this error and a little further down some information telling us that we received an expected message type.

Clicking the **Messages** tab shows us exactly what this errant message is. This is shown in the following screenshot:

It is in fact a SOAP Fault message and our solution currently does not know what to do about it. The bad news is that our send port service instance is complete. This message is now stuck. We cannot resume it; we must save the original message out and terminate this instance. This is generally not an acceptable solution.

Why is this happening?

If you're interested in the details of how we ended up here, we can briefly look at the subscriptions query we used before, but this time query on subscriptions with **Subscription Type** set to **Instance Subscription**. We can see a stopped XLANGs subscription and if we look at the expression, it is similar to the following:

```
http://schemas.microsoft.com/BizTalk/2003/system-properties.Correla-
tionToken == d1e5e9a0-5806-4dc1-8c4d-398f7a2537d9.
```

The GUID will be different each time, but this is simply showing us that this subscription is explicitly waiting for a message with a property called **CorrelationToken** set to the expected value. If you examine the suspended orchestration's messages, you will see that the SOAP Fault does have this property and it is set to this value. This is because the service did return a message, it just wasn't the message that the service contract said it would be. This is a good demonstration of how decoupled all the parts of BizTalk are. This orchestration and port may appear coupled in our minds, but they are not as coupled as we think. We have no choice but to terminate the existing service instances.

Using a scope to catch the fault

We quickly realize that any outage in the **Discount Service** results in the non-resumable orchestration instances that must be resolved manually by the Operations team. We decide to add some error handling to the orchestration, so that the instances can simply be resumed. The steps for this are as follows:

1. Open the orchestration **OrderProcessing**.

2. Add a scope shape named **Discount Service Scope** between the send and receive for the **Discount Service Call**.

3. Set the **Transaction Type** to **None** in the properties window.

4. Move both the **Snd_PurchaseOrder** and **Rcv_OrderDiscount** shapes for the Discount Service into this scope.

5. Add a **Reference** to the Orchestrations project for **System.Web.Services**.

6. Right-click **Discount Service Scope** and click **New Exception Handler**; name this new exception handler **SOAP Exception**.

7. Change the new handler's properties as follows:
    ° For the **Exception Object Type** click **<.NET Exception>** and browse to **System.Web.Services.SoapException** (if **System.Web.Services** is not already referenced in your project you may need to add a new reference)
    ° Set **Exception Object Name** to **ExSoapException**

8. Build the solution and see why it is failing. This makes sense, as our scope has not assigned the message definitively, which orchestration will not allow.

9. Move the **Construct_MsgDiscountedOrder** and **Snd_PriorityPurchaseOrder** shapes into the **Discount Service Scope** after the **Rcv_DiscountResponse_PurchaseOrder** shape.

Our solution will now build and we can catch the SOAP exception returned by the discount server. Now we have to decide what to do about it. Ultimately, we want a way to safely retry the service even if a fault is returned. Because our orchestration cannot proceed without this service response, retrying is our only real option.

Using a loop to retry the request

A simple way to accomplish this is with a loop shape inside the orchestration. The loop will bring us back around to the service request in the event of a fault. The steps for this are as follows:

1. Drag a loop shape named **Service Loop** above the **Discount Service Scope**.

2. Move the **Discount Service Scope** into **Service Loop**.

3. Create an orchestration variable called **Complete** of type **boolean** with an initial value of **False** (in the orchestration view).

4. Click the condition for **Service Loop** and set it to **Complete == false**.

5. Drag an expression shape after the shape **Rcv_OrderDiscount**; name it **Discount Complete**.

6. In **Discount Complete** add the expression: **Complete = true;**.

We now have crude and dangerous retry capabilities. The solution as it stands will indeed retry when there is a fault, but it will retry instantly and it will retry indefinitely. If the service we're calling is throwing a fault, it is unlikely to be resolved instantly. Assuming our request is correct, which can be validated in the send port, we should be getting a legitimate response back. Because most platforms are not as robust or parallel as BizTalk, they are unlikely to be able to handle the request flood that a solution like this can cause. We must put in some sort of safety net to this solution.

Breaking out of retry loop

To do this, we will use another orchestration variable to control how many times we actually attempt retry in the case of a SOAP Fault:

1. Create a variable at the orchestration level called **RetryCount** of type **Int32** with **Initial Value** of **0**.

2. Drag a decision shape into the exception handler **SOAP Exception** and call it **Retry Count Exceeded**:

    ° Label the **Rule_1** side as **Yes** with an expression **RetryCount > 1**

    ° Drag a suspend shape into the **Yes** branch named **Retry Exceeded Suspend** with an **Error Message "The Retry Count has been exceeded for a service call, this Instance can be resumed and will try again";** – note that the quotes and semicolon are required

    ° Drag an expression shape after the suspend named **Clear Count** with expression **RetryCount = 0;**

    ° Drag an expression shape to the **Else** side of the decide named **Increment Retry Count** with expression **RetryCount = RetryCount + 1;**

3. Deploy the solution (remember this will restart the host instances for us).

4. Update the Send Port **OP_Wcf_Send_DiscountService** to have a **Retry Count** of **0** (this is for demonstration only).

5. Run the **CanRoutePriorityOrder** (it will fail) and look at **All In-Progress Service Instances** and you will see what has happened.

6. Change the **web.config** element from earlier back to **False** and resume the suspended orchestration.

The suspended orchestration should resume and complete as we expect. This solution is by no means perfect, but it does allow us to use some of the BizTalk features like port level, retry in the case of transport failures, and still trap generic SOAP Faults. The business requirement is met here by making sure we're able to complete the business process, but the side effect is that we get failed messages from the send port. This is because the send port itself does receive a response from the service that is the fault, but it's a response that it does not understand and now has nowhere to send it to.

Over time, these failed messages will accumulate in our message box (in the suspended queue) and slow down our system. They make debugging and tracking on a live system much more difficult. Our goal in BizTalk should really be that solutions clean up after themselves. For a variety of reasons this isn't always the case. One possible solution is **Failed Message Routing**.

Implementing Failed Message Routing

Failed Message Routing is an error handling capability built into BizTalk that allows us to automate how we handle failures in either send or receive ports. Unlike the suspended messages we have seen in the BizTalk Administration console thus far, which are moved out of the work queues and into the suspended queue, failed messages marked for routing do not suspend, but make a second pass, looking for a new set of subscribers with a new set of properties promoted. The old promoted properties are demoted during this failed routing process.

These newly promoted properties include a failure code and the send or receive port names. There are others, but these are generally the most useful to us. Enabling failed message routing is done at the port level.

We will now simply send our failed messages to a file send port, so as to keep them out of the message box as follows:

1. Create the directory **C:\BizTalk\PRP\ErrorLocation** (if it does not already exist).

2. On the send port **OP_Wcf_Send_DiscountService**, go to **Transport Advanced Options** and check **Enable routing for failed messages**.

3. Create a new Static One-way send port named **OP_File_Send_FailedMessages**.

4. Use **FILE** as the type.

5. Use the location: **C:\BizTalk\PRP\ErrorLocation** and **Fault.xml** as the name. Be sure to change the **Copy Mode** to **Overwrite**.

6. Under **Filter**, create the following filter **ErrorReport.SendPortName == OP_Wcf_Send_DiscountService**.

7. Start the new port.

8. Repeat our forced failure test by toggling the **web.config** back to **True** for the **ThrowFault** setting.

9. Toggle **ThrowFault** back to **False** and resume the instance.

This solution does work and doesn't even interfere with our BAM, and because we overwrite our failure message, we even avoid overhead maintenance of having to clean the faulted messages out of the file location. This solution does, however, carry some very serious caveats. So far, we have focused heavily on how BizTalk never loses messages, but this is a direct way to make BizTalk appear as if it is, in fact, losing messages. A quick look at the tracked service instances will show this not to be the case, but it will appear that way; especially to the inexperienced who have yet to fully embrace the reliability of BizTalk. The other and quite possibly more serious issue is that failed messages contain the entire content of the message and this could include sensitive information. The solution presented previously may not be appropriate for handling sensitive information. A similar solution can be created in orchestration that avoids having to write out to disk.

One of the most useful ways to utilize failed message routing is to use it for message repair scenarios. The ESB Framework for BizTalk does this extensively and even provides a generic portal for it. The steps to do this would be to route a failed message out to disk, or SharePoint, and to allow a user to repair and resubmit them to a new receive location on the existing receive port.

Finally, it is also important to understand that although we are using failed message routing within an orchestration, it is not actually an orchestration concept. It is a messaging feature and we can use it completely outside of orchestration.

Summary

In this chapter, we learned how to use orchestration for service composition to consume existing services. We also learned how to make orchestrations that can recover from errors and also how to route failed messages. This is really just the beginning of our journey with orchestration, but already we can see how powerful it is. Later chapters will build on orchestration techniques and cover advanced orchestration concepts.

8

The WCF-SQL Adapter and WCF Services

The current solution is a robust real-world scenario that does a good job demonstrating some basic capabilities of BizTalk Server 2010. We have orchestration, messaging, BAM, and unit tests. This chapter introduces the WCF-SQL adapter and how to use it to pull data from upstream systems as well as send data and requests to downstream ones. We will finish with how to expose WCF services from BizTalk.

Polling a database with the WCF-SQL Adapter

Our application is running well and it is now time to connect our solution to the site that receives sales orders from the web. This website uses a SQL Server backend to store sales orders. We must now automatically retrieve orders from the website's database and flow them into our solution. The name of the website database is AlphaOrders. The data structure of orders is a fairly standard parent-child relationship. The tables that hold an order are Order and OrderLine.

An order has one or more order lines. This schema closely resembles our current understanding of what a purchase order is.

Polling is a technique used by many BizTalk adapters to periodically check on a system that does not provide outbound notifications. On a set interval, a polling operation reaches out to the source system and checks for messages. This is how the FTP and file adapters work internally. The adapter is responsible for when the polling will occur and decouples our applications from the entire concept of time. Although polling involves proactive operations, such as reading a file from an FTP site, it appears to BizTalk purely as a receive operation.

The WCF-SQL Adapter allows us many options when it comes to retrieving data from a database, but the polling approach most closely resembles the majority of other adapters like DB2 and Oracle, so we will use this approach to build up our skillset. In previous versions of BizTalk, this type of polling was the only option in the classic SQL Adapter. We're going to use a stored procedure to pull the records from the website database and we will base our solution on the same pattern as classic SQL Adapter, but we will use the new WCF-SQL Adapter at runtime. Although we could use inline SQL in performing a polling query, the stored procedure approach allows us to have yet another controlled contact point in our solution. The stored procedure acts as an endpoint and contract between the `AlphaSales` database and our solution. As long as the signature of the stored procedure doesn't change, the team maintaining it is free to change the other artifacts in the database.

Constructing XML from SQL using FOR XML

The classic SQL Adapter required us to use an often overlooked feature of SQL Server in order to use stored procedures. This feature is called FOR XML and is used to construct XML results instead of the traditional rowset provided by the SQL Server. FOR XML is added to a `select` query, simply by adding the words FOR XML and a directive, such as AUTO, which instructs SQL Server to use heuristics based on the `select` statement specified.

In the `AlphaSales` database, this can be accomplished with the following query:

```
select * from [order] join orderline on id = orderid for xml auto,
elements
```

The join part of the query is standard T-SQL and the elements directive at the end instructs SQL Server to use element normal XML; meaning that it will make child node's elements rather than attributes. Running this query in SQL Management Studio returns an XML result that shows the following XML document:

```
<order>
  <Id>25</Id>
  <OrderNumber>4321</OrderNumber>
  <CustomerName>Dan</CustomerName>
  <CustomerAddress1>123 Fake St</CustomerAddress1>
  <CustomerState>CA</CustomerState>
  <CustomerZip>94101</CustomerZip>
  <CustomerCity>San Francisco</CustomerCity>
  <OrderTotal>1000.00</OrderTotal>
  <ReadStatus>1</ReadStatus>
  <PhoneNumber>555-1212</PhoneNumber>
  <OrderDate>2011-05-08</OrderDate>
  <orderline>
    <OrderLine>25</OrderLine>
    <OrderId>25</OrderId>
    <ItemNumber>1234       </ItemNumber>
    <Quantity>1</Quantity>
    <UnitCost>1.000000000000000e+002</UnitCost>
    <Description>test</Description>
  </orderline>
  <orderline>
    <OrderLine>28</OrderLine>
    <OrderId>25</OrderId>
    <ItemNumber>3332       </ItemNumber>
    <Quantity>2</Quantity>
    <UnitCost>7.500000000000000e+001</UnitCost>
    <Description>another</Description>
  </orderline>
</order>
```

The XML listed previously, closely resembles our order schema already. Note, how the SQL query engine inferred the structure of the resulting XML, based on the parent- child relationship of the Order and OrderLine tables. This is evident, because the order node is the parent of the orderline nodes. Without using the FOR XML technique, we would need to run two separate queries: one to get the order and one to get the orderlines. SQL XML is a great technique for getting rich records out of SQL Server that are stored in a normalized form, while making only one query to the database.

A stored procedure named ReadUnprocessedOrders exists in the AlphaSales database that contains a modified version of the previous query. These modifications are subtle, but significant. This stored procedure is shown as follows:

```
CREATE PROCEDURE [dbo].[ReadUnprocessedOrders]
AS
BEGIN
update TOP (500) [order] set readstatus = 1  where  readstatus = 0
```

```
select TOP 500 * from [order] join orderline on id = orderid where
readstatus = 1 for xml auto, elements--, xmldata

update TOP (500) [order] set readstatus = 2  where readstatus = 1
END
```

The modifications are as follows:

- A `readStatus` column is used to determine if a record has been read or not, and this is handled via a `where` clause. This technique uses a three state read status with the following meanings:
  - ○ Ready: This status indicates that the record is to be read
  - ○ Locked: This status indicates that the record is in the process of being read
  - ○ Done: This status indicates that the record has been read
- Two `update` queries are added before and after the `select`, to update the records that are to be read. This allows the query to mark records as having been read and also allows multiple host instances running the WCF-SQL receive handler to safely read from the same table. This can greatly increase our throughput.
- All the queries use a `TOP` clause to limit how many records will be read at any time. This is always a good idea to keep from overloading our solutions with large numbers of records, when systems are first turned on or data imports are performed on the source database. The limit shown in the previous code is 500, which is quite small, but it is large enough for most scenarios.
- There is a subtle part of the query that is commented out: `, xmldata`. This directive tells SQL Server to return an inline schema with the results and is required in the next section, when we generate the schema for this stored procedure.

Creating the SQL message schema

The steps for creating the SQL message schema are as follows:

1. Uncomment the **--,xmldata** directive in the stored procedure `ReadUnprocessedOrders` in the `AlphaSales` database by deleting the two dashes.
2. Right-click **Add | Generated Items | Add Adapter Metadata**.
3. Click **Add**.
4. Select **SQL** from the adapter list.
5. Click **Set** in the upper right to set the connection string for the database.

6. Enter **localhost** for the server, **Use Windows NT Integrated Security**, and select `AlphaSales` as the database.

7. Click **OK**.

8. Click **Next**.

9. Keep the radio button on **Receive port** and enter the value **http://performanceracingparts.com/schemas/PurchaseOrder/sql/2011-05** for the namespace and **WebSiteOrders** for the root element name.

10. Click **Next**, select **Stored Procedure** and click **Next** again.

11. Click the dropdown and select **ReadUnprocessedOrders**. Click the **Generate** button, and you will see the text appear in a read-only textbox.

12. Click **Next**.

13. Click **Finish**.

14. Rename the schema **SQLService__x32011_x2d05.xsd** (or whatever it is) to **WebSiteOrders.xsd** and be sure to rename the **Type Name** as well to **WebSiteOrders**.

15. Also, because we're not actually using the classic SQL Adapter, we must change the setting for the schema root node **Element Form Default** from qualified to unqualified (or default, which is the same).

16. Delete the orchestration that this wizard made for us automatically — **BizTalk Orchestration.odx** — as we will not be using it.

We can see here some of the reasons this adapter was retired, the artifacts it made for us were not only not terribly useful; they had terrible autogenerated names as well.

17. Finally, we must edit `ReadUnprocessedOrders` to remove the , `xmldata` directive; delete, or comment it out.

> The `xmldata` statement was required when running the classic SQL wizard, but it cannot be used after the wizard is run. This is because it will return an inline schema that BizTalk is not expecting and it will cause an error. Be sure to comment out or delete this statement after running the wizard.

Our schema is now complete and ready to be used in our solution. Fortunately for us, all we have to do is create a map and a receive location within our existing receive port to make this happen.

Creating the map for the website orders

The steps for creating the map for the website orders are as follows:

1. Create a map from **WebSiteOrders** to **PurchaseOrder**, name it
   Ext_WebSiteOrders_To_PurchaseOrder.btm.

2. Like we did for the InfoPath order, map the customer information to the
   BillTo and **ShipTo** nodes.

3. Map **CustomerAddress1** to **Street** and **CustomerZip** to **PostalCode**.

4. On the orderline, map **ItemNumber** to **CatalogNumber**.

5. Finally, for the **SalesChannel** we will again use a **String Concatenate
   Functoid** and this time use the value **Website**.

6. Deploy the solution.

The map turns out to be very similar to what we did in *Chapter 5, Basic Messaging
Solution*, in the section, *Creating Maps*. Please refer to that section for screenshots and
other information about maps.

Creating the new WCF-SQL receive location

The steps for creating the new WCF-SQL receive location are as follows:

1. Create a receive location called **OP_SQL_Receive_PurchaseOrders**, selecting
   OP_Receive_PurchaseOrders as the parent receive port.

2. Select **WCF-SQL** for the type and **XMLReceive** for the receive pipeline.

3. Click **Configure**.

4. Enter **mssql://localhost/sqlexpress/alphasales?** as the **Address (URI)** in the
   General tab, which can also be done via the **Configure** button.

5. Switch to the **Bindings** tab.

6. Set **XmlStoredProcedureRootNodeName** to **WebSiteOrders**.

7. Set **XmlStoredProcedureRootNodeNamespace** to **http://
   performanceracingparts.com/schemas/PurchaseOrder/sql/2011-05**.

8. Set **Inbound Operation Type** to **XmlPolling**.

9. Set the **PolledDataAvailableStatement** to **select COUNT(*) from [order]
   where readstatus = 0**.

10. Set the **PollingStatement** to **exec ReadUnprocessedOrders**.

11. Update the **OP_Receive_PurchaseOrders** to also have the new map
    Ext_WebSiteOrders_To_PurchaseOrder in **Inbound Maps**.

We have now added the capability of handling a completely new and much more complex data source to our current solution. Our BAM profile continues to function, unaffected by these changes, and we can see a real-world example really developing in our solution.

Most organizations are already storing their data in databases and most of the adapters we'll work with will be able to return complex record structures that we will want to work with in the manner we have seen here. With only the addition of a single column to a table and a stored procedure, we are able to integrate easily with SQL Server-based applications.

Creating the unit test for website order

Arguably, we should have done this first, but now is as good a time as ever. This unit test will be a little more real-world than our previous ones. This unit test will clearly have to work with SQL Server in order to accomplish our test objectives, but as we'll now see, BizUnit makes this easy, as explained in the following points:

1. Be sure your `TestEntities.dtd` has an accurate value for the `AlphaSales` database connection string as follows:

   ```
   <!ENTITY AlphaSalesDb "Server=localhost\sqlexpress;Database=AlphaS
   ales;Trusted_Connection=True;">
   ```

2. Create a new XML document in the **BizUnitTests** folder called **CanRouteStandardWebsiteOrder.xml**.

3. Copy the contents of **CanRouteStandardPurchaseOrder.xml** into **CanRouteStandardWebsiteOrder.xml**.

4. Rename the **testName** attribute **CanRouteStandardWebsiteOrder**.

5. In the test setup, add the following two test steps after the `FileDeleteMultiStep` as follows:

   ```
   <TestStep assemblyPath="" typeName="BizUnit.DatabaseDeleteStep">
      <ConnectionString>&AlphaSalesDb;</ConnectionString>
      <Table>OrderLine</Table>
      <Condition>OrderLine >= 0</Condition>
   </TestStep>
   <TestStep assemblyPath="" typeName="BizUnit.DatabaseDeleteStep">
      <ConnectionString>&AlphaSalesDb;</ConnectionString>
      <Table>[Order]</Table>
      <Condition>Id >= 0</Condition>
   </TestStep>
   ```

If we look at these steps, the power of BizUnit becomes immediately clear. These simple steps simply take a connection string, a table name, and a condition, they then delete all the records in that table matching that condition. We leverage another entity in the DTD to make this connection string only exist in a single place as follows:

1. Copy these two steps to the test cleanup as well, again after the FileDeleteMultiStep.

 Please note that the order these are in is significant because of the foreign key relationship that exists between these tables.

2. Replace the FileCreateStep in the test setup with the following test step:

```
<TestStep assemblyPath="" typeName="BizUnit.
DBExecuteNonQueryStep">
    <DelayBeforeExecution>1</DelayBeforeExecution>
    <ConnectionString>&AlphaSalesDb;</ConnectionString>
    <NumberOfRowsAffected>1</NumberOfRowsAffected>
    <SQLQuery>
        <RawSQLQuery>INSERT INTO [Order] (OrderNumber, CustomerName,
CustomerAddress1, CustomerState, CustomerZip, CustomerCity,
OrderTotal, ReadStatus, OrderDate, PhoneNumber) VALUES
('3774632','John Doe','123 Fake
St','IL','60611','Chicago','247.54',    '0','2010-03-26','312-555-
1234')
        </RawSQLQuery>
    </SQLQuery>
</TestStep>
```

This DBExecuteNonQuery step, as the name implies, runs a raw SQL statement that does not return results. In this case, it is an insert into the order table. It allows us to specify the number of seconds to wait before executing the query, the connection string, and the number of rows affected by the query. We also specify the query itself. This step creates the row in the order table. We will now insert a record into the OrderLine table as follows:

1. Copy the DBExecuteNonQuery step from the previous code and paste it directly in the following code.

2. Paste the query in the following code into the RawSQLQuery element of the newly copied step:

```
INSERT INTO OrderLine (OrderId, ItemNumber, Quantity, UnitCost,
[Description])
VALUES ((SELECT TOP 1 id FROM [Order]), '54346',
'1','247.54','Some Item')
```

We now have our test setup and cleanup complete. This test will create new records in the `AlphaSales` database and delete them when it is complete. We will now modify the text execution stage of the unit test as follows:

1. Increase the **Timeout** value of the first step in the test execution stage—which is the **FileExistStep**—to 50,000. This parameter is measured in microseconds.

2. Update the **Number** in the **XmlValidateValidationStep** to 3774632 and the **Total** to 247.54.

3. Create a new test harness method in **BizUnitTests.cs** with the following code:

```
[TestMethod]
public void CanRouteStandardWebsiteOrder()
{
BizUnit.BizUnit test = new
    BizUnit.BizUnit("CanRouteStandardWebsiteOrder.xml");
      test.RunTest();
}
```

Our test is now complete and, in those few steps, we replaced trivial file operations with realistic database ones.

Performing imperative queries with the WCF-SQL Adapter

The WCF-SQL Adapter can also be used for send ports and performing imperative queries, rather than just polling read operations, like we just accomplished. Our `AlphaSales` database also contains customer information that we, and other teams in the enterprise, are interested in accessing. We are asked to create a customer WCF service for accessing this information. Like always in BizTalk solutions, we will use a canonical schema to provide isolation and decoupling. To accomplish this, we must perform the following steps:

1. Create WCF-SQL endpoint schema
2. Create an external schema to expose as a service
3. Create an internal, canonical schema to build our solution
4. Create maps to tie the schemas together
5. Publish our service endpoint

Creating the schemas to communicate with the database

Our first step is to use the WCF-SQL Adapter to consume services from the `AlphaSales` database. This will allow us to access the SQL artifacts from within BizTalk and expose them as we choose other consumers, as shown in the following steps:

1. Right-click **ExternalSchemas** and select **Add | Generated Items | Consume Adapter Service** to launch the Adapter Framework wizard.

2. Select the **sqlBinding** and enter the following URI: **mssql://localhost/sqlexpress/AlphaSales?**

3. Click **Connect**.

4. Expand the **Tables** category on the left and click the **Customer** table, below **Tables**.

5. Select **Insert**, **Select**, **Update**, operations in the **Available categories and operations** section on the right and click **Add**.

We can see that the three operations were added to the section **Added categories and operations**.

1. At the bottom of the dialog, enter **AlphaCustomer_** as the **Filename Prefix**.

2. The **Consume Adapter Service** dialog should look similar to the following screenshot, before we click **OK**:

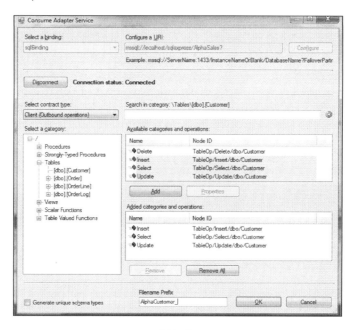

3. Click **OK**.

4. We can see that the following files were added to the solution:

   ° `AlphaCustomer_SimpleTypeArray.xsd`

   ° `AlphaCustomer_Table.dbo.xsd`

   ° `AlphaCustomer_TableOperation.dbo.Customer.xsd`

   ° `WcfSendPort_SqlAdapterBinding_Custom.bindinginfo.xml`

Of these, `AlphaCustomer_TableOperation.dbo.Customer.xsd` is the most interesting to us as it is where the operations and their responses are defined. `WcfSendPort_SqlAdapterBinding_Custom.bindinginfo.xml` is a bindings file that we can use to create a new send port in the administration console.

Creating the external schema for the service request

Now, we must create the external schema that we will expose as our actual service. Our goal is to make this service simple for our consumers, so exposing the schemas from the WCF-SQL Adapter would not be ideal. We are trying to decouple the consumer from the details of SQL and the WCF-SQL Adapter. The steps for creating the external schema for the service request are as follows:

1. Create a new schema `CustomerRead.xsd` in **ExternalSchemas**.

2. Change the namespace to the following: **http://performanceracingparts.com/ schemas/customer/2011-05**.

3. Rename the **Root** node **CustomerReadRequest**.

4. Add a child element called **Name**.

5. Create a new root node called **CustomerReadResponse**.

6. Add the following nodes to the response record:

   ° Name

   ° Status

   ° TotalOrderedAmount (set the Data Type to `xs:decimal`)

   ° PhoneNumber

   ° State

   ° LastOrderDate (set the Data Type to `xs:date`)

Creating the internal schema for the service request

Because we always want to isolate our internal and external schemas, we now need to create an internal schema that directly matches our external customer read request, as shown in the following steps:

1. Add an existing item to the **InternalSchemas** project and select the `CustomerRead.xsd` from the **ExternalSchemas** project.

2. Change the namespace to the following: **http://performanceracingparts.com/ schemas/customer/internal/2011-05**.

3. Expand the **CustomerReadRequest** and add an **Action** element after **Name**.

4. Right-click the **Action** node, select **Promote | Show Promotions** with the **Microsoft.BizTalk.GlobalProperties** schema. Click the **Property Fields** tab and click the folder icon to add a new property schema. Select **BTS.bts_ system_properties** on the Operation property, as shown in the following screenshot:

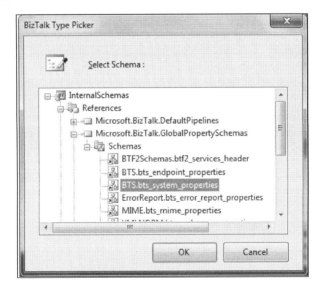

5. Click **OK**.

6. Click **Add >>** to assign the property to the right and select **ns0:Operation**, as shown in the following screenshot:

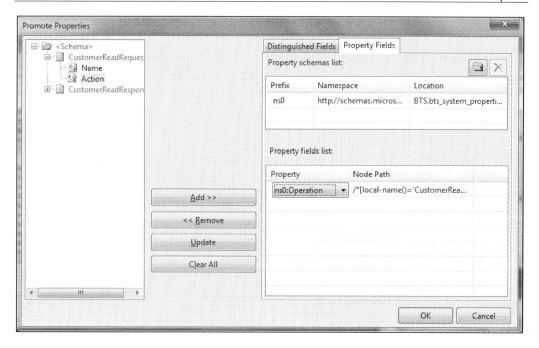

7. Click **OK**.

System properties

There are many existing system properties within BizTalk that are used internally and are vital to the functioning of the platform. We are free to use some of these, as we do in this example, to inject functionality into the platform. In this case, we are using the BTS.Operation system property, which will later be used to control the WCF action that is called.

Creating maps for the service

Our last development task is to create maps to tie the request, the internal messages, and the response together. This is a two-way service, so we will require four maps to do this; two on each direction. All of these will be added to the Maps project. The steps for creating maps for the service are as follows:

1. Create a map **Ext_CustomerReadRequest_To_CustomerReadRequest.btm**. Select the external **CustomerReadRequest** for the source and the internal one for the destination.

2. Map **Name** to **Name**.

3. Map **Select** to the **Action** node using a **String Concatenate Functoid**.

4. Create a map **Int_CustomerReadRequest_To_AlphaCustomerSelect.btm**, selecting the internal **CustomerReadRequest** schema for the source and **AlphaCustomer_TableOperation.dbo.Customer** as the destination; when the dialog appears asking you which root node to use, click **Select**.

5. Drop two String Concatenate Functoids onto the grid, one above the other.

6. Enter * as the value in one and connect it to **Columns**.

7. Connect the **Name** input to the other Functoid.

8. Click the **+** sign to add a constant valued **Functoid** and enter **WHERE Name ='**, use the up arrow to move this constant to the top of the list. Add another constant value at the bottom and enter a single quote **'** in the other (the result will come out as **WHERE Name = '<NameValue>'**).

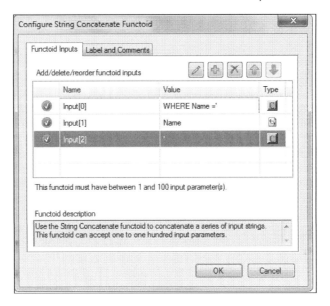

9. Create a map, **Ext_AlphaCustomerSelectResponse_To_CustomerReadResponse.btm**, using the **SelectResponse** root element from the **AlphaCustomer_TableOperation.dbo.Customer** schema and the internal **CustomerReadResponse** as the destination.

10. Drag **Customer** to **CustomerReadResponse** and select **Link by Name**.

11. Create map **Int_CustomerReadResponse_To_CustomerReadResponse.btm**. Recall that, by the naming convention, we know that the schema on the source (left) will be the internal and the destination (right) will be the external.

12. Drag **CustomerReadResponse** to **CustomerReadResponse** and select **Link by Name**.

13. Deploy the solution.

We now have all the artifacts that we need for our service to be published to the broader world. It required a few more steps in the beginning, but this service follows the same principles that all of our solutions have up to this point.

Publishing the schemas as a WCF service

BizTalk comes with a tool that will help us publish WCF services and we will now use that tool to expose our new schemas as services. This tool makes exposing WCF services very simple and allows us a great deal of control over the resulting service. The steps for publishing the schemas as a WCF service are as follows:

1. Launch the **WCF Service Publishing Wizard** by clicking **Start | All Programs | Microsoft BizTalk Server 2010 | WCF Service Publishing Wizard**.

2. Click **Next**.

3. Select the **ServiceEndpoint** radio button (the default) and **Wcf-BasicHttp** as the Adapter name (Transport type). Check **Enable on-premise metadata exchange** or (**Enable metadata endpoint**, if you do not have the AppFabric extensions installed) and create **BizTalk Receive locations** by selecting **Order Processing** as the application.

4. Click **Next**. If you have the AppFabric add-on installed, then skip the **AppFabric** settings and click **Next** again.

5. Change the radio button to **Publish Schemas as WCF service**.

> It is a good idea to avoid the first option, **Publish BizTalk orchestrations as WCF service**; this is because it would expose our internal schemas to the outside world and break our carefully crafted isolation model. Although there are great features like fault contracts that we miss out on, there are other ways to accomplish these; namely WCF interceptors.

6. Rename **Web Service Description** from **BizTalkWcfService** to **CustomerServices**, rename the service from **Service1** to **CustomerService** and **Operation1** to **GetCustomer**.

7. Set **Request** and **Response** to appropriate schemas by right-clicking them. Click **Select schema type** and navigate to **ExternalSchemas\bin\Debug\ PRP.OrderProcessing.ExternalSchemas.dll**. Select **CustomerReadRequest** for request and **CustomerReadResponse** for response.

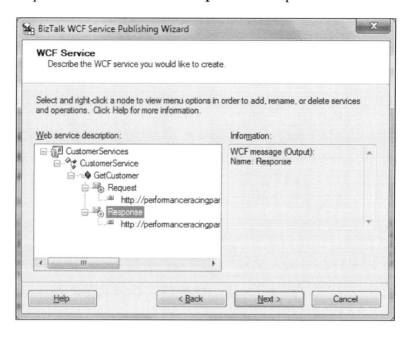

8. Click **Next** and change the Target namespace of **WCF service** to **http://performanceracingparts.com/interfaces/customer/2011-05**.

9. Check **Allow anonymous access to WCF service** and click **Next**.

10. Click **Create**.

11. Click **Finish**.

12. After deployment, rename the port and location as the following:

    ° **OP_Receive_CustomerService**

    ° **OP_Wcf_Receive_CustomerService**

13. Enable the **Location**.

14. Set the Maps on the Receive Port as **Ext_CustomerReadRequest_To_ CustomerReadRequest** (Inbound) and **Int_CustomerReadResponse_To_ CustomerReadResponse** (Outbound).

Changing the IIS AppPool

We have created all of the artifacts that will be used by our solution and, at this point, we have two more steps. The first is to change the AppPool that was assigned to our service during the deployment wizard. The service must run in an AppPool that has access to BizTalk through an Isolated Host Instance. The steps for this are as follows:

1. Start the Internet Information Services Manager by clicking **Start** and typing `inetmgr` in the search box (you can also use the computer management console if you like).

2. This console is another MMS Snap-In. On the left, expand the root (local computer) node and expand the sites node.

3. Expand the **Default Website** node.

4. Click on the **CustomerServices** site.

5. On the right, in the action pane, click **Basic Settings**.

6. Change the **Application pool** on the Virtual Directory to **BizTalk Isolated Host AppPool**, as shown in the following screenshot:

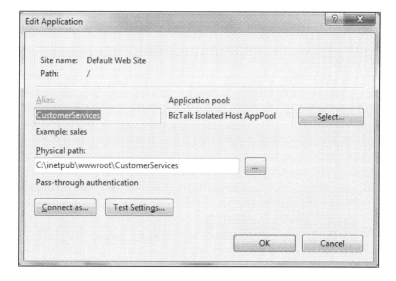

This will assign an AppPool that is capable of communicating with the message box to the IIS application. This AppPool was created when we configured BizTalk on the machine. Skipping this step will cause an error when we browse to the service. This step can also be performed via the command line as shown in the following line of code:

```
C:\Windows\System32\inetsrv\appcmd set app /app.name: "Default Web Site/
CustomerServices" /applicationPool:"BizTalk Isolated Host AppPool"
```

Using the command line is often much faster and can be used to automate processes as well.

Creating the send port for the SQL request

The last step is to create the send port that will send our customer service requests to the SQL Server. This will tie together the WCF service request that we receive to the SQL Server. The steps for this are as follows:

1. In the BizTalk Administration console, right-click the application **Order Processing** and select **Import | Bindings**.

2. Browse to the bindings file **WcfSendPort_SqlAdapterBinding_Custom. bindinginfo.xml** that was created by the consume adapter service wizard.

3. Click on **send ports** and double-click the send port **WcfSendPort_ SqlAdapterBinding_TableOp_dbo_Customer_Custom** and rename it as **OP_WcfSql_Send_AlphaCustomer**.

4. Attach the maps **Ext_AlphaCustomerSelectResponse_To_ CustomerReadResponse** (Inbound) and **Int_CustomerReadRequest_To_ AlphaCustomerSelect** (Outbound).

5. Add a filter **BTS.ReceivePortName == OP_Receive_CustomerService**.

6. Start the **send port**.

Testing the service

Don't worry, we're not going to make an automated test for this service, but it would be easy to do. We will simply test this service with SoapUI.

> SoapUI is a freely available web services testing tool, available at http://www.soapui.org. It is a great tool for testing services, and is especially compatible with non-.NET systems.

1. Launch Soap UI and click **File | New soapUI Project**.

2. Enter the location of the WSDL for our new service **http://localhost/ CustomerServices/CustomerService.svc?wsdl** in the **Initial WSDL/WADL** textbox and click **OK**, as shown in the following screenshot:

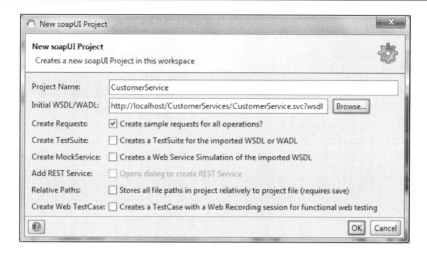

3. The new project contains a sample request for our service called **Request1**, as shown in the following screenshot:

4. Double-click **Request1** and edit the request, so that the name element contains Dan and click the Green arrow to perform a customer read for Dan. The AlphaSales database already has a record for a customer named Dan in it, so this will work. There are a few other customers we can use too, but seeing who they are is left as an exercise for the reader, as shown in the following screenshot:

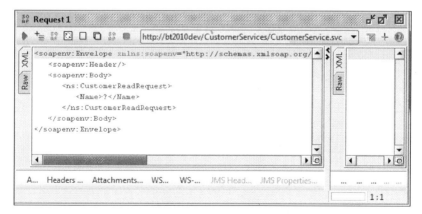

5. Bask in the glory.

This last step is especially important. We have just exposed a WCF service, compatible with Java (as SoapUI is a Java-based tool) that provides access to SQL Server artifacts without writing a single line of code. This is a pretty amazing feat if you think about it. We can easily add other operations and thus create a service layer over our databases to further abstract data consumers from the underlying storage. If we were to switch to another data source or backend system altogether, our service consumers would never need to even know about it.

Summary

In this chapter, we learned how to respond to database changes via the polling technique that is minimally intrusive to our source and scales well. We also learned how to perform imperative queries to SQL databases using the WCF-SQL Adapter. We ended with how to expose WCF services from BizTalk to provide access to these SQL resources. In the next chapter, we will expand our solution by consuming this customer information and using the Business Rules Engine to add rich processing logic.

Expanding the Solution with Services and Rules

9

This chapter starts with consuming the customer service that we previously exposed. We will use this information in making a discount decision for orders. We will explore different ways to do this and introduce the Business Rule Engine as a way to provide rich, loosely coupled business decisions.

Topics covered in this chapter include the following:

- Consuming WCF-SQL services
- Creating policies, rules, and vocabularies
- Looping in a policy
- Versioning policies

Consuming the customer service

Now that we have exposed the customer service to other consumers, we are asked to use it ourselves when calculating an order discount. We need to use the customer service that we built in the last chapter from inside of our Order Processing orchestration. Our goal is to produce better discount calculations based on this information.

Creating a new map

The first task will be to create a new map that translates from our canonical purchase order format to the customer select request, and is shown as follows:

1. Create a new map **Int_PurchaseOrder_To_ AlphaCustomerSelect.btm**.

2. Drop two **String Concatenate** functoids onto the grid, one above the other.

3. Enter * as the value in one and connect it to **Columns**.

4. Connect the **Name** input to the other Functoid.

5. Click the **+** sign to add a constant valued Functoid and enter **WHERE Name ='**, using the up arrow to move this constant to the top of the list. Add another constant value at the bottom and enter a single quote **'** in the other column (the result will come out **WHERE Name = '<NameValue>'**).

The result is shown in the following screenshot:

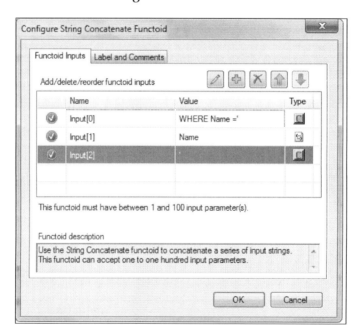

Our map is now complete and we don't even need to add a new port for the service. Both the subscription and the orchestration can use the existing port to send messages.

Adding the data query to the orchestration

Now that we have the way to call our customer service and we already have the canonical format for the customer response, we must connect our Order Processing orchestration to the actual endpoint itself.

Creating the logical port

The first step is to add a logical port that is later bound to the existing WCF-SQL send port. The steps for this are as follows:

1. Open the **Order Processing Orchestration** and add a new port.

2. Name the port **AlphaCustomerPort** and click **Next**.

3. Name the port type: **AlphaCustomerPortType** and be sure to select **Request-Response**.

4. Select **Always be Sending and Specify Later** and click **Next**.

5. Create a new multipart message called **CustomerType**, rename **Part1** as **Body** and select the schema **CustomerReadResponse** as the type.

6. Update the new port in the type browser of the orchestration view.

7. Change the **Operation** to **OP_Send_GetCustomer**.

8. Change the **Request Message Type** to our **PurchaseOrderType** multipart message.

9. Change the **Response Message Type** to **CustomerType** multipart message type.

Adding the new send and receive shapes

With our orchestration port in place, we must now add send and receive shapes to connect to it, which we do as follows:

1. Add new send and receive shapes, **Snd_GetCustomer** and **Rcv_Customer**, and put these after the **Rcv_OrderDiscount**.

2. Connect these to the port **AlphaCustomerPort** that we created previously (note that a new message called **Message_1** of **CustomerType** was added, but not a **PurchaseOrder**).

3. Rename **Message_1** as **Customer**.

4. Select **PurchaseOrder** as the message for **Snd_GetCustomer**.

Enhancing the discount calculation

We have successfully connected this WCF-SQL service to our orchestration and we did it in the best practice manner; that is, we do not have an internal map, and the orchestration is still largely decoupled from the service. We now need to use the data returned by this service to perform some sort of processing.

There are many ways we could use this newly retrieved information in our orchestration, but following the model of the current solution, we decide to use the expression editor to create a progressive discount calculation as follows:

1. Distinguish the element **TotalAmountOrdered** in the internal **CustomerReadResponse** schema.

2. Update the **Assign_DiscountedPurchaseOrder** expression to contain the following:

    ```
    DiscountedServiceOrder.Body.Total = OrderDiscount.Body.Total -
    ((Customer.Body.TotalOrderedAmount / OrderDiscount.Body.Total) *
    OrderDiscount.Body.Total);
    ```

3. Deploy the solution.

We are done coding our new solution changes and we can see that this wasn't really all that much work. Granted our canonical customer schemas did exist before we began this phase, but this is a good demonstration for why canonical schemas should always be created anyway; they encourage reuse and foster a big picture view, which makes it easier for us to pick and choose which functionality we want to add to a solution. Besides being able to help us enforce our separation of concerns and a clean architectural model, we are also able to easily provide services to outside consumers or use the schemas ourselves.

Updating the WCF-SQL Send Port

We have only a few minor changes to make for our solution to work with the new service. We must bind the new orchestration port, create a new entry in the WCF Action map, and attach the new map, as follows:

1. Configure the Orchestration to now use our new Send Port **OP_WcfSql_Send_AlphaCustomer**.

2. Update **OP_WcfSql_Send_AlphaCustomer** to have a new Action map entry:

    ```
    <Operation Name="OP_Send_GetCustomer" Action="TableOp/Select/dbo/
    Customer" />
    ```

Action map

The Action map in a WCF Send Port is used to specify which WCF Action (similar to a SOAP Action) will be used at runtime. The action is similar to a method or operation name. In the previous example, the Action map is used to translate from BTS.Operation (the name of our logical send operation in the orchestration) to the WCF action that will be called. This helps to keep us decoupled from our endpoint as our orchestration does not internally use the external action names.

3. Add the map, **Int_PurchaseOrder_To_ AlphaCustomerSelect** as an Outbound map.

Our current solution will run and the tests will actually still pass because the customer used for this purchase has a new status, which basically makes the calculation apply no additional discount. We can quickly see from the previous assignment that using code to perform our pricing is becoming burdensome. The solution for pricing and discounts currently requires us to recompile and redeploy in order to make any changes. The expression window that the calculation is typed into is also limiting; recall that it is intentional.

We could simply put that logic in a .NET assembly and call the assembly from the orchestration, but we would still have the fundamental problem of having the GAC assemblies on every server and having to restart the host instances for the changes to appear. This is not very scalable and for most systems not very practical. The more frequently our discounting policy changes, the more painful it will be. This is completely contrary to our IT promise to enable Business; we would actually be a hindrance.

Using Business Rules to improve our process

We decide with our business users that having the customer information and the discount should allow us much more flexibility and power in our pricing and discount calculations than we currently have. Our users express a desire to be able to more quickly change pricing and discount models to incorporate more dynamic decisions. They also do not like the way relatively simple calculations look inside our expression window, because the use of parenthesis to provide scoping makes reading the formulas more difficult.

You are aware that the Business Rule Engine can help out with these types of situations and decide to use it to meet the requirements. The business team wants to use the customer loyalty status returned by the customer lookup in the price calculation.

Introduction to the Business Rules Editor

The primary tool for working with BRE is the **Business Rules Composer** that is part of the BizTalk solution stack. The composer is a separate UI outside of Visual Studio and can be installed and used on machines that are not running the full BizTalk Developer edition.

The tool is partitioned into the following three major parts:

- **Explorers** on the left
- **Conditions** on the top right
- **Actions** on the bottom right

These three parts are shown in the following screenshot:

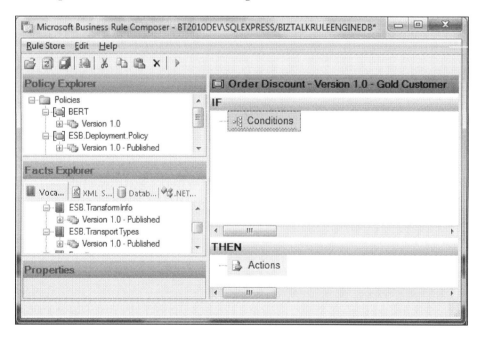

The **Explorers** allow us to see **Policies** (with their rules) as well as **Vocabularies**. There is also a **Properties** window. These artifacts were introduced in *Chapter 2, Introduction to BizTalk Development*.

Creating a vocabulary

We will now create a vocabulary, the base element of the BRE. The vocabulary, as the name implies, is the language of the business we are creating rules for. This could almost be looked at as a domain-specific language. It will allow our users to express rules in terms that they are familiar with rather than with element, property, or column names that developers may have specified. Although not explicitly required, especially when working with .NET-based artifacts, a vocabulary is a useful layer of abstraction in most BRE scenarios that allows us to translate from technical code type concepts to business concepts. The steps for creating a vocabulary are as follows:

1. Start the **Business Rule Composer (Start | All Programs | Microsoft BizTalk Server 2010 | Business Rule Composer)**.

2. Create a new vocabulary called **Order Processing** by right-clicking **Vocabularies** on the left and selecting **Add New Vocabulary**.

Adding a new set of values called definition

Right-click the **Version 1.0** below new vocabulary and click **Add New Definition Customer Loyalty Level** as a Set of Values (string) {New, Silver, Gold}.

 If you happen to name a definition or a rule incorrectly, simply highlight it and press *F2*. You will now be able to edit the value.

The first page of the wizard shows us several options which we have when creating new definitions in the vocabulary. Here we can choose the type of definition that we are creating, namely: constant value, XML, and Database.

After selecting the type of definition and clicking **Next**, we are presented with another dialog that will allow us to name the definition as well as to further define it, which in the case of constant values means the type of constant value to create. There are three types of constant values which are as follows:

- **Constant**: This is simply a value that is always the same no matter what. These are used to stand in for the values themselves. In our solution thus far, we could use a constant value of 1000 called Priority Order, instead of typing the value 1000 into the places we use it. This allows us to name this value and to define it only in one place and use it in many. If we ever have to change the value, we only change the definition, not every rule using the definition.

- **Range of values**: This defines a bound range that can be used for more fuzzy definitions like defining a large order or good credit.

- **Set of Values**: This is a list of values that are possible for a particular definition. States are a good example. We can define a set of values that can be used to describe something in our business. In this case, state could be used to help us determine routing, shipping, or discount information and we would have a single list of valid states for use across our rules.

We will be using a set of values, which will function very much like an enumeration in the rules.

The final dialog lets us enter the details for the subtype that we have selected. Here, it is the specific values of the enumeration that we are defining. Our values Gold, Silver, and New all correspond not only to values within the customer table (which is important by itself), but to concepts within the business context in which we are working. Vocabularies really are the common language we need to establish with business users in order to create effective solutions. This is true in BizTalk or any other platform. The following image shows this final dialog in the **Vocabulary Definition Wizard**:

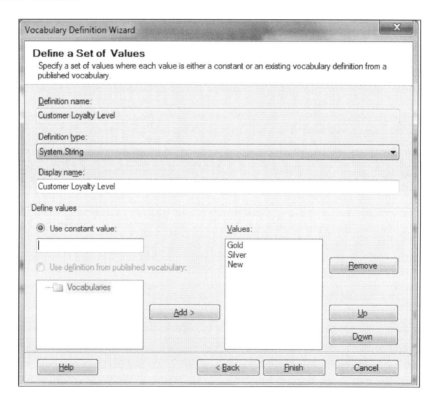

Creating XML definitions in a vocabulary

Some definitions are useful on their own, such as the previous constant values, but very often we need data from our messages or even .NET classes or databases in order to perform useful comparisons. Vocabulary definitions can help us here as well by functioning as shorthand for XPath or .NET properties that would normally not be well understood by business users. Now we will create several XML vocabulary definitions that will be used to interact with the messages in our solution, as follows:

1. Create a new definition and select **XML Document Element or Attribute**, click **Next**.

2. Use the name **Get Customer Loyalty Level** and browse to **InternalSchemas\ CustomerRead.xsd** (ignore the warning about the imported schema, you don't need to browse for it).

3. In the schema, use the **CustomerReadResponse** root node and select **Status**. Also be sure to change the radio button at the bottom to **Perform "Get" operation**.

The first page of the XML document element or attribute definition wizard is shown in the following screenshot:

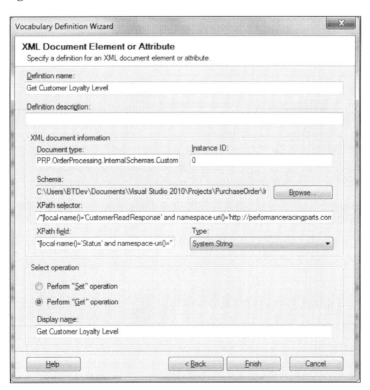

1. Create another XML definition called **Get Order Total**. Again, be sure you select **Get** at the bottom. This time you will use the **PurchaseOrder** schema and select **Total**.

2. Create a final definition called **Set Order Total** and again use the **Total** element of the **PurchaseOrder**, but this time select **Perform "Set" operation** at the bottom of the definition wizard.

3. Right-click the vocabulary and select **Publish**.

We now have our basic vocabulary. This will be used to create a policy that contains individual rules. Again this vocabulary is our translation layer between our solution and the business users.

Creating a policy

Policies are sets of rules that work together in one functional unit. We'll explore the mechanics shortly, but for now, we just need to think of them as the conditions and actions that will produce our outcome. Here, we will create a policy for calculating the order discount for a specific customer. The basic logic is as follows:

- Gold Customers receive a 10 percent discount
- Silver customers get a 5 percent discount
- New customers do not get a discount

We will now create a policy that implements this logic in BRE as follows:

1. Right-click the **Policies** folder in the policy explorer and select **Add New Policy**.

2. Name the new policy **Order Discount**.

3. Right-click the **Version 1.0** below **Order Discount** and select **Add New Rule** (Right-Click version) called **Gold Customer**.

4. In the upper center of the editor, right-click **Conditions** and at the bottom select **Predicates | Equal**.

5. Drag **Get Customer Loyalty Level** to **argument 1** and **Customer Loyalty Level** to **argument 2**. Click the drop down to the right of **Customer Loyalty Level** and set it to **Gold**.

6. Drag **Set Order Total** to **Actions** (near bottom under **THEN**).

7. Right-click the **0** and select **Functions Multiply**.

8. Drag **Get Order Total** to **Value 1** and **.90** to **Value 2**.

9. Add a new rule called **Silver Customer**.

10. Do the same as previously, but make the multiplication **.95**.

11. Create a rule named **New Customer**.

12. Set the **equals to** check for **New**.

13. Set the **Set Order Total** at the bottom to **Get Order Total**.

14. Right-click to publish and then again to deploy the policy.

Because the policies are stored in a central database, many different people can contribute to them or test them before they are finalized. Publish and deploy are separate steps because publish allows others to see and test the policy without making it available to rules' consuming applications like orchestrations. The policies become finalized and available to orchestrations, only when they are deployed. This is also because the Business Rules Engine stores policies and vocabularies in a central database, which allows many consumers to access it concurrently. Publishing allows us to make policies available for testing and review by other users without allowing them to be used by running applications.

Updating the orchestration to call this policy

The final task facing us is to call the rules from the order processing orchestration. This turns out to be quite easy as there is already a Call Rules shape in the orchestration toolbox. The steps for this are as follows:

1. Add a Call Rules shape to the **OrderProcessing** orchestration above **Construct_DiscountedPurchaseOrder** and name it **Call Discount Policy**.

2. Configure the shape to call the Policy and add the following messages:
    ○ **Customer.Body**
    ○ **PurchaseOrder.Body**

3. Redeploy and test.

The priority order test will now break and that's OK, because we expect it to. We can see the reason for the failure is because the amounts do not match. This makes sense because we're not applying the 5 percent discount returned by the discount web service.

We now have a policy driving our decision on discount pricing and fixing the previous error. This turns out to be much easier than before where our only option was to redeploy the orchestration.

Performing a simple update to the policy

We want to slightly adjust the way the prices are calculated. The discount for new customers, which is currently none, must be set to 0.95. We must update the policy to do this. We cannot simply go and change our policy though, because it is already in the enterprise and is being used. To do this, we must version our policy. Versioning, which is done to both policies and vocabularies, allows us to keep a history of what rules were active in what timeframe. By default, the `Call Rules` shape in orchestration always uses the latest version of a given policy. The old policies remain, unless we explicitly delete them, so that we can run them explicitly if we need to and audit when they were changed. It turns out that modifying policies is quite easy.

In order to modify our policy, all we have to do is create a new version of the policy, make our change, and publish/deploy the new policy that is shown as follows:

1. In the **Policy Explorer**, right-click **Version 1.0** of the **Order Discount** policy and click **Copy**. This context menu is shown in the following screenshot.

2. With our policy copied into the clipboard, we next paste the just copied version into the policy. This is shown in the following screenshot as the **Paste Policy Version** menu option:

3. Right-click the **Order Discount** policy (from **Version 1.0**) and click **Paste Policy Version**.

4. Edit the **New Customer** rule, so that instead of assigning the **Get Order Total**, we use the multiplication function like the other rules and multiply by **0.95**.

5. Publish and deploy the modified version.

As always, test to make sure that your policy is working as expected by running the BizUnit tests; specifically the priority purchase order test.

Understanding how business rules work

The basics of the BRE were covered in *Chapter 2, Introduction to BizTalk Development*, but some important aspects were not covered and probably are not immediately clear from the example we just completed. This is because BRE does not use an imperative programming model like procedural or even OOP languages. The BRE uses a **forward chaining** technique, which is a modified Rete algorithm. These types of algorithms are amazingly fast, much faster than pure .NET, but they come with some costs, including memory costs.

Perhaps most importantly, they do not execute like procedural .NET code at all; it is a totally different paradigm. You will notice that there is no Else concept to these rules. The way this works is that when the engine starts, it loads all the artifacts it needs into memory; in this case the two messages it is expecting. This is done via an `assert` command, which asserted them into the memory. Then all the rule predicates are loosely evaluated to look for potential matches. Each condition is not assessed, but each condition that might be true is. Part of the power of BRE is that instead of independently assessing each rule in code iteratively—like you would in .NET—the engine assesses separate facts then evaluates them, once sharing the results with rules that also use that fact. These rules are then placed on an agenda, which runs them in order of their priority (which can be assigned a number in the editor).

If no changes are made to the memory of the rule engine, then the process ends when the last rule is executed. This is the case in our policy as it sits. Only one rule is ever true and all it does is change a value. Other actions, which can be viewed by right-clicking **Actions** in the lower part of the rule editor, actually change the state of the rule engine's memory. This causes a second sweep of rules and the creation of another agenda. This is the whole concept of forward chaining. The policy executes until there are no more changes made to the memory.

This may be easier to understand in terms of a graph. The policy is really a graph that is dynamically built and run until a leaf node, that is, a node with no children, is reached. The leaf is being no more memory changes.

Expanding the policy

With the current state of our rules, we are making extremely poor use of the BRE. The rules may be easier to read than code and they are certainly easier to change, in that they don't require us to compile anything, but we have really just scratched the surface of the BRE. It is the forward chaining that is both the most difficult to understand and the most powerful part of the engine. This section demonstrates forward chaining.

Looping in BRE

One issue always encountered by those new to the BRE is that there seems to be no way to loop over collections, even if you include your own custom classes in a policy. This causes most developers to either not use BRE or to assume that they need to call a policy, once for every item in a collection; both of which are unnecessary. The developers of BRE did not overlook a major commonly used feature of programming languages, it is just implemented differently because of the Rete nature of the rules engine.

In order to demonstrate basic looping in the BRE, we are going to define a class that contains a product. This will also serve to help us see how to use custom classes from within orchestrations:

1. Right-click the **PurchaseOrder** solution and select **Add | New Project**.
2. Select **C# Class Library** as the project type and name it **Library**.
3. Right-click **Library** and select **Properties**.
4. In the **Application** section, rename the assembly name and default namespace both to **PRP.OrderProcessing.Library**.
5. In the **Signing** section, check **Sign the assembly** and under **Choose**—a strong name key file—browse to the key **PurchaseOrder.snk**, which is in the **Build** folder of the solution.
6. Delete the `Class1.cs` file that was created with the project.
7. Right-click **Library** and select **Add | Class** using the name **Product.cs**.

The following code listing for this class shows that there is nothing significant in this class, just some properties, two constructors, and a method. One of the more important features of this class is that it is decorated with the `SerializableAttribute`; this allows the .NET Framework to serialize instances of the class and makes them useable in the durable orchestration environment. In order for a .NET class to be used from within an orchestration, it must either be marked explicitly as serializable or it must be used within an atomic scope, shown as follows:

```
using System;

namespace PRP.OrderProcessing.Library
{
    [Serializable]
    public class Product
    {
        public Product()
        {
```

```
        }
        public Product(string number, int quantitySold, decimal
profitMargin)
        {
            Number = number;
            QuantitySold = quantitySold;
            ProfitMargin = profitMargin;
        }
        public string Number { get; set; }
        public int QuantitySold { get; set; }
        public decimal ProfitMargin { get; set; }

        public void OrderMore()
        {
            System.Diagnostics.Trace.WriteLine("This product is
selling, we should order more: " + Number);
        }
    }
}
```

Building the Library project

We now need to build the **Library** project that we just created. We will also need to register this assembly in the GAC. To do so, click **Start | All Programs | Microsoft Visual Studio 2010 | Visual Studio Tools | Visual Studio Command Prompt** to open a visual studio command prompt.

Browse to the **PurchaseOrder\Library\bin\Debug** directory and type the following command:

```
gacutil /i PRP.OrderProcessing.Library.dll
```

The assembly is now in the GAC and is accessible to other applications including the Business Rule Composer from which we will now consume it.

Using the product class from BRE

Open the business rule composer. In the **.NET Classes** section of the Business Rules Composer (a tab near vocabularies), right-click the folder **.NET Assemblies** and click **Browse** and add **PRP.OrderProcessing.Library**.

Repeat the processing this time adding **mscorlib** (then main .NET assembly) and be sure to select the **Version 4.0**. We will now create a new policy explicitly for the purpose of demonstrating iteration over collections inside BRE as follows:

1. Add a new policy in the Business Rules Composer and name this policy **Product Policy**.
2. Add a new rule called **Assert Collection**.
3. Set the condition to **1 is equal to 1**.
4. Right-click **Actions** at the bottom and select **Assert**.
5. Browse to the **ArrayList** class in **mscorlib 4.0.0.0** and drag the method **ArrayList.GetEnumerator** to the right of the assert statement.
6. Create another rule called **Iterate**.
7. Navigate to the **IEnumerator** interface in **mscorlib** and drag the **MoveNext** method to the **Conditions** of the rule.
8. Add an assert to the actions list and drag **IEnumerator.get_Current** to the assert.
9. Add an update to the actions, below the assert, and drag the **IEnumerator** class to the right of the update.
10. Add a third rule named **Evaluate Purchase**.
11. Right-click **Conditions** and select is greater than.
12. Go to the **Product** class in **PRP.OrderProcessing.Library** and drag **Product. get_ProfitMargin** onto the left of the condition and type **.1** on the right.
13. Drag the **OrderMore** method of the **Product** class onto the **Actions** at the bottom.

We are now ready to use our policy to iterate a collection of the .NET class **Product**. To do this, we will need to create an **ArrayList** of products from within our orchestration. Having access to the **Product** class requires us to add a project reference to the orchestrations project. Right-click the **orchestrations** project and click **Add Reference**. Navigate to the **Projects** tab and double-click **Libraries**.

Open the **OrderProcessing** orchestration and add a new orchestration level variable called **Products**. Select **<.NET Class>** and browse to **ArrayList** as the type.

Drag an **expression** shape to the top of the **If_Priority** branch of our **decision** shape. Name it **Populate Products**. Enter the following expression:

```
Products.Add(new PRP.OrderProcessing.Library.Product("1234", 100,
.1M));
Products.Add(new PRP.OrderProcessing.Library.Product("4321", 50,
.2M));
Products.Add(new PRP.OrderProcessing.Library.Product("2222", 100,
.3M));
```

This just adds some products to our product list. If we were really extending this solution, we would probably want to do something more useful, such as possibly getting the products from our order as follows:

1. Drag a **Call Rules** shape onto the orchestration, directly below **Populate Products** and double-click this shape to configure it.

2. Select the **Product Policy** that we just created.

3. If you click the **Parameter Name** dropdown, you will see that the **Products** variable is already specified. Select it and click **OK**.

4. Deploy the solution.

5. Start **DebugView** and make sure all the options except **Log Boot** are enabled.

6. Run the priority test again (or drop the priority file in the receive location).

You will see that the diagnostics trace writes out twice. As can be seen here, the policy does not even show the concept of iteration as we normally know it. There is no `for` loop, but we can see that it is happening when the policy itself executes. We can also see that the concept of a variable is different in BRE as well. Anything asserted or changed in the memory of the policy is a "variable", but the specific rules are written against a seemingly disconnected type rather than against a variable. This is different from the normal case in C#, which would use a `foreach` loop to process any logic against a single variable instance that functions as the current place of the iterator.

The BRE works this same way with XML as well. Looping is a concept that is built into the BRE by default, but it's not always clear to us how or whether it is really there. This example shows quite clearly how different BRE is from our normal environments. All this said, recall that BRE was designed to run large rules' sets very quickly and it is very good at doing that.

Deploying policies

We saw earlier how the Business Rules Composer can be used to deploy and publish policies and vocabularies, but normally the process much more closely resembles the rest of the BizTalk development and deployment pattern.

Just like in BizTalk when the "developers" of policies are finished (that's in quotes because they may not be developers like you) the policy and any vocabularies it uses are exported from the BRE as XML files, which are then imported into the next server. This isn't the only way to do this, you can include policies as resources in your BizTalk MSI, but this is the most common approach to deploying newer versions of policies.

As we discussed before, it is this ability to decouple policies from a BizTalk solution which uses them that makes the whole BRE proposition so compelling. Just like we were able to correct our new customer pricing rule, our business users can also make changes as needed.

The simple wizard used to export and import vocabularies and policies is called the Business Rules Engine Deployment Wizard. When this wizard starts, we are presented with the following four options from which to choose:

- Import and publish Policy/Vocabulary to the database from the file
- Export Policy/Vocabulary to the file from the database
- Deploy Policy
- Undeploy Policy

When the wizard starts, you simply choose if you wish to import, export, deploy, or undeploy. From here you can choose the rule store by providing a server and database name. The resulting file from an export of either policy or vocabulary is an XML file that contains the parts of that vocabulary or policy. It is really a rather simple file, but there are few needs to edit the files directly and if you do, please be careful.

The following is an extract from the vocabulary we created earlier. As we can see, the vocabulary contains the definitions we created, the version numbers, and in the case of Get Discount Amount, the schema and XPath for the underlying definition:

```xml
<?xml version="1.0" encoding="utf-8"?>
<brl xmlns="http://schemas.microsoft.com/businessruleslanguage/2002">
  <vocabulary id="fdd61fdc-6e8b-47e8-ad5c-75e60fea849c" name="Order
Processing" uri="" description="">
    <version major="1" minor="0" description="" modifiedby="BT2010Dev\
BTDev" date="2011-05-11T16:07:42.153784-05:00" />

    <vocabularydefinition id="45203a3e-8943-49a4-9695-4eec3f9dfd00"
name="Customer Loyalty Level" description="">
      <setdefinition type="string">
        <element>
          <valuedefinitionliteral type="string">
            <string>New</string>
```

```
            </valuedefinitionliteral>
          </element>

          ...

      </setdefinition>
      <formatstring language="en-US" string="Customer Loyalty Level"
/>

   </vocabularydefinition>


   <vocabularydefinition id="8b19038c-f4a5-48e5-8207-9a8ae8271d42"
name="Get Discount Amount" description="">
      <bindingdefinition>
         <documentelementbindingdefinition field="*[local-
name()='Total' and namespace-uri()='']" fieldalias="Total"
type="decimal">

            <documentinfo schema="C:\Users\BTDev\Documents\Visual
Studio 2010\Projects\PurchaseOrder\InternalSchemas\PurchaseOrder.
xsd" documenttype="PRP.OrderProcessing.InternalSchemas.PurchaseOrder"
selector="/*[local-name()='PurchaseOrder' and namespace-uri()='http://
performanceracingparts.com/schemas/PurchaseOrder/internal/2011-
05']" selectoralias="/*[local-name()='PurchaseOrder' and namespace-
uri()='http://performanceracingparts.com/schemas/PurchaseOrder/
internal/2011-05']" instance="0" />

         </documentelementbindingdefinition>
      </bindingdefinition>
      <formatstring language="en-US" string="Get Discount Amount" />
   </vocabularydefinition>
  </vocabulary>
</brl>
```

Although we cannot edit deployed vocabularies, we can export their definition, manually make changes if absolutely necessary, and then redeploy them with the deployment wizard. This can be a very risky and dangerous activity and should be avoided if at all possible. Policies are very similar in structure to vocabularies and can also be manipulated in a similar fashion as a last resort. This is perhaps more pertinent to policies because, as you version them, they will keep references to the original vocabularies that were used to create them. This can result in a policy that requires multiple versions of a vocabulary deployed to function properly.

Summary

This chapter showed us how to consume WCF-SQL services from within an orchestration and how our solution structure facilitates reuse. We were also introduced to the Business Rules Engine and shown how to create vocabularies and policies, how to version and deploy policies, and how to iterate over collections in the BRE.

10
Envelopes, Flat Files, and Batching

At this point, we have a very well-developed real-world solution built according to the best practices with some of the latest technologies. But the fact of the matter is that many data interactions in our industry still involve batches or flat file formats, such as EDI and HL7, or custom formats that have been in operational use for a very long time. This legacy of computing is not going away any time soon, and despite the rise of services and SOAP, we will be required to work with flat files and batches for a very long time. The good news is that BizTalk can really help us here. In this chapter, we will cover the following topics:

- Delimited flat files
- Positional flat files
- Header and footer records
- XML envelopes
- Testing envelopes and pipelines

Understanding delimited flat files

Delimited flat files are files that use a specific symbol or character to mark the delineation between two elements in the file. Comma Separated Value (CSV) is a very common example of a delimited file format. The file `CatalogOrders.csv` (available at `http://biztalk2010patterns.com//documents/order-processing/CatalogOrders.csv`) contains sales orders from one of PRP's catalog outsourcers. The file has two types of records within it: orders and lines. Each order has one or more lines after it that belongs to the order directly before it. The file itself can contain many different orders in a batch. Our current solution processes orders individually and we need to break this file apart into individual orders.

Fortunately, this is very easy in BizTalk. The flat file processing features of BizTalk are well suited to a variety of processing tasks.

Creating the delimited flat file schema

Our first task will be to use the Flat File Schema Wizard to generate a schema that represents the delimited file we're dealing with. A wizard will walk us through defining the format and will ultimately result in an XSD schema being created that components in BizTalk can use to translate to and from text/XML:

1. Right-click **ExternalSchemas** and click **Add | New Item**.

2. Select **Flat File Schema Wizard** and name the file `CatalogOrderCsv.xsd`.

3. Browse to the instance file being sure to change the filter to **All Files (*.*)**.

4. Rename the root as **CatalogOrderCsv**.

Namespaces are slightly different for flat files because the files themselves do not contain the namespace within them. This gives us a lot more latitude when selecting namespaces for flat file schemas. It is still a good idea to follow the naming conventions of this book so for this schema I have selected the namespace: `http://performanceracingparts.com/schemas/PurchaseOrder/external/2011-05`.

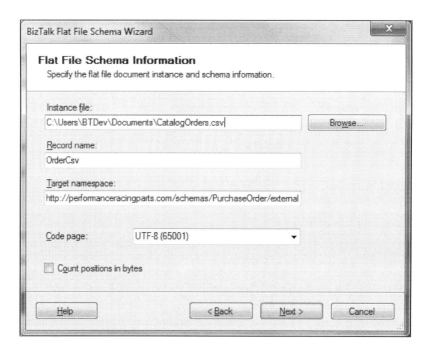

The wizard now highlights the entire document and asks us to highlight the area we are interested in defining a schema for. Since we are making a schema for the entire document do not change the highlighting.

5. Keep the full highlighting and click **Next**.

6. Keep **By delimiter symbol** radio button checked and click **Next**.

7. Keep {CR}{LF} as the delimiter and click **Next** again.

 Some delimiters mark the dividing point between records and some mark the dividing point between fields in a record. In this case, it is the former. Each record is delimited with a carriage return line feed, the new line standard of Windows files.

8. Rename the first row as **Order a**nd change its element type to **Record**.

9. Rename the second row as **Line** and change its element type to **Repeating Record**.

Change the element type to **Ignore** for the rest of the rows as these are merely repeats of the two we have just named. This tells the flat file parser to skip these parts of the file in the rest of the wizard. The **Record** type we specified before tells the parser that a given record will occur exactly once. The **Repeating record** element type specifies an element with a **Max Occurs** set to unbounded. The other two options: **Record element** and **Record attribute** both specify a field-level data point that will either become an element or attribute in the resulting XML schema. This dialog also allows us to select an XSD data type for a data point of an element or attribute. This data type is then used in file validation and allows us to provide strong typing to flat files. Elements and attributes are leaves in the XSD, that is they have no child elements.

The following screenshot shows the **Child Elements** dialog filled out for this step in our flat file generation:

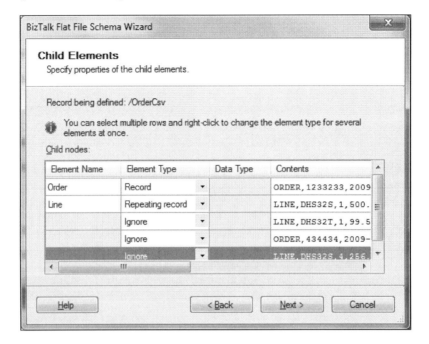

10. Click **Next**.

11. Click **Next** again to define the **Order** record.

12. Keep the **By delimiter symbol** radio button selected and click **Next**.

    As we can see in the following screenshot, the entire line is highlighted. If we scroll to the right, we will see that the CR LF has been excluded, as that is a part of the parent record.

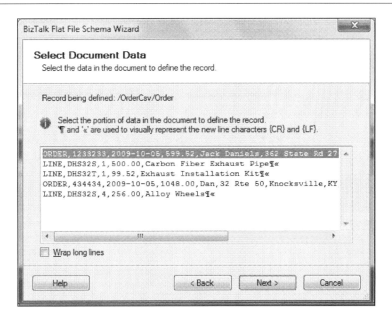

13. Type in a comma (,) as the child delimiter.

14. Check the **Record has tag identifier** checkbox and type in **ORDER** as the tag. You can see that each line begins with either **ORDER** or **LINE**. This is how the parser in BizTalk will know which lines are orders and which are lines. This is shown in the following screenshot:

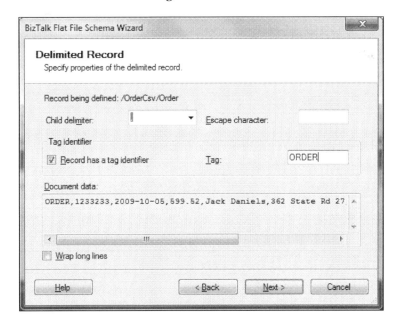

15. Click **Next**.

    Notice how the fields are already broken out, albeit with non-expressive names. We have the chance here to name the fields however we like and also to set their type. Notice in the following screenshot how this is the same **Child Elements** dialog that we have walked through once already. This wizard allows us to model complex nested structures very easily.

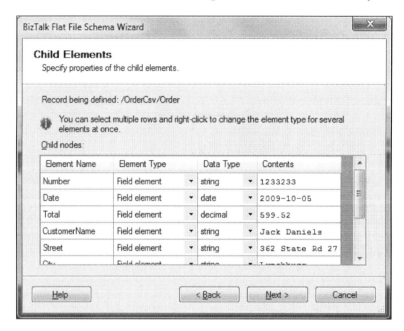

16. Name the elements as follows:
    - **Number**: string
    - **Date**: date
    - **Total**: decimal
    - **CustomerName**: string
    - **Street**: string
    - **City**: string
    - **Zip**: string
    - **Phone**: string
    - **Click next**: string

17. Click **Next** and you will see the schema view displayed again, this time highlighting the **Line**. Click **Next** again.

18. Repeat the process for **Line** using **LINE** as the tag identifier.

19. Name the elements and set their types as follows:

    ○ **ItemNumber**: **string**

    ○ **Quantity**: **int**

    ○ **UnitCost**: **decimal**

    ○ **Description**: **string**

20. Click **Next**.

21. Click **Finish.**

The completed schema will now be in your external schemas project and if you right-click the schema, you can validate the input instance that we used to generate the schema.

If we do this, we are presented with the same type of output window we saw when testing maps:

```
Invoking component...
Validation generated XML output <file:///C:\Users\BTDev\AppData\Local\
Temp\_SchemaData\CatalogOrderCsv_output.xml>.
Validate Instance succeeded for schema CatalogOrderCsv.xsd, file:
<file:///C:\Users\BTDev\Documents\CatalogOrders.csv>.
Component invocation succeeded.
```

We can click on the upper link and be shown the output from the validation, which is shown as follows:

```
<CatalogOrderCsv xmlns="http://performanceracingparts.com/schemas/
PurchaseOrder/external/2011-05">
  <Order xmlns="">
    <Number>1233233</Number>
    <Date>2009-10-05</Date>
    <Total>599.52</Total>
    <CustomerName>Jack Daniels</CustomerName>
    <Street>362 State Rd 27</Street>
    <City>Lynchburg</City>
    <State>TN</State>
    <Zip>53823</Zip>
    <PhoneNumber>312-555-1212</PhoneNumber>
  </Order>
  <Line xmlns="">
    <ItemNumber>DHS32S</ItemNumber>
    <Quantity>1</Quantity>
    <UnitCost>500.00</UnitCost>
```

```
      <Description>Carbon Fiber Exhaust Pipe</Description>
   </Line>
   <Line xmlns="">
      <ItemNumber>DHS32T</ItemNumber>
      <Quantity>1</Quantity>
      <UnitCost>99.52</UnitCost>
      <Description>Exhaust Installation Kit</Description>
   </Line>
</CatalogOrderCsv>
```

Interestingly, despite the fact that this file contained two orders, we only see one in the output. This is because the flat file parser was specifically designed to make our job easier in this case; namely to transform batches of data into individual transactions. This file is broken apart because we set the **Order** to be a record, which equates to maximum occurrence being set to one (or more precisely to the default, which is one). This instructs the parser to break the file every time it encounters an **Order** record after reading **Line** records.

BizTalk really is a transaction-based system and although you can do batch processing with it, it is really designed for live transaction processing. This particular schema is actually quite complex compared to most flat files, which contain only a single record structure. With files of that type, we don't have to break the file apart.

There is something else going on here that is really quite impressive as well. Recall that we set the order date to be a **date** field; defined as **xs:date** in the schema. If we go into `CatalogOrders.csv` and change one of these order date values to **2011-09-31**, the schema validation will now fail. This is because there are only 30 days in September and we have provided an invalid date. The same is true for the order total or any other field we wish to put constraints on. We have the entire validation framework of XSD, including regular expressions, at our disposal for validating flat files that we are sent. This greatly simplifies working with flat files when using BizTalk, as field validation is almost always the first step performed by custom solutions that interact with flat files. This is a feature that should be heavily leveraged.

Mapping the delimited flat file

Now that we have our XML representation of the flat file schema, we are ready to map it into our canonical order schema. This map, `Ext_CatalogOrderCsv_To_PurchaseOrder.btm`, is fairly simple and many of the fields will map by using the **Link by Name** feature of the mapper. Importantly, map the customer and address information to both the `BillTo` and `ShipTo` nodes. Also, map the `ItemNumber` to the `CatalogNumber`. Finally, we still need to set the source for this file, so again use a `String Concatenate` functoid with the value `Mail Order`.

Using the flat file schema

We have our external format defined and our map to translate from the flat file XML to our canonical XML. Now we need a way to actually apply our flat file schema so that it can convert the text into XML. This is done in a pipeline. Pipelines were introduced in *Chapter 2, Introduction to BizTalk Development*, and are a core component of BizTalk's architecture. Their stream-based programming model makes working with even large data sets keep a small memory footprint, which helps BizTalk scale and process both larger files and more files:

1. Right-click the **Pipelines Project** and click **Add | New Item**.

2. Select **Receive Pipeline** from the list of BizTalk components and name the pipeline **CatalogOrderCsvReceive.btp**.

3. When the pipeline appears (double-click it to open it if it does not) look for the **Flat file disassembler** component in the **Toolbox** and drag it onto the **Disassemble** stage of the pipeline.

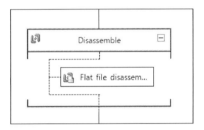

If you now click the **Flat file disassembler** component and look at its properties you will see a section for **Document schema**. We need to specify a document schema here to instruct this disassembler as to what schema to apply to the flat file data stream that it receives.

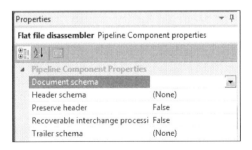

Click on **Document schema** and the drop-down list will be filled with all the schemas on this BizTalk environment. It is a long list and we will be thankful that we have used a naming convention to make selecting the appropriate schema easier. Select the schema that begins with **PRP.OrderProcessing.ExternalSchemas. CatalogOrderCsv**.

 Setting the document schema is required in the flat file disassembler, but it can be overwritten in any receive location, so that you don't have to create a new pipeline for each flat file that is received. That can help keep your solution free of artifact clutter.

Compile and deploy the solution

With the solution complete, all we need to do now is add a receive location to pick up the catalog files. This new location will still use the same port, OP_Receive_ PurchaseOrders, and will be named OP_File_Receive_MailOrderCsv. We will reuse the existing call center order location and this time use a file mask of *.csv (the URI in the Administration Console will be: C:\BizTalk\PRP\CallCenterOrders*.csv).

We also need to select our pipeline **CatalogOrderCsvReceive** as the receive pipeline. If this pipeline does not appear in the Administration Console, remember that you must refresh it after deploying new artifacts.

Finally, we must add the map Ext_CatalogOrderCsv_To_PurchaseOrder to the receive port OP_Receive_PurchaseOrders. Now if you copy CatalogOrders.csv to C:\BizTalk\PRP\CallCenterOrders, the file will be picked up and one order will route to the priority SendInventoryPriorityPurchaseOrder and the other to SendInventoryPurchaseOrder.

Working with positional flat files

Not all flat files are delimited. Some systems, particularly mainframe and AS400, send files by a different method altogether. These are positional flat files that do not use delimiters between fields, but use their character position within a line of the file. These files are called positional files.

BizTalk is capable of dealing with positional flat files as well and we happen to have such a file from one of our mail order resellers that we must incorporate. The file is available at http://biztalk2010patterns.com//documents/order-processing/ CatalogOrders.txt. This file contains very similar data to the delimited flat file, but as can be seen, it is in fact positional. We will now create the schema for this file.

1. Right-click external schemas and select **Add | New Item**. Again, we will select the Flat File Schema Wizard and this time name the schema **CatalogOrderPositional.xsd**.

2. Click **Add**, then click **Next**.

3. Browse to CatalogOrders.txt.

4. Name the root node **CatalogOrderPositional** and change the namespace to http://performanceracingparts.com/schemas/PurchaseOrder/external/2011-05.

5. Click **Next**.

6. Keep the entire file highlighted and click **Next**.

7. Despite the fact that this is a positional flat file, each line is still delimited with a CR LF (carriage return, line feed) so keep the radio button selection of **By delimiter symbol**.

8. Click **Next**.

9. Keep the CR LF default and click **Next** again.

10. Like before, name the first line **Order** and set the **Element Type** to **Record**. Name the second one **Line** and set the **Element Type** to **Repeating Record**.

11. Set the other records to **Ignore** for **Element Type** and click **Next**.

If you are given real files to work with to generate your flat file schemas via the wizard, you should delete most of the file, so as not to have to mark many records to be ignored. If you're going to do this, please be aware that you should delete the middle of the file, not the end because the last CR LF will dictate if the file is Infix or Postfix. Postfix files will have a blank line at the end because the delimiter is always affixed post record, rather than between records.

We will now define the elements for the order. This starts out in a similar way as before so click **Next** twice so that you reach the **Select Record Format** page of the dialog:

1. Select the **By relative positions** radio button and click **Next**.

   We are now presented with a new dialog that allows us to graphically select where to split the elements as well as define a tag identifier.

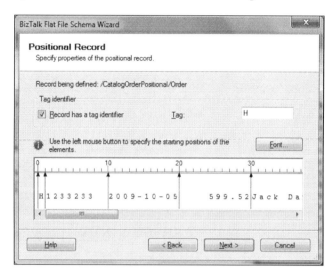

2. Check the **Record has a tag identifier** checkbox and enter **H** as the tag.

3. Click on the record displayed in the text window at positions: **1**, **10**, **20**, **30**, **53**, **77**, **101**, **106**, and **111**.

4. Click **Next**.

5. Rename the elements as we did before:

   - **Tag**: string
   - **Number**: string
   - **Date**: date
   - **Total**: decimal
   - **CustomerName**: string
   - **Street**: string
   - **City**: string
   - **Zip**: string
   - **Phone**: string
   - **Click Next**: string

6. Repeat the process for the line defining the tag as **D** and the break positions at: **1, 7, 9, 18**.

7. Name the elements and set their types appropriately:
    ◦   **Tag**: string
    ◦   **ItemNumber**: string
    ◦   **Quantity**: int
    ◦   **UnitCost**: decimal
    ◦   **Description**: string

8. Click **Next** and **Finish**.

We now have a completed positional schema and are ready to use it in our solution. This is left as an exercise to the reader as it works exactly like the previous example. We need only a map, a pipeline, and a receive location (again, it can be in the same path due to the new file mask `.txt`).

Grasping important flat file schema concepts

Flat files have many rules governing them that have been developed and refined over decades. BizTalk goes a long way towards making flat files easy to work with.

Justification: In a positional flat file, the justification will control which side the value in that field is set against. The default justification is left, but it is common for monetary values to be right justified. This is controlled through an attribute on the individual elements in the schema. The following is an example:

*   Left-justified elements are often strings as in the following example: "3X2H63   "
*   Right justification is common in number fields as in the following example: "   29.55"

Pad character: When values do not fill the entire available area in the positional structure, a padding character must be selected to be used when filling out a file. This value can be set at the element level, but one of the options is **Default Pad Character**, which uses the pad character defined at the schema level (the folder above the root node). A pad character can be any character, but is commonly a space or a zero. If we had a value of "29.55" and it needs to be padded with leading zeros to result in a 10-digit number, we would set the justification to right and the pad character to "0" for a positional field we specified with a length of 10. The result would be "0000029.55" and we would not need to write any code to get it.

Wrap character: The wrap character is used with the wrap character type to define special characters that enclose, or qualify, values. This is commonly a double quote in CSV files, as in the following line:

"Bob", "1234", "ABC"

If you're working with CSV files that are quote wrapped like this, you can specify the wrap character to enclose the values. The wrap characters are automatically stripped from the value when it is converted into XML and automatically inserted when XML is converted to text.

Importantly, although we saw examples of converting text flat files into XML, these same schema definitions are used to do the opposite: convert XML into flat files. The only difference is that instead of using a receive pipeline you use a send pipeline, and instead of using a disassembler, you use an assembler. Finally, there are other options available at the root level of a flat file schema that impact how the flat file parser performs; of particular note are the Lookahead Depth which controls how far ahead in the file the parser will search for matching data and the parser optimization which can either be set to speed (the default) or complexity. Complexity enables the parser to handle more ambiguous formats, but this comes at the price of speed.

Using flat file headers and trailers

Some flat files will contain records in the beginning or the end that are simply unrelated header and trailer records. Often these will contain counts and totals, but aren't necessary for the processing of records within the file. These fields tend to be holdovers from the bad old days of networking and data transmission, when we had much less certainty in the reliability of networks or even computer systems. Records at the first and last lines would contain counts or checksums to ensure that the file had not been truncated. Although these are not really necessary anymore, they are still there.

We can define header and trailer records to remove these lines from our message. Header and trailer schemas are defined exactly like normal flat file schemas, but in the pipeline they are selected for the header or trailer schema, rather than the document schema. The default behavior is to simply remove these parts of the message, but they can be subscribed to individually if you like (although they won't cause a failed routing error if they are not). We can also preserve the header in the message context if we choose, but I have found this to be of limited use.

Alternatively, we can define the header and trailer inline (within the document schema) if we would rather keep them as part of the message. A great walkthrough of using header and trailer schemas exists on MSDN at `http://msdn.microsoft.com/en-us/library/aa560774(BTS.70).aspx`.

Processing XML envelopes

If we look carefully at our SQL solution for receiving website orders, we will notice that there is actually a problem with it. In its current form, the solution only works correctly with one order. Clearly, our query is capable of returning more than one record. We could use a TOP 1 clause in the stored procedure to only return one record, but that would be terribly inefficient and not scale well at all. We can also use an envelope to accomplish this.

Envelopes are special schemas that instruct the XML Disassembler to break apart matching messages. The XMLReceive pipeline that we're already using extensively has an XML Disassembler built into it, so this change is relatively easy. This all works through message probing using the message type (`namespace#rootnodename`).

If we were to look at our current solution and the XML it produces (which can be done by changing the receive pipeline on `OP_SQL_Receive_WebsiteOrders` to the `PassThruReceive`) we would see that the message contains the following content:

```
<WebSiteOrders xmlns="http://performanceracingparts.com/schemas/
PurchaseOrder/sql/2011-05">
  <order xmlns="">
    <Id>44</Id>
    <OrderNumber>3774632</OrderNumber>
    <CustomerName>John Doe</CustomerName>
    <CustomerAddress1>123 Fake St</CustomerAddress1>
    <CustomerState>IL</CustomerState>
    <CustomerZip>60610</CustomerZip>
    <CustomerCity>Chicago</CustomerCity>
    <OrderTotal>247.54</OrderTotal>
    <ReadStatus>1</ReadStatus>
    <PhoneNumber>312-555-1234</PhoneNumber>
    <OrderDate>2010-03-26</OrderDate>
    <orderline>
      <OrderLine>46</OrderLine>
      <OrderId>44</OrderId>
      <ItemNumber>54346   </ItemNumber>
      <Quantity>1</Quantity>
      <UnitCost>2.475400000000000e+002</UnitCost>
      <Description>Some Item</Description>
    </orderline>
  </order>
</WebSiteOrders>
```

It is a good practice to keep external sample data in the `TestData\External` directory of the **UnitTests** project. Save the preceding file to that directory and add it as an existing item so it can be used by other developers.

If there were multiple orders, there would simply be more order nodes. This is the reason why we needed to specify a root element node name as well as a namespace in the adapter configuration, because the adapter wraps the returned XML document fragments in an outer element to form valid XML. What we really want is just the order itself, not the envelope that contains the orders. This turns out to be fairly easy:

1. Open the SQL Adapter generated schema and click on the schema node (the small folder). Scroll down to the reference section of the **Properties** and look for a property called **Envelope**. Change this property to **Yes**. This instructs BizTalk to use this schema for breaking apart messages.

2. Click on the **WebSiteOrders** node and look for the property **Body XPath**. This is where we instruct BizTalk how to break the message. BizTalk will look for sub-messages below this node. Click the ellipsis on the right of this property and a dialog will be presented to you.

3. Set this property to be the root node: **WebSiteOrders**.

   You can see that the property is now populated with the fully qualified `xpath` of the node that you selected. In this case it is the following:

   ```
   /*[local-name()='WebSiteOrders' and namespace-uri()='http://
   performanceracingparts.com/schemas/PurchaseOrder/sql/2011-05']
   ```

4. Create a new schema called **WebSiteOrder.xsd** (via **Add | New Item** in external schemas) and delete the value from the **Target namespace** property.

5. Rename the **Root** node as **order**.

 Since there is a change to the way the SQL Adapters work, we need to use a blank target namespace in this new schema because the XML itself has an explicit `xmlns=""` in it. Remember the parser is looking for exact matches and it will not work properly if it does not find one.

6. Import the `WebSiteOrders` schema by browsing for the **Imports** property and clicking the ellipsis.

7. Change the **Data Structure Type** of **order** to **orderType** which is now available in the drop-down thanks to our import.

8. Modify the map `Ext_WebSiteOrders_To_PurchaseOrder` to use our new schema. This is quite easy if you open the map and right-click the top node of the source. On the left, the schema folder, there is an option **Replace Schema**. If you click this you can browse for the source schema again. This time pick `PRP.OrderProcessing.ExternalSchemas.WebSiteOrder`.

Fortunately for us, the schema didn't really change that much, so the mapper is actually able to reconnect all of the links that were there before. This turns out to be all we have to do to make the new envelope processing work for us. If you want to see it in action run the website order test again. It will still pass. If you change the test to make two records (or just insert more records) you will see that the disassembly happens as we expect it to.

Testing envelopes and pipelines

Although the preceding solution does work, figuring out exactly how pipelines and envelopes will function at runtime can be tedious if you have to deploy your solution every time in order to test them. The developers of BizTalk thought the same and provided us with plenty of tools to make working with envelopes and pipelines much easier. These are available in the following directory:

```
<InstallDir>\Microsoft BizTalk Server 2010\SDK\Utilities\
PipelineTools
```

 Add this to the path of your development workstation so that working with these tools is easier. The easiest way to do this is to click the **Start** button, right-click **Computer**, and select **Properties**. Click **Advanced System Settings** on the left, then click **Environment Variables**.

XML Disassmbler

The tool we would use to test the envelope above is `xmldasm`, the XML Disassembler. This is a command-line tool that wraps much of the BizTalk infrastructure of the XML Disassembler pipeline component. The interactive help for this tool is as follows:

```
Microsoft BizTalk XML Document Disassembler. Version 1.0
Copyright (C) Microsoft Corporation. All rights reserved.

usage: xmldasm document -ds documentSchema... [ -es envelopeSchema...
] [ -s ] [
 -c ] [ -p ] [ -sd ] [ -se ] [ -m filenamemask ] [ -en encoding ] [ -v
] [ -ri ]
```

```
where:
  document              XML document
  documentSchema        XML document schema(s)
  envelopeSchema        XML envelope schema(s)
  -s                    Validate document structure
  -c                  Display disassembled XML message on the console
  -p                  Display promoted properties on the console
  -sd                   Set document schema(s) as design-time property
  -se                   Set envelope schema(s) as design-time property
  -m                  Output file name mask (default is %MessageID%)
  encoding            Input message body part encoding name (e.g.
windows-1252) o
r code page (e.g. 936)
  -v                    Verbose mode
  -ri                   Recoverable Interchange

file name macros:
  %MessageID%           XML message identifier (Guid)
  %MessagePartID%       XML message part identifier (Guid)
  %MessageNumber%       XML message number
```

If you open a command prompt and change directories into the external schemas folder of the solution, you can run the following command to watch this message be disassembled.

```
xmldasm ..\UnitTests\TestData\External\WebSiteOrders.xml -ds
WebSiteOrder.xsd -es WebSiteOrders.xsd -v
Creating objects.
Creating message.
Adding message to a pipeline.
Executing pipeline.
Getting processed message(s).
Doing output for a message 1.
```

You can see here that I have specified the WebSiteOrders.xml file as input, the WebSiteOrder.xsd as the document schema (for the single external order) and the WebSiteOrders.xsd as the envelope (the schema we marked as an envelope and gave a body xpath to). I also added the –v (verbose) parameter to see more output. For each message that is debatched in the envelope, one line of Doing output for a message n. will be listed on the console.

If we copy the order element in the source message and run this command again, we will see two messages written out. We can also see that new files named with GUIDs have been created. Each output message will be displayed this way.

Flat file disassembler

A very similar tool, FFDASM.exe, provides the same functionality for flat file disassembly. This tool basically works the same way and running the command with no parameters lists the help (as it does with all of the pipeline tools). The primary difference is that you use –bs for body schema, –hs for header schema, and –ts for trailer schema.

```
ffdasm ..\UnitTests\TestData\External\CatalogOrder.csv -bs
CatalogOrdersCsv.xsd -v
Creating objects.
Creating message.
Adding message to a pipeline.
Executing pipeline.
Getting processed message(s).
Doing output for a message 1.
Doing output for a message 2.
```

We can see that the disassembler does, in fact, create two output messages for our disassembled flat file.

XML assembler / flat file assembler

There are also tools that allow us to deal with the reverse process, which is document assembly. This will enable us to assemble many messages into a single document (XML or flat file) or to test that our flat files are being created the way we want without having to deploy the solution. These tools, XMLASM.exe and FFASM.exe, work almost identically.

```
Microsoft BizTalk XML Document Assembler. Version 1.0
Copyright (C) Microsoft Corporation. All rights reserved.

usage: xmlasm document... [ -dm documentMask... ] -ds
documentSchema... [ -es en
velopeSchema... ] [ -c ] [ -d ] [ -sd ] [ -m filenamemask ] [ -v ]

where:
  document        XML document(s)
  documentMask    XML document(s) file mask, e.g. c:\\documents\\*.xml
  documentSchema  XML document schema(s)
  envelopeSchema  XML envelope schema(s)
  -c              Display assembled XML message on the console
  -d              Demote properties
  -sd             Set document schema(s) as design-time property
  -d              Demote properties
  -m              Output file name mask (default is %MessageID%)
  -v              Verbose mode
```

```
file name macros:
    %MessageID%          XML message identifier (Guid)
    %MessagePartID%      XML message part identifier (Guid)
```

Much like their disassembler cousins, these tools allow you to specify a document and the schemas to use for the assembly. You can even use the documents that are output by the FFDASM and XMLDASM as input to XMLASM and FFASM. You can also use a document mask (-dm) if you want to assemble multiple messages into a single output message.

Pipeline testing

There is a final tool, again similar to the ones before, `pipeline.exe`, which allows for testing full `.btp` files (like the `CatalogOrderCvsReceive.btp` that we created earlier). This tool takes a few more parameters and will test every stage of the pipeline, not just assembly and disassembly.

`Pipeline.exe` can also be connected to the Visual Studio Debugger to allow us to step into custom pipeline components. This is useful for testing components that have not yet been deployed to a BizTalk server. To do this, you simply set your pipeline project as the startup project in the solution and change the debug values properties. Select **Start External program** and browse to `pipeline.exe`. Now you set the **Command line arguments** like you would for using `pipeline.exe` directly from the command line. Additionally, like with maps and schemas, you can set the **Enable Unit Testing** property to true, which will wrap the pipeline in the `TestablePipeline` class and this then makes it available for code-based unit testing.

If you put a breakpoint in your custom pipeline component, Visual Studio will stop at the breakpoint when the pipeline executes.

Alternatively, you can also attach to the `BTSNTSvc.exe` process and debug from there. This allows you to see everything going on inside BizTalk at the time the pipeline executes. For more information on using the Visual Studio Debugger to attach to processes, please see `http://msdn.microsoft.com/en-us/library/c6wf8e4z.aspx`.

Summary

In this chapter, we have learned how BizTalk can help us work with flat files and batches of data. We learned how to incorporate these legacy formats into our modern real-time solution architecture and how to be a producer or consumer of these formats. We also learned about debatching data files and testing pipelines, flat files, and XML envelopes. In the next chapter, we will expose the current service as a WCF service, learn about solution bindings, create a build script, and create advanced BAM views.

11
Completing the Order Processing Solution

This chapter rounds out our solution by exposing it to web service consumers, providing a walkthrough of build and deployment strategies, and creating advanced BAM views. This chapter concludes our initial project and we will soon start a second solution: inventory management.

Topics covered in this chapter include:

- Exposing our current solution as a web service
- BizTalk bindings
- BizTalk resources
- MSI deployment
- BAM continuations and aggregations

Exposing the process to web service clients

In an effort to modernize their B2B channels, we have been asked to provide a real-time service for our customers. We want to expose the InfoPath order format as a message type that service clients can submit to us directly via a web service request.

Expose the schema as a service endpoint

We've already used the BizTalk WCF service publishing wizard once before, but we can also use it now to expose our current solution as a WCF service for a variety of consumers. We must now use this wizard to create a service endpoint.

1. Launch the wizard.

2. Click **Next**.

3. Select **Service Endpoint** and check the checkbox **Enable metadata publishing**.

4. Click **Next**.

5. Select **Publish Schemas** and click **Next**.

6. Rename the service description to **PrpOrderServices.**

7. Rename the service to **OrderService**.

8. Add a new one-way operation.

9. Delete the **operation1** web method.

10. Right-click **Request** and specify the message type for this new operation as the **InfoPath**.

11. Click **Next**.

12. Replace the namespace **http://tempuri.org** with **http://performanceracingparts/interfaces/orderprocessing**.

13. Check **Allow anonymous access to WCF service** and click **Next**.

14. Review the service summary and click **Create**.

15. Click **Finish**.

Creating a new one-way receive location

We will now create a receive location on our OP_Receive_PurchaseOrders port to receive these messages and flow them into our existing solution. Unlike before we did not let the wizard create our receive location; we will do it manually to understand how it works:

1. Select **OP_Receive_PurchaseOrders** as the port.

2. Name the location **OP_Wcf_Receive_PurchaseOrders**.

3. Select the **WSHttp** as the **Type**.

4. Click **Configure** and set the **URI** to **/PrpOrderServices/OrderService.svc**.

5. Click **OK**.

6. Select the **XMLReceive** pipeline.

7. Click **OK**.

8. Enable the new location.

9. Run the following command:

```
C:\Windows\System32\inetsrv\appcmd set app /app.name: "Default Web
Site/PrpOrderServices" /applicationPool:"BizTalk Isolated Host
AppPool"
```

 Setting the AppPool can also be performed via the Internet Information Services (IIS) Management Console.

Our solution is now exposed as a web service endpoint on our local machine. We can test this in SoapUI or even in InfoPath.

 InfoPath is a very good tool for using with BizTalk as it can allow us to return results (i.e. submit forms) via SOAP or even e-mail.

Examining the solution bindings

Although we have created many artifacts in Visual Studio and other tools, the solution is largely comprised of the configurations of ports, locations, and settings that we configured in the BizTalk Administration console. This configuration is called the **bindings** for a BizTalk solution.

The bindings are critical for any BizTalk solution because they bind together everything that we created. Without the bindings our solution simply won't work; it won't do anything or even know where to look to do anything.

Exporting the bindings

We can export the bindings from the BizTalk Administration console and we will do that now in order to explore them further:

1. Expand the **Applications** node in the group and right-click **Order Processing,** then click **Export | Bindings**.

2. The wizard will ask you for a location to save the bindings to, so save them to `Bindings\LocalDev_OrderProcessing.BindingInfo.xml` at the solution root and click **OK**.

Don't be surprised if it takes a moment to export the bindings, there is actually a lot of information in the bindings and it is being serialized into XML during this process. What you will now have is a relatively large XML file that very verbosely describes our entire solution. Add the bindings as an existing item to the `Bindings` folder of the solution.

 For security reasons, passwords are removed from bindings when they are exported. If you use adapters or locations that include their own usernames and passwords, the passwords will have to be manually set after importing the bindings or updating in the bindings file. For security reasons, it is best to manually update them.

Understanding bindings

Open the newly added bindings file in Visual Studio as we can see all the details of this application. Don't worry, we don't need to know what all this XML means, but we will take a brief tour of it.

There are five major sections within the bindings document introduced as follows:

- **ModuleRefCollection:** This section contains information about the application as a whole, including all the assemblies, schemas, and orchestrations within the solution. Some of the information for the application as a whole is as follows. As can be seen, the schemas are listed below the `TrackedSchemas` element, which is a slightly misleading name.

```
<ModuleRefCollection>
  <ModuleRef Name="[Application:Order Processing]" Version=""
Culture="" PublicKeyToken="" FullName="[Application:Order
Processing], Version=, Culture=, PublicKeyToken=">
    <Services />
    <TrackedSchemas>
     <Schema FullName="PRP.OrderProcessing.ExternalSchemas.
WebSiteOrder" RootName="order" AssemblyQualifiedName="PRP.
OrderProcessing.ExternalSchemas.WebSiteOrder,PRP.OrderProcessing.
ExternalSchemas, Version=1.0.0.0, Culture=neutral, PublicKeyToken=
0e3c97569ac5667e" AlwaysTrackAllProperties="false">
      <TrackedPropertyNames />
    </Schema>
   </TrackedSchemas>
  </ModuleRef>
  ...
</ModuleRefCollection>
```

More interestingly, a little further down the `ModuleRef` for the orchestrations project shows us some things we actually set up ourselves in the BizTalk Administration console. We can see some highlighted sections of this part of the bindings as follows. Under `Services`, there are `Service` elements that detail orchestration bindings. Critically, we can see the `Ports` and for each `Port` the orchestration name and the reference to the actual BizTalk port.

```
<ModuleRef Name="PRP.OrderProcessing.Orchestrations"
Version="1.0.0.0" Culture="neutral" PublicKeyToken="0e3c97569ac566
7e" FullName="PRP.OrderProcessing.Orchestrations, Version=1.0.0.0,
Culture=neutral, PublicKeyToken=0e3c97569ac5667e">
    <Services>
     <Service Name="PRP.OrderProcessing.Orchestrations.
OrderProcessing" State="Started" TrackingOption="ServiceStartEnd
MessageSendReceive OrchestrationEvents" Description="">
        <Ports>
         <Port Name="ProcessPurchaseOrderPort" Modifier="2"
BindingOption="1">
            <SendPortRef xsi:nil="true" />
            <DistributionListRef xsi:nil="true" />
            <ReceivePortRef Name="OP_Receive_PurchaseOrders" />
         </Port>
         ...
        <Roles />
        <Host Name="BizTalkServerApplication"
NTGroupName="BizTalk Application Users" Type="1" Trusted="false"
/>
       </Service>
    </Services>
   </ModuleRef>
```

Recall that we configured all of these settings graphically within the BizTalk Administration console.

- **SendPortCollection:** This collection is named more appropriately and it is fairly straightforward, albeit quite verbose. Some of the following listing has been removed for simplicity, but if you examine the file on your own screen you will see that all of the elements correspond to the settings in the administration console that we are free to change.

The file adapter is a rather trivial example, but we can see the highlighted `Address` node would be likely to be changed between environments.

```
<SendPort Name="OP_File_Send_CRM_SalesOrder" IsStatic="true"
IsTwoWay="false" BindingOption="0">
    <Description xsi:nil="true" />
```

```
    <TransmitPipeline Name="Microsoft.BizTalk.DefaultPipelines.
PassThruTransmit" REMOVED TrackingOption="ServiceStartEnd
MessageSendReceive PipelineEvents" Description="" />
    <PrimaryTransport>
    <Address>C:\BizTalk\PRP\CRM\%MessageID%.xml</Address>
    <TransportType Name="FILE" Capabilities="11" ConfigurationClsi
d="5e49e3a6-b4fc-4077-b44c-22f34a242fdb" />
    <TransportTypeData>&lt;CustomProps&gt; REMOVED lt;/
CustomProps&gt;</TransportTypeData>
    <RetryCount>3</RetryCount>
    <RetryInterval>5</RetryInterval>
    <ServiceWindowEnabled>false</ServiceWindowEnabled>
```

We can also see the SendHandler lists the Host that is configured for this send port.

```
    <SendHandler Name="BizTalkServerApplication"
HostTrusted="false">
    <TransportType Name="FILE" Capabilities="11" ConfigurationClsid
="5e49e3a6-b4fc-4077-b44c-22f34a242fdb" />
    </SendHandler>
</PrimaryTransport>
<SecondaryTransport>
```

We can see that this port has a filter in place on it and we can also see that this filter is stored in the bindings as escaped XML. This allows the filters to be arbitrarily complex, but it also introduces some caveats. For one, the filter must not have any whitespace at the beginning. If you paste this port's information into a new XML document in Visual Studio, it will add a new line after the opening Filter tag. This will break your filters and you will be unable to start the port in the administration console.

```
</SecondaryTransport>
<ReceivePipelineData xsi:nil="true" />
<Tracking>0</Tracking>
<Filter>&lt;?xml version="1.0" encoding="utf-16"?&gt;
&lt;Filter xmlns:xsi="http://www.w3.org/2001/XMLSchema-instance"
xmlns:xsd="http://www.w3.org/2001/XMLSchema"&gt;
  &lt;Group&gt;
    &lt;Statement Property="BTS.ReceivePortName" Operator="0"
Value="OP_Receive_PurchaseOrders" /&gt;
    &lt;Statement Property="BTS.MessageType" Operator="0"
Value="http://performanceracingparts.com/schemas/PurchaseOrder/
internal/2011-05#PurchaseOrder" /&gt;
  &lt;/Group&gt;
&lt;/Filter&gt;</Filter>
```

We can also see any transforms listed on this port. Again, this has been truncated to make reading easier in the book.

```
<Transforms>
  <Transform FullName="PRP.OrderProcessing.Maps.Int_
PurchaseOrder_To_SalesOrder" REMOVED />
</Transforms>
```

Finally, we can also see the application that this port is destined for. This is useful because we can use bindings files to add just a single port to an application. We did this a few chapters ago and we were warned about the application names not matching because the WCF wizard did not specify a value in this element.

```
<RouteFailedMessage>false</RouteFailedMessage>
<ApplicationName>Order Processing</ApplicationName>
</SendPort>
```

- **DistributionListCollection:** The distribution list is the name for send port groups. We don't have any in our application, but if we did they'd be listed here. They can have their own filters and a list of send ports that belong to them.

- **ReceivePortCollection:** Again this is a fairly straightforward section named appropriately and clear in intent. This section is very similar to `ReceivePortCollection` and contains many of the same values and structure applied to send rather than receive ports.

- **PartyCollection:** This section contains any party information used by the application. Again, we're not using parties in this application, but if we did they would be listed here.

The bindings are stored inside the management database with sensitive information, like passwords, stored in the SSO system used by BizTalk. In order to deploy our solution to another machine, including another developer who is working on the project with us, we should provide the bindings so that they can quickly setup and run the project. These would be developer targeted bindings.

Modifying bindings

As we can see, these are very tight bindings and would very likely need to be changed as we move the solution from our developer workstation to an integration server, UAT, and ultimately production. As we learned in *Chapter 4, Operating BizTalk*, we want to use MSIs to perform this installation and they will give us the opportunity to bundle bindings within them for each target environment that we plan to deploy to.

Creating bindings for each environment

The key part to this aspect of BizTalk management and development is to know which settings are going to change between environments and how. There are two primary ways to approach this. One is to make the changes manually in the administration console and export them for specific environments. The other is to manually change the binding XML files. Either way, you will want to create a `Bindings` file for each environment that you plan to deploy this solution onto. This should be at least two and hopefully more. The `Bindings` folder exists in our solution so that the bindings are organized in a place we will remember and so that they can be managed in source control, which is also an important part of changing management with BizTalk. Other than the settings within the bindings, the names of the files are also a good key to help keep them different. In this solution, we will prepend the environment names to our `Bindings` files.

In Windows Explorer, navigate to the solution directory and open the `Bindings` folder. Make two copies of `LocalDev_OrderProcessing.BindingInfo.xml` in that same folder naming them `UAT_OrderProcessing.BindingInfo.xml` and `Production_OrderProcessing.BindingInfo.xml`. Then add these files as existing items to the `Build` solution folder. If this were a real solution, we would now go and change the appropriate values, but this is left as an exercise to the user.

Building and deploying the solution

Now that our solution is complete, we have to be able to deploy it to other server environments in our enterprise such as UAT/Staging and production. The best practice for deploying BizTalk solutions is MSI installation. MSIs are binary installation packages used for deploying software in Windows environments. The MSI approach helps us to be certain that the artifacts we approve in a testing environment are the ones deployed to a production environment.

Building an MSI manually

We can create an MSI directly from the BizTalk Administration console and we'll walk through that process right now:

1. Right-click the **Order Processing** application and select **Export | MSI file....**

    A welcome screen will greet us that explains how this wizard works.

2. Click **Next**. From here we are shown a list of all the resources within this application which is displayed in the following screenshot:

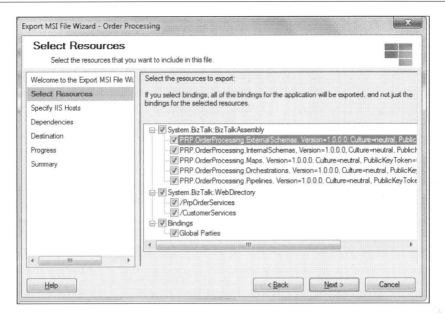

We can select which resources we want to include in the package here.

3. Click **Next**.

    We can now see which IIS hosts (or virtual directories) will be exported as well.

4. Click **Next**.

    The next screen shows us dependencies to other BizTalk applications. Since we don't have any, only `BizTalk.System` is shown.

5. Click **Next**.

    Here we can set the application name we wish this application to be installed to and the destination on the filesystem on which to construct the MSI file.

6. Click **Export**.

    The wizard shows us status as it bundles up all the selected resources and creates an MSI for them.

7. Click **Finish**.

We now have an MSI that we can use to install our package onto other environments. This is pretty useful, but it's not ideal yet. For one, our bindings are not in this package and worse still, even if they were, because we did not uncheck the **Bindings** checkbox at the bottom of the **Select Resources** dialog, we wouldn't be able to use them anyway. If we don't uncheck that box, then the bindings from the current server get packaged into the MSI and if the next server has any different settings, the installation will simply fail. Different settings could be as simple as a different send hander (host) for an adapter. Clearly this is problematic.

We can add our bindings to the BizTalk server as resources using the administration console. All we have to do is right-click **Resources** and select **Add**. This presents another problem altogether. The bindings will be a snapshot at the time they were added to the BizTalk application as resources. If we then go and make changes to them, we would need to re-add them to the application. Obviously, this is a hassle and something that just won't work for automated building, which if you recall is something we should all strive towards.

Examining how the MSI is built

Before we automate this entire BizTalk build process, it is worth considering exactly what is going on. When we walked through the wizard before, we could see that there were certain boxes we could check (or uncheck) to tell the administration console how to construct our MSI package. It turns out there is a second administration tool that is a command-line utility: `btstask.exe`.

`Btstask.exe` provides nearly all the same features as the BizTalk Administration console, but in a command-line form. This links to the past of BizTalk when there was no administration console, but also exists to help us with exactly these types of automated tasks we are trying to achieve here.

The steps involved in our build will be:

- Updating the bindings in the application
- Packaging all resources, except the installed bindings
- Exporting an MSI from BizTalk

Automating MSI builds

Considering the steps we need to perform, this turns out to be quite easy. We're going to use a `.bat` file to hold a few commands to `btstask.exe` that will perform the three preceding tasks. This batch file should be created in the `Build` directory of the solution and named `BuildMSI.bat`. The commands that should be in this file are listed as follows:

```
btstask addresource /ApplicationName:"Order Processing" /Type:
System.BizTalk:BizTalkBinding /Property:TargetEnvironment="Producti
on" /Source:"bindings\Production_OrderProcessing.BindingInfo.xml" /
Overwrite

btstask addresource /ApplicationName:"Order Processing" /Type:
System.BizTalk:BizTalkBinding /Property:TargetEnvironment="UAT" /
Source:"build\UAT_OrderProcessing.BindingInfo.xml" /Overwrite

btstask exportapp /ApplicationName:"Order Processing" /Package:
OrderProcessing.msi /ResourceSpec:Build/OrderProcessingResourceSpec.
xml
```

The first two commands will add our `Bindings` files to the application.
The `/overwrite` switch will overwrite previous versions of these resources.

The last command will actually perform the export of the MSI. We specify the name
of the MSI to export as well as the `ResourceSpec` which is an XML file listing the
resources we want to export. This is analogous to the **Select Resources** dialog we
saw earlier.

We do have a little bit of setup to do before this becomes seamlessly repeatable, but
it only needs to be done once. We need to run the first two commands that add the
resources and then generate the `ResourceSpec`:

1. Open a Visual Studio command prompt and change directories into your
   solution directory.

2. Run the two `btstask addresource` commands.

3. Change directories into the `Build` directory.

4. Run the following command:

   ```
   btstask listapp -ApplicationName:"Order Processing" -ResourceSpec:
   OrderProcessingResourceSpec.xml
   ```

   If we open the `OrderProcessingResourceSpec.xml` file, we will see the
   listing as follows:

   ```
   <?xml version="1.0" encoding="utf-16"?>
   <ResourceSpec xmlns:xsi="http://www.w3.org/2001/XMLSchema-
   instance" xmlns:xsd="http://www.w3.org/2001/XMLSchema"
   ApplicationName="Order Processing" xmlns="http://schemas.
   microsoft.com/BizTalk/ApplicationDeployment/ResourceSpec/2004/12">
     <Resources>
       <Resource Type="System.BizTalk:BizTalkAssembly" Luid="PRP.
   OrderProcessing.ExternalSchemas, Version=1.0.0.0, Culture=neutral,
   PublicKeyToken=0e3c97569ac5667e" />
   ```

```
      <Resource Type="System.BizTalk:BizTalkAssembly" Luid="PRP.
OrderProcessing.InternalSchemas, Version=1.0.0.0, Culture=neutral,
PublicKeyToken=0e3c97569ac5667e" />
      <Resource Type="System.BizTalk:BizTalkAssembly" Luid="PRP.
OrderProcessing.Maps, Version=1.0.0.0, Culture=neutral, PublicKeyT
oken=0e3c97569ac5667e" />
      <Resource Type="System.BizTalk:BizTalkAssembly" Luid="PRP.
OrderProcessing.Orchestrations, Version=1.0.0.0, Culture=neutral,
PublicKeyToken=0e3c97569ac5667e" />
      <Resource Type="System.BizTalk:BizTalkAssembly" Luid="PRP.
OrderProcessing.Pipelines, Version=1.0.0.0, Culture=neutral, Publi
cKeyToken=0e3c97569ac5667e" />
      <Resource Type="System.BizTalk:BizTalkBinding"
Luid="Production_OrderProcessing.BindingInfo.xml" />
      <Resource Type="System.BizTalk:BizTalkBinding" Luid="UAT_
OrderProcessing.BindingInfo.xml" />
  <Resource Type="System.BizTalk:BizTalkBinding"
Luid="Application/Order Processing" />
      <Resource Type="System.BizTalk:WebDirectory" Luid="/
CustomerServices" Source="http://localhost/CustomerServices" />
    </Resources>
</ResourceSpec>
```

The highlighted line is the equivalent of the checkbox we saw before for bindings that are always applied. We need to remove that line from the file. Above it we can see the two bindings that we added to the application.

From now on, we can build our MSI with updated resources and bindings by simply running `build\buildmsi.bat` from our solution root. This makes it very easy to do this from TFS, MSBuild, or CruiseControl.NET. The only tasks we would need for any of these is a Visual Studio deploy task and a command-line task to run `BuildMSI.bat`. We could also add in a copy task to move the MSI somewhere from where it can be installed.

If we added custom assemblies to our application and wanted to deploy them, we can also add them via `BtsTask`. We would then want to regenerate our resource spec or add a line in it for them so that they are bundled into our MSI. We can even add policies and BAM definitions and profiles this way. For more information on using `BtsTask` see: `http://msdn.microsoft.com/en-us/library/aa559686(BTS.70).aspx`.

Using advanced BAM features

Our solution is now functionally complete and we even have an automated build and self-contained MSI that is used for deployment. The last missing part is in depth monitoring. Our current BAM is woefully inadequate for almost all intents and purposes. It contains no aggregations and only tracks when the solution receives orders, not when it sends them out. It is also tracking inaccurate price information because it does not take the discount into consideration. We will now update our BAM definition and profile to address these issues.

Updating BAM activities

Before we can update a BAM activity, there are a few things that are happening that we need to be aware of. Since the entire BAM infrastructure is dynamic, we need to be aware of what our update is going to do. Adding new fields to an activity is not a problem, but taking them away will be and so may changing aliases. Importantly, changing views is going to cause problems. You will get an error updating the view. The solution to this is to delete the views, which are only views anyway, not stored data. We can then perform a BAM update and the views will be recreated along with any new fields:

1. Open the `OrderProcessing.xlsx` file in Excel and click the **Add-Ins** tab and then the **BAM** menu. Select **BAM Activity**.

2. Click **Edit Activity**.

3. Create a new item called **Discounted Total** of type **Decimal**.

4. Create a new item called **Priority Order Sent** of type **Business Milestone**.

5. Create a new item called **Standard Order Sent** of type **Business Milestone**.

6. Click **OK**, then click **OK** again.

This will launch the **View Creation** wizard:

1. Click **Next**.

2. Keep the **Create a new view** selection and click **Next**.

3. Name the view **Sales View** and check the **Purchase Orders** activity.

4. Click **Next**.

5. Click **Select all items** and click **Next**.

Defining groups for BAM milestones

We can group milestones together when only one of a given action is expected to happen, which is conveniently the case in our solution. An order will either be priority or not.

1. At the **View Items** page click **New Group**.

2. Name the new group (milestone alias) as **Order Sent** and select **Priority Order Sent** and **Standard Order Sent** from the available milestones, then click **OK**.

3. Click **New Duration** and name the duration **Processing Time** selecting **Order Received (Purchase Orders)** as the start milestone and **Order Sent (Purchase Orders)** as the end milestone.

4. Click **OK** and then click **Next**.

Creating dimensions

We're now at the Aggregations and Dimensions dialog and we will create both to improve our visibility and understanding of the solution.

1. Click **New Dimension**.

2. Name the dimension **Date Received** and set the **Dimension type** as **Time Dimension** with **Display Settings** as **Year, week, day, hour, minute** (the option at the bottom).

3. Create another dimension and name it **Sales Channel** and choose **Data Dimension**.

4. Select **Sales Channel** from the **Available data items** and click **Add**.

5. The dialog should look similar to the following screenshot:

6. Click **OK**.

7. Create another data dimension named **Billing State** using the **Billing State** as the **Available data item**.

8. Create a new dimension named **Order Size** and this time select **Numeric Range Dimension** selecting **Order Total** as **the Base data item**.

9. Click **New Range** and name this range **Small** and set **0** as the **From** and **250** as the **To** values.

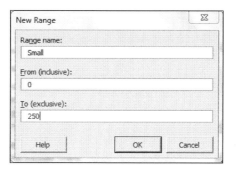

10. Click **OK**.

11. Create another range in that same dimension called **Medium** and use **From** and **To** values of **250** and **1000**, respectively.

This tool is actually smart enough to know if you're creating overlapping ranges and it will prevent you from doing so.

12. Create a final range called **Large** using **To** and **From** values of **1000** and **100000000**. Your final configuration for the **Order Size** dimension should look similar to the following screenshot:

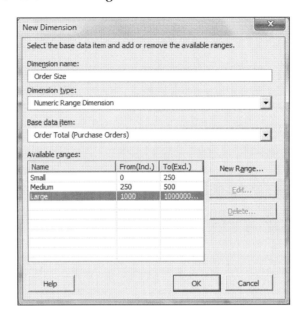

13. Click **OK**.

Defining measures in BAM views

Measures allow us to see aggregated metrics based upon certain underlying data within a BAM activity; some are based on numbers in the data and others are based on the number of individual activities.

1. Back at the **Aggregations and Dimensions** dialog, click **New Measure**.

2. Name this measure **Order Count** and select **Count** as the **Aggregation Type** as shown in the following screenshot.

3. Click **OK**.

4. Create another measure called **Order Sum** and use **Sum** as the **Aggregation Type** and **Order Total** as the **Base activity**.

5. Click **Next** at the **Aggregations and Dimensions** dialog.

6. Click **Next** at the **Summary** dialog, then click **Finish**.

It will now become much more clear why Excel was chosen as the tool for creating BAM definitions as we can see the base of a pivot table in the workbook now.

7. Drag the **Date Received** dimension from the right to the left-hand side of the pivot table as shown in the following screenshot:

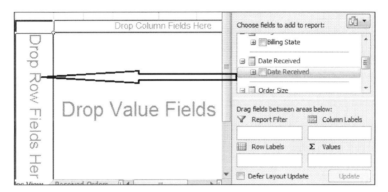

8. Drag the **Sales Channel** to the top of the pivot table.

9. Check the **Order Count** and **Order Sum** checkboxes in **the ∑ Values** list.

Your final pivot table should look similar to the following screenshot:

	Sales Channel ▾	Data				
	Sales Channel_1		Sales Channel_2		Sales Channel_3
Year ▾	Order Count	Order Sum	Order Count	Order Sum	Order Count
⊞ 2010	13.	2642609238.	6.	852916661.9	4.
⊞ 2011	6.	959729724.8	5.	493796555.4	1.
Grand Total	19.	3602338962.8	11.	1346713217.3	5.

Excel is actually creating fake or stub values for us to see what our pivot table will actually look like. This is only sample data at this time.

10. Rename `PivotTable1` in the upper left to `Sales` just to be kind to our users and avoid embarrassment.

11. Save and close the workbook.

12. Deploy our updated activity with the following command:

```
bm update-all -definitionfile:orderprocessing.xlsx
```

The activity and views (there are two now) then update and if we go back into the BAM portal we can see more than we did before. We now have our new **Sales** view and amazingly enough, there are already records in this view, albeit incomplete.

We now need to update our tracking profile to show us the Order Sent as well as Discounted Total fields. If we open the Tracking Profile Editor, we can click the **Click here to import a BAM Activity Definition** link. Select **Purchase Orders** and be sure to check the box **Retrieve the current tracking settings for this activity** at the bottom of the list of activity. Click **OK**.

We can now see that there are three new nodes in our activity on the left and we need to connect them.

1. Drag the **PortEndTime Messaging Property** onto both **Priority Order Sent** and **Standard Order Sent**.

2. Right-click **Priority Order Sent** and click **Set Port Mappings**.

3. Map this to the send port OP_File_Send_Fulfillment_ PrioritySalesOrder.

4. Map **Standard Order Sent** to OP_File_Send_Fulfillment_SalesOrder.

We're now left with the discounted order total. To track this, we actually need to use the external schema PRP.OrderProcessing.ExternalSchemas.SalesOrder rather than our internal schema. This makes sense because we could very well have done a calculation in our map and this way we can monitor the actual value that was sent out post mapping. We map this element to both OP_File_Send_Fulfillment_ SalesOrder and OP_File_Send_Fulfillment_PrioritySalesOrder.

Leveraging BAM continuation

We now have a bit of a problem because those send ports are not the same as the port we used before to bind our profile. If we run the solution now, we will actually end up with two records in our BAM. One for the receive port and the information bound to it, and another for the send port and its information. We need to bridge these two parts of the business process. The way we do that is with a **continuation**. A continuation is a part of two elements in a tracking profile that connect with each other using the same piece of data. It can be something from within the schema, or something else entirely:

1. Right-click the **Purchase Orders** folder in the left of the TPE and click **New Continuation**.

2. Name this new continuation **InterchangeID**.

3. Right-click **Purchase Orders** again and this time click **New ContinuationID**. Also, name this one **InterchangeID**.

> **Critical**
>
> It is imperative that the names of Continuation and ContinuationID are the exact same and that the values that will link the two are unique during their active runtime (that is, before the process completes).

4. Drag (associate) the **Messaging Property** named **InterchangeID** to both the continuation and continuationID.

5. Map the Continuation to the port OP_Receive_PurchaseOrders and map the ContinuationID to both OP_File_Send_Fulfillment_PrioritySalesOrder and OP_File_Send_Fulfillment_SalesOrder. This allows the profile to be bound to either of these events, functioning almost like our group did in the view.

Exploring the improved view

The new **Sales** view we have created not only shows us more tracking data, it shows it as it is updated; meaning as the continuation populates more records. This allows us to have a single tracking view over multiple discreet parts of a process, rather than using orchestrations to provide a tracking view. Better still, it also creates aggregations that we can view either from Excel or from the BAM portal directly. Before we can see these though, we must run the SSIS package that processes them.

Running the SSIS package to process aggregations

Connect to **Integration Services** on your local machine. Browse to **Stored Packages** in MSDB and look for **BAM_AN_Sales View**. This package was created by BAM when we deployed our new definition. Right-click this package and select **Run Package**. When the dialog appears click **Execute**. When the package is done click **Close** and then click **Close** again. This package will use the data in the activity tables to populate the analysis cubes that we defined and used in the pivot table.

This package, which takes no parameters, should be scheduled to run as a SQL job on a regular basis in your environments. How often to run this is a function of the volume, time sensitivity, and processing power available to you. Most aggregations can be defined as real time within the Excel Plug-In when creating them. This allows users to dynamically run the aggregation without the need for the SSIS package, but it also places extra strain on the SQL Servers running BAM.

Viewing the aggregation results

Go back to the BAM portal and expand **Aggregations** node under the **Sales** view then click **Sales** (which is what we called our pivot table). Here we get a screen split into two parts, upper and lower. The upper part is a tabular view of our dimensions and measures (aggregations). This is called the **Pivot Table** view. The lower part is a chart of the same information and is the **Chart** view. The two parts of the screen stay in sync and if you expand the time dimension on the left and open the **Year**, **Week**, and **Day** you will see the pivot table resembles the following screenshot:

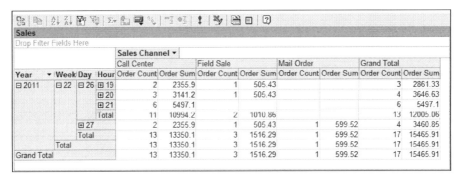

The lower chart view will resemble the following screenshot:

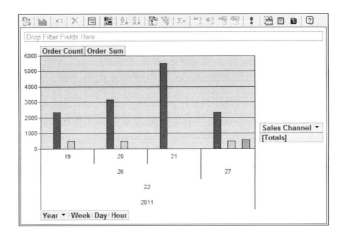

The two views stay synchronized with each other and, no matter which you change, the other reflects the changes. From this window, you can also change dimensions and measures.

Users can also view this data in Excel outside of the BAM portal. When we deployed the tracking profile, BAM actually created a spreadsheet already connected to the live data feed. The spreadsheet is named the same as the BAM definition spreadsheet with `_LiveData` appended to the filename.

Finally, users can also create BAM alerts based on this aggregated information. If you want to set an alert for a specific aggregate condition (or composite aggregate condition) it occurs just as easily as the previous alerts. The user simply right-clicks the cell they want to create an alert based on (the aggregate) and selects **Create Alert**. These alerts can use the aggregation as a threshold and restrict the alert based on a dimension (normally a time dimension). These alerts can be used for expressing complex business scenarios like 'notify anytime a particular sales channel has more than $X in sales in any hour'.

The really cool part is we're getting full analysis services here with charts, alerts, and interactive Excel access and we didn't have to work with SSAS or MDX directly at all. We didn't even have to write any code for all of this. This type of capability is amazingly powerful and is generally an epiphany for executives and business leaders when they are presented with this level of monitoring capability. It is also at the forefront of self-service business intelligence that is really gaining momentum.

Summary

This chapter rounded out and completed our order processing application. We exposed our primary ordering process, examined how bindings hold a solution together, and even built an automated script for creating deployment packages. We then improved our monitoring capabilities by updating our activity and creating an entirely new view. This solution which we have just completed should now serve as a reference architecture for all BizTalk solutions we have to create in the future. Every solution will be different, but they should exhibit the same architectural principles laid down in this solution: organized, loosely coupled, controlled dependencies, automated testing, high reusability, and ample monitoring.

The next chapter, *Asynchronous Solutions*, introduces tools and techniques used for dealing with solutions that cannot rely on centralized timing and control.

12
Asynchronous Solutions

This chapter breaks out from the previous solution and creates a completely new solution to address a different aspect of the business, that of inventory management. As our previous solution processes sales, products are removed from our inventory and need to be replenished when it is appropriate. We break this into a separate BizTalk application (and Visual Studio solution) so as to keep the applications isolated and allow them to evolve separately.

The following topics are discussed in the chapter:

- Receiving SQL broker notifications
- Using correlations
- Composite SQL operations
- Processing missed notifications
- Using polling instead of notifications

Introducing the inventory management solution

The operations team wants to be notified when the inventory of any product falls below a given threshold value. To streamline operations, they want the notification to send out a quote request to their primary supplier and then send the quote to a person for approval via an InfoPath form. At the end of the process, regardless of whether the order is approved and sent, we must update the inventory system to reflect that the product is on back order or has been discontinued.

Inventory notification with approval

The database `AlphaInventory` contains a table `Products` that we are to monitor for conditions that require inventory orders. We must do so without creating any database artifacts or making changes to the database. This means we cannot use the stored procedure approach that we used earlier.

We need to:

- Receive the product notification from the database
- Send the quote request to the web service of the supplier (vendor)
- Send the quote out for approval
- Receive the approval response
- Send the inventory order
- Update the inventory system

We have to decide how we want to proceed with this and the clearest solution is to use an orchestration. We will need to call some web services and also wait for an approval from a person who reviews the order; which is an asynchronous operation that can take any length of time to complete.

We also have two choices as to how we should receive the inventory notifications from the `AlphaInventory` database in the first place. We could use a polling approach like we did in the previous example, but we also have access to notifications delivered via SQL Broker. Notifications fire when the results of the query that specifies the notification change. Unlike polling, SQL Server itself actively sends out these notifications immediately.

These notifications have some benefits over the polling approach, but also some drawbacks. The greatest benefit is that events are sent out in real time as they happen, so we don't need a polling interval or the overhead of repeated polling for empty data. This can be critical in low latency applications. The drawbacks will be detailed later in this chapter. We will build this solution using the notification features of the WCF-SQL adapter.

Creating the notification schema with the WCF SQL adapter

The first step to using SQL notifications is to create a schema that will deliver the notifications to us. This is a fairly simple schema, but it will also show us some more of how to use the WCF-SQL adapter tool:

1. Right-click **External Schemas** and select **Add Generated Item | Consume Adapter Service**.

2. Choose **slqBinding**.

3. Set the connection settings to **mssql://localhost/sqlexpress/AlphaInventory? InboundId=InventoryNotification** and click **Connect**.

 The preceding URI is broken down according to the following pattern: the adapter type—MSSQL, the machine name— localhost, the SQL instance—SQLExpress, the database name— AlphaInventory, and an InboundId parameter that we can use to specify exactly which notification we are receiving.

4. Change the **Select contract type** drop-down to **Service (Inbound operations)**.

5. Place your cursor in the **Search in category** textbox and press the **Tab** button on your keyboard; this will populate the list **Search in categories and operations**.

6. Double-click **Notification** to add the operation to the **Added categories and operations list**.

7. Type **AlphaInventory_** into the **Filename Prefix** textbox and click **OK.**

A schema named AlphaInventory_Notification.xsd was created in our external schemas project and if we examine it, or better still right-click it and select **Generate Instance**, we can see the XML will look similar to the following:

```
<ns0:Notification xmlns:ns0="http://schemas.microsoft.com/Sql/2008/05/
Notification/">
  <ns0:Info>Update</ns0:Info>
  <ns0:Source>Data</ns0:Source>
  <ns0:Type>Change</ns0:Type>
</ns0:Notification>
```

Unfortunately, this schema does not give a lot of information. We can see that it was an update that caused this, rather than an insert, and that the source was a data change event. The other type of event we can receive is a startup event, which we will discuss shortly.

All this really does is tells us that something has "changed"; we now have to decide what to do after a "change". We could make an orchestration to receive these notifications, but that will fairly quickly couple us to the notification concept. We may want to be able to change to polling that will use a direct subscription to retrieve the product details as well as to instantiate our new orchestration.

Using SQL table operations

As we can see from the XML example before, we cannot see what record was actually changed. We will have to perform a separate operation to actually retrieve the product record itself. We will again use the WCF-SQL adapter and this time we will perform a select operation to retrieve this data. But we'll also use this adapter to perform other operations, so now we must generate another set of schemas using the wizard again:

1. Right-click **External Schemas** and click **Add | Generated Items**.

2. Select **Consume Adapter Service** and click **OK**.

3. Use the URI: `mssql://localhost/sqlexpress/AlphaInventory?`.

4. Click **Connect**.

5. Use the default **Client (Outbound operations)** and expand **Tables** and **[dbo].[Products]** and add **Select** and **Update**.

6. Once selected click the **Add** button.

7. Again use the prefix **AlphaInventory_**.

8. Click **OK**.

The preceding operations will let us perform the database operations that are required for the rest of our solution. We can see three schemas and a binding file were added to our project; the schemas are as follows:

- `AlphaInventory_Table.dbo.xsd`

- `AlphaInventory_TableOperation.dbo.Products.xsd`

- `AlphaInventory_TableOperation.dbo.Vendors.xsd`

We will now need to connect our notification to our select operation from the database. Despite the fact that we know we should not create maps that map from external schema to external schema, we will now violate this guideline for the sake of brevity. This is also because what we ultimately want to do is combine these two WCF-SQL operations in a chain to retrieve the record we are actually interested in. The process for this is as follows:

1. Create a new map **Ext_AlphaInventory_Notification_To_AlphaInventory_ProductsSelect.btm**.

2. Select **PRP.InventoryManagement.ExternalSchemas.AlphaInventory_Notification** as the source schema.

3. Select **PRP.InventoryManagement.ExternalSchemas. AlphaInventory_TableOperation.dbo.Products** as the destination schema and choose **Select** as the root element.

4. Drag two **String Concatenate** Functoids onto the canvas.

5. Use * as the constant value for one Functoid and connect it to the **Select\ Columns** element in the destination.

6. Use **WHERE Stock = 'Low' and OrderStatus = 'Filled'** as the constant value input for the other and connect it to the **Select\Query** element.

Finally, we want to transform this product message into an inventory notification format we can build our solution with. The **InternalSchemas** project contains a schema InventoryNotification.xsd that will model what we want to accomplish in this application.

Create a map **Ext_AlphaProduct_To_InventoryNotification.btm** that maps SelectResponse to InventoryNotification. If you drag from **Products** on the left to **Products** on the right and select **Link by Name** many of the fields will map automatically.

Map LastOrderDate to Product/PreviousOrder/Date, LastUnitCost to Product/ PreviousOrder/UnitCost, and LastVendorNumber to Product/PreviousOrder/ Vendor.

The final field **IsValidProduct** is going to be used internally by our application to help us distinguish between data change and startup events. To make this work, we need to implement the map equivalent of if/then/else logic which we will do now:

1. Drag a **Logical Existence [?]** functoid onto the canvas.

2. Drag **a Logical Not [!]** functoid to the lower-right of the logical existence.

3. Drag two **Value Mapping** functoids onto the canvas to the right of the previous two functoids (one above the other).

4. Connect the output of the **[?]** functoid to the logical not **[!]** and also to one of the value mapping functoids; for this value mapping, use type in the value **true** for the second parameter as shown in the following screenshot:

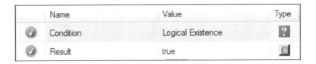

	Name	Value	Type
✓	Condition	Logical Existence	?
✓	Result	true	

5. Connect the output of the logical not **[!]** to the input of the other value mapping functoid and use the hardcoded value **false** for the second parameter of this functoid.

6. Connect the output of both the value mapping functoids to the **IsValidProduct** element on the right side (destination) schema. Your completed functoids should look similar to the following screenshot:

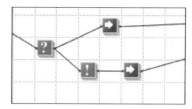

This arrangement will allow us to use `IsValidProduct` as a distinguished property, which we will do shortly.

Consuming the vendor order service

For the sake of brevity, the schemas necessary to consume the vendor order service have already been added to the external schemas project. The service itself is located at: `http://localhost/ItalianMotorImports/ItalianMotorOrderService.svc?wsdl`.

 For more details about how to consume WCF services see *Chapter 7, Leveraging Orchestration.*

Creating the orchestration

We are now ready to begin processing of our notification messages and, as we have already discussed, we will be using an orchestration to do so. This orchestration is fairly simple and will start when it receives our canonical `InventoryNotification` message.

Right-click the orchestration project and select **Add** | **New item**. Select **Orchestration** and use the name `ProductInventory.odx`.

Creating messages

Before we get too far into our orchestration design, we'll create the three messages that we know we need to execute this process:

1. Right-click the **Multi-part Message Types** folder and click **New Multi-part Message Type**.

2. Name the type **InventoryNotificationType**, rename the **MessagePart_1** to **Body** and select **PRP.InventoryManagement.InternalSchemas. InventoryNotification** from **Schemas** as the body type.

3. Add a second message type called **ProductQuoteType**; again rename the **MessagePart_1** to **Body** and this time use the schema **PRP. InventoryManagement.InternalSchemas.ProductQuote** as the body type.

4. Add a third message **VoidResponseType** and this time for the body select **.NET Classes** and **<Select from referenced assembly...>**. When the browse dialog appears browse to the type **System.Xml.XmlDocument**.

5. Recall that in *Chapter 3*, *BizTalk Development Guidelines*, we covered how bad an idea it is to use XmlDocument, even in this simple limited fashion. If we were to put this code into production it would be much better to simply create a void, or empty, type schema. This is left as an exercise for the reader.

Finally create three messages that correspond to the three types we just created: **InventoryNotification**, **ProductQuote**, and **VoidResponse**.

Laying out the shapes

With our messages created we are ready to layout the shapes that will exist in this orchestration. Recall that we will receive completed inventory notification message (corresponding to the products table) not the un-typed SQL notification:

1. Drag a receive shape on the canvas named **Rcv_InventoryNotification**.

2. Assign **InventoryNotification** as the message for this receive shape, then set the **Activate** property to **True** and click the ellipsis (**...**) next to the **Filter** property. Then use **BTS.LastInterchangeMessage** as the **Property** and the value **true** as shown in the following screenshot:

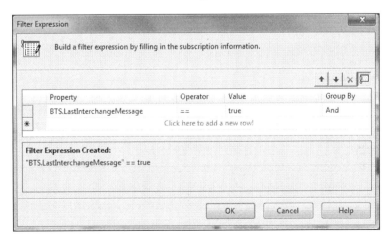

3. Click **OK** to close the dialog.

 `BTS.LastInterchange` is a property that describes if a message is the last in a related group of messages. With a batch of messages it is the last in a batch, with a two-way adapter call it is the second message.

Just like we used filters in send ports before, we can also use them in orchestrations. This allows us to activate (start) our orchestration when any arbitrary conditions of a message are met. This also allows us to receive messages from many ports or even to daisy chain multiple orchestrations together in a very loosely coupled manner.

Filters in Orchestrations

Creating filters is subtly different inside of orchestration. This is largely because orchestration is a strongly typed environment, unlike the BizTalk Administration console. Notice that the value **true** used above does not have quotes around it. This is because the `BTS.LastInterchangeMessage` property is a `Boolean` property. If we chose a different property that is a string, such as `BTS.Operation`, we would need to enclose the value in quotes. Not doing so will cause compilation errors that aren't always the easiest to figure out. You can see a visual cue to this by the **Filter Expression Created** part of the dialog.

One important note about this filter is that it will be triggered by any message with the message type that matches the underlying message type of `InventoryNotification` and has the `BTS.LastInterchangeMessage` property set to true. If we did not use this filter our very first send shape would also match the subscription and we would have a new instance of our orchestration spawned in a perpetual chain. It happened to me when writing this chapter. You must be careful to avoid these types of conditions:

1. Drag a decide shape onto the canvas and name it **Is Valid Product Order**. Rename **Rule_1** as **Yes** and set the **Expression** to be `InventoryNotification.Body.IsValidProduct == true`.

2. Drag a send shape named **Snd_QuoteRequest** onto the canvas in the **Yes** branch of the decide.

3. Drag a receive shape named **Rcv_Quote** below the send shape.

4. Drag another send shape below **Rcv_Quote** and name it **Snd_ApprovalRequest**.

5. Drag a receive shape below **Snd_ApprovalRequest** and name it **Rcv_Approval0**.

6. Drag another decide shape below **Rcv_Approval**; name it **Approved** and rename **Rule_1** as **Yes** and set expression to `ProductQuote.Body.Approved == true`.

7. Drag a send shape into this new **Yes** branch and name it **Snd_Order**.

8. Drag a receive shape below **Snd_Order** and name it **Rcv_OrderResponse**.

9. Drag a final send shape **Snd_OrderComplete** after the **Approved** decide shape, but still inside the **Yes** branch of the **Is Valid Product Order**.

Your completed orchestration outline should resemble the following screenshot:

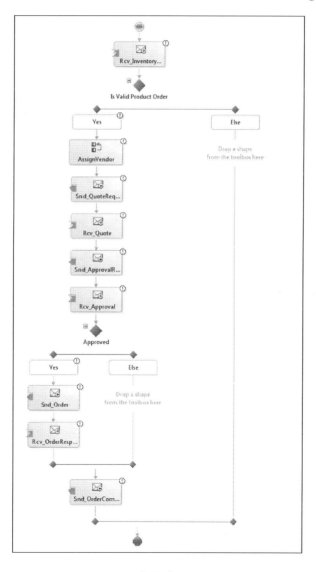

Creating the logical ports

With our message types and schema layout complete, we can create the ports necessary for this solution. The following tables list each port that needs to be created and the properties for each of them.

Property	Value
Name	InventoryNotificationPort
Type	InventoryNotificationPortType
Communication Pattern	One-Way
Port Direction	I'll always be receiving messages on this port
Binding	Direct (routing between ports will be defined by filter expressions on incoming)
Operation	IM_Receive_InventoryNotification
Message Type	InventoryNotificationType

Wire this receive port to the shape **Rcv_InventoryNotification** and assign the message **InventoryNotification** to the shape.

Property	Value
Name	ProductQuotePort
Type	ProductQuotePortType
Communication Pattern	Request-Response
Port Direction	I'll be sending a request and receiving a response
Binding	Specify Later
Operation	IM_Send_ProductQuote
Message Type	InventoryNotificationType (Request) ProductQuoteType (Response)

Wire up the port to **Snd_QuoteRequest** using message **InventoryNotification** and **Rcv_Quote** using the **ProductQuote** message.

We now need to create two ports that will handle the sending and receiving on the notification. Since this is an asynchronous event and we very well may send and receive these messages with separate transports, we will be using two one-way ports for send and receive. This first port is to send out the approval request.

Property	Value
Name	QuoteApprovalRequestPort
Type	QuoteApprovalRequestPortType
Communication Pattern	One-Way
Port Direction	I'll always be sending messages on this port
Binding	Specify Later
Operation	IM_Send_QuoteApprovalRequest
Message	ProductQuoteType

Connect the send shape **Snd_ApprovalRequest** to the operation **IM_Send_ QuoteApprovalRequest** on this port and assign the message **ProductQuote** to the send shape.

This second port is to receive the approval responses.

Property	Value
Name	QuoteApprovalResponsePort
Type	QuoteApprovalResponsePortType
Communication Pattern	One-Way
Port Direction	I'll always be receiving messages on this port
Binding	Specify Later
Operation	IM_Receive_QuoteApprovalResponse
Message	ProductQuoteType

Connect the send shape **Rcv_Approval** to the operation **IM_Receive_ QuoteApprovalResponse** of this new port and assign the message **ProductQuote** as the message for the shape.

Messages are immutable

Remember that we are completely overwriting the ProductQuote message. Since messages are immutable we are actually creating a completely new message that will not have any of the context properties of the originally received message. Often it is better to create a new location to hold a new message if you need some of the context of the original message later on.

We also need a way to send out the web service request to place our order, but we don't have to (and should not) create a new port for this, as we can simply reuse the existing port `ProductQuotePort`.

Right-click this port and click **New Operation** as shown in the following screenshot:

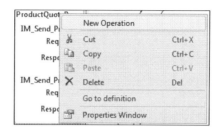

Name the new operation **IM_Send_ProductOrder** and assign **PRP. InventoryManagement.Orchestrations.ProductQuoteType** as the request message type and **PRP.InventoryManagement.Orchestrations.VoidResponse** as the response message type. Connect **Snd_Order** to the request using the message **ProductQuote** and **Rcv_OrderResponse** to the response using the message **VoidResponse**.

We need one final port and that is to send out the completed product quote and update the `AlphaInventory` database accordingly. Like the first port we created, we will be using direct binding to send messages directly to the message box.

Property	Value
Name	ProductOrderCompletePort
Type	ProductOrderPortCompleteType
Communication Pattern	One-Way
Port Direction	I'll always be receiving messages on this port
Binding	Direct
Operation	IM_Send_ProductOrder
Message	ProductQuoteType

If we build the solution, we will see the following error and may then wonder exactly what has gone wrong:

```
you must specify at least one already-initialized correlation set for
a non-activation receive that is on a non-selfcorrelating port
```

If we double-click this error, the shape **Rcv_Approval** is highlighted in the orchestration canvas. Once we know what this error means it does make perfect sense. Recall how we have always had to set the first receive shape in our orchestrations to have the `Activate` property set to `True`. This is so that BizTalk knows to create a subscription that will activate the orchestration. The orchestration compiler is warning us right now that it does not have a way to connect `Rcv_Approval` to the shapes before it. We need to find a way to correlate an approval message to the specific orchestration instances that sent it out. The mechanism we use to do this is called a **correlation**.

Creating the correlation

So far we have only seen orchestrations use request-response ports to perform two-way communications. We already know that internally BizTalk uses instance subscriptions to make this work and it is in fact asynchronous behind the scenes, but we can actually do this ourselves explicitly with a correlation and we will do that now.

The `Id` element of the `ProductInventoryQuote` schema has already been promoted for us into the `QuoteId`, which was done exactly as we did before via the wizard. Now we will use this property for correlation:

1. Right-click the **Correlation Types** in the orchestration view and select **New Correlation Type**.

2. Name this correlation type **QuoteIdCorrelationType**.

3. Right-click **Correlation Sets** in the orchestration section (upper part) of the orchestration view and click **New Correlation Set**.

4. Name this correlation **QuoteIdCorrelation** and select the type **QuoteIdCorrelationType** as the **Correlation Type**.

5. On the send shape **Snd_QuoteApprovalRequest** set the property **Initializing Correlation Set** by selecting **QuoteIdCorrelation** from the drop-down.

6. On the shape **Rcv_QuoteApprovalResponse** set the property **Following Correlation Set** by selecting **QuoteIdCorrelation** from the drop-down.

7. Build the solution, which should now succeed.

Updating the inventory

We are nearing the end of our solution, but we do have one final challenge to address. We must update the products table that launched our notification, as well as conditionally updating the vendors table if the order was approved and placed.

We could perform these in separate send operations from our orchestration, but this could result in inconsistent states in our database if the first operation succeeds and the second one does not. We could handle these with compensating actions or other approaches, but it is far easier to simply use the transactional nature of the WCF-SQL adapter itself to accomplish these goals for us. We are going to do this with a composite operation on the WCF-SQL adapter, which allows us to group any set of operations together in a single operation.

> Critically composite operations do not support table-based select operations.

Creating a composite operation schema

In order to execute a composite operation, we need to create a composite schema that will both update the product record to reflect the order status (In **Progress** or **Discontinued**) as well as to update the last order date of the vendor if the order was approved. Recall that when we ran the WCF-SQL wizard we generated update operations for both the products and vendors tables, so all we have to do now is make a schema that includes both of these operations:

1. Add a new item to external schemas named **Alpha_CompositeOperation. xsd**.

2. Click the schema root and in the properties window click the ellipsis (...) in the **Imports** property.

3. In the **Imports** dialog click **Add**.

4. Add the schema **PRP.InventoryManagement. ExternalSchemas. AlphaInventory_TableOperation.dbo.Products**.

5. Rename the **Root** node as **CompositeRequest**.

6. Add a child node to **CompositeRequest**.

7. Click this new node and change the **Data Structure Type** to **ns0:Update (Reference)**. Notice how the node was renamed for us.

8. Add another child node to **CompositeRequest** and change the **Data Structure Type** of this new node to **ns1:Update (Reference)**. We can see how the node now reflects the fields of the vendors update.

9. Create a new root node called **CompositeRequestResponse**.

We can name the request and response nodes whatever we like, especially in this case because we won't actually use the response schema, but the name of the response root node must be the same as the request with the word **Response** appended.

10. Add a child record to **CompositeRequestResponse** and change its **Data Structure Type** to **ns0:UpdateResponse**.

11. Add a second child record to **CompositeRequestResponse** and change its **Data Structure Type** to **ns1:UpdateResponse**.

We now have the vehicle that will perform the two operations against the WCF-SQL adapter that we require in one single DTC transaction. We could add as many operations as we want to this composite schema and perform complex database operations. The order in which the nodes appear in the XML dictates the order that they execute against the database as well.

Creating the composite operation map

The last task we have to address is to create a map that will use this new composite schema to actually perform the updates in the AlphaInventory database:

1. Right-click the **Maps** project and click **Add | New Item** and select a map using the name **Int_ProductQuote_To_AlphaCompositeOperation.btm**.

2. Select **PRP.InventoryManagement.InternalSchemas.ProductQuote** as the source schema and **PRP.InventoryManagement.ExternalSchemas.Alpha_CompositeOperation** as the destination schema.

3. Expand all the XML tree nodes so that you can see the complete source and destination formats.

   We can see that each update on the right has an **Update/Rows/RowPair** node with **After** and **Before** children. **Before** functions like a where clause and **After** like the set clauses in a query against a table.

4. Click the map grid to get to the map properties and change **Ignore Namespaces for Links** to **False**.

5. Connect **ProductInventoryQuote/Product/CatalogNumber** to **CompositeRequest/ns0:Update/ns0:Rows/ns0:RowPair/ns0:Before/CatalogNumber**.

The previous step will allow us to map to destinations with the same name, but different namespaces, which is what we have in this case. This last step will effectively produce a where clause using the catalog number column of the products table.

6. Drag a **Logical Equal** functiod [=] onto the upper part of the canvas.

7. Connect **ProductInventoryQuote/Approved** to the **equal** functoid and enter **true** as the hardcoded second parameter.

8. Drag a **Logical NOT** functoid onto the canvas to the upper right of the equal and connect the output of [=] to the input of the [!].

9. Drag a **Value Mapping** functoid [->] to the right of the logical not [!] and connect the [!] to [->] then set the second parameter of the value mapping to **Discontinued**.

10. Drag another **Value Mapping** functoid [->] to the right of the logical equal [=] and connect the output of [=] to this new value mapping and set the second parameter of the value mapping to the value **In Progress**.

11. Connect both of the value mapping functoids to the output element **CompositeRequest/ns0:Update/ns0:Rows/ns0:RowPair/ns0:Before/OrderStatus**.

Your map should resemble the following screenshot:

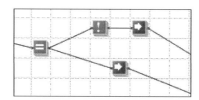

The rest of the fields we want to map are conditional based upon the result of the approval, which we already have a logical equal to determine and drive our mapping.

12. Drag another **Value Mapping** functoid onto the canvas below the previous functoids and connect [=] to the input of it.

13. Drag the **Product\UnitCost** node from the left to this new value mapping (it will be the second argument).

14. Connect this new value mapping to the **LastUnitCost** element in the **After** node.

The order of inputs to the **Value Mapping** functoid is significant. The first value should either be true or false (or a logical functoid) and will determine if the second parameter is mapped or not. In the preceding arrangement, the **LastUnitCost** is only updated if the order was approved (meaning it was placed).

15. Drag a **Date** functoid onto the canvas below this latest value mapping.

16. Drag another **Value Mapping** functoid to the right of the **Date** functoid and connect [=] to this new value mapping as the first parameter and the **Date** as the second.

17. Connect this latest **Value Mapping** functoid to the **LastOrderDate** of the **After** record in the destination then connect this same value mapping to the **ns1:Update\ns1:Rows\ns1:RowPair\ns1:After\LastOrderDate** (of the vendors table, which only has three nodes in the **After** element.

18. Drag a final **Value Mapping** functoid onto the canvas below the **Date** functoid.

19. Connect the output of [=] to this last **Value Mapping** functoid as the first parameter and the **Vendor\Name** element from the source schema as the second.

20. Connect the output of this final **Value Mapping** functoid to **ns0:After\ LastVendorNumber ns1:After\VendorNumber** and **ns1:Before\ VendorNumber**.

The final map should resemble the following screenshot:

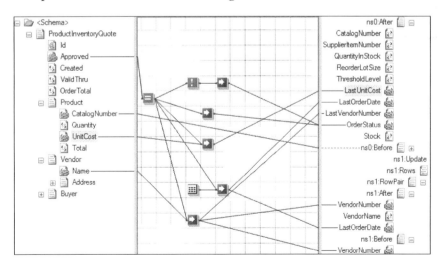

Creating the other maps

We have created three maps thus far, but we have a few more to go. Fortunately, these are fairly straightforward and some are extremely simple. Create a map **Int_ProductInventoryNotification_To_QuoteRequest.btm** with **PRP. InventoryManagement.InternalSchemas.InventoryNotification** as the source and **PRP.InventoryManagement.ExternalSchemas.ItalianMotorOrderService_tempuri_ org** as the destination schemas.

Map only **CatalogNumber** and **ReorderLotSize** from **InventoryNotification\ Product** to **ItemNumber** and **Quantity** of **GetQuote\requestForQuote\Products\ Product** respectively.

Create the map **Ext_Quote_To_ProductQuote.btm** using **PRP. InventoryManagement.ExternalSchemas.ItalianMotorOrderService_tempuri_org** as the source and **PRP.InventoryManagement.InternalSchemas.ProductQuote** as the destination schemas. Every element in the source has a name matched element in the destination schema with the following exceptions that should be matched: **Number** to **Id**, **ValidUnit** to **ValidThru**, and **Approved** (destination) which should be mapped with the constant value false in a **String Concatenate** functoid.

We also need two more maps, **Int_ProductQuote_To_ProductQuote.btm** and **Ext_ProductQuote_To_ProductQuote.btm** which are one-to-one direct maps where every field maps exactly by name or structure.

The final map, **Int_ProductQuote_To_PlaceOrderRequest.btm**, maps directly just like **Ext_Quote_To_ProductQuote.btm**.

Our solution is now complete and should be built and deployed.

Binding the solution

Now that the solution is deployed, it is time to bind it all together. We have several binding files that were generated for us by the consume adapter service wizard. We can use these and then customize the ports to fit our specific needs. For several other ports we will have to create them manually. The rest of this will be performed in the BizTalk Administration console.

Importing the notification bindings

We can now import the bindings that were created by the consume adapter service wizard for our notification:

1. Right-click the **InventoryManagement** application and click **Import | Bindings** and browse to **WcfReceivePort_SqlAdapterBinding_Custom. bindinginfo.xml**.

2. Rename the new port as **IM_Receive_InventoryNotification**.

3. Rename the location as **IM_WCFSQL_Receive_InventoryNotification**.

4. Click the **Configure** button for the transport.

5. On the **Bindings** tab change **inboundOperationType** to **Notification**.

6. Set the notification statement to **select CatalogNumber, SupplierItemNumber, QuantityInStock, from dbo.Products where Stock = 'Low' and OrderStatus = 'Filled'**.

> The database schema, **dbo** in this case, is required and the columns must be explicitly listed because wildcards are not allowed in SQL notifications.

We can now enable this receive location and we will begin receiving messages as soon as changes occur to the underlying source table.

> **Service Broker** must be enabled on the database from which you intend to receive notifications. This can be enabled in the database options, which can be accessed by right-clicking the database in **Management Studio**, clicking **Properties** and navigating to the **Options** section.

Importing the WCF-SQL send bindings

We will now create the send port that will perform the select statement that retrieves the product details for us:

1. Right-click the **InventoryManagement** application and click **Import | Bindings** and browse to **WcfSendPort_SqlAdapterBinding_Custom. bindinginfo.xml**.

2. Rename this send port as **IM_WcfSql_Send_AlphaProductSelect**.

3. Click the **Configure** button and set the **Action** to **TableOp/Select/dbo/ Products** and click **OK**.

4. Set the outbound map to **Ext_AlphaInventoryNotification_To_ AlphaProductSelect**.

5. Set the inbound map to **Ext_AlphaProduct_To_InventoryNotification**.

6. Set the **Filter** to **BTS.ReceivePortName == IM_SQL_Receive_ InventoryNotification**.

7. Click **OK**.

This third step is used to hardcode the WCF Action of the port. Because we are not using an orchestration and didn't promote a special property like we did previously, we need a way to tell the adapter which action to perform.

Manually creating a WCF-SQL send port

We need another WCF-SQL send port to provide our final update:

1. Right-click **Send Ports** and select **Static One-way Send Port**.

2. Name the port **IM_WcfSql_Send_AlphaProductVendorUpdate** and select **WCF-SQL** as the **Type** then click **Configure**.

3. Set the **Address (URI)** to **mssql://localhost/sqlexpress/AlphaInventory?** and the **Action** to **CompositeOperation** and click **OK**.

> CompositeOperation is a special operation that tells the adapter to look one node lower in the message for the actual operations to perform. The WCF SQL Adapter uses name matching to perform this. We must use the value CompositeOperation to make this work.

4. Set the outbound map to **Int_ProductQuote_To_AlphaCompositeOperation**.

5. Set the Filter to **BTS.Operation == IM_Send_ProductOrderComplete**.

6. Click **OK**.

This port was fairly easy to configure and you can see that not all of these parameters are as complicated as they at first appear.

Creating the approval physical ports

Finally we need to create the two ports that will send and receive the approvals for the solution. For simplicity we will use the file adapter for both ports. In reality, SMTP and WCF would be much better options, but incorporating them is left as an exercise for the reader.

Property	Value
Name	IM_File_Send_ApprovalRequest
Type	Static One-way Send Port
Address (Destination Folder)	C:\BizTalk\PRP\ApprovalRequest
Filename	%MessageID%.xml
Map	Int_ProductQuote_To_ProductQuote

This second port receives the actual approval response.

Property	Value
Port Name	IM_Receive_ApprovalResponse
Location Name	IM_File_Receive_ApprovalResponse
Type	Static One-way Receive
Address	C:\BizTalk\PRP\ApprovalResponse
Mask	*.xml
Map	Ext_ProductQuote_To_ProductQuote

Manually creating a web service send port

Our final port to create is a WCF send port to call the vendor order service and we could simply import the bindings that the wizard created for us, but in an effort to better understand these bindings, we will create this port manually:

1. Right-click **Sent Ports** and select **New Static Solicit-Response Port**. Name it **IM_Wcf_SendPort_ItalianMotorOrderService**.

2. Select **WCF-BasicHttp** as the **Type**.

3. Set the **Receive pipeline** to **XMLReceive**.

4. Click **Configure** and set the **Address (URI)** to **http://localhost/ItalianMotorImports/ItalianMotorOrderService.svc**.

5. Set the **Action** to include the following action mapping which translates BTS. Operation (that is, logical send port name from an orchestration) into a WCF Action.

```
<BtsActionMapping xmlns:xsi="http://www.w3.org/2001/XMLSchema-
instance" xmlns:xsd="http://www.w3.org/2001/XMLSchema">
 <Operation Name="IM_Send_ProductQuote" Action="http://tempuri.
org/ItalianMotorOrderService/GetQuote" />
 <Operation Name="IM_Send_ProductOrder" Action="http://tempuri.
org/ItalianMotorOrderService/PlaceOrder" />
</BtsActionMapping>
```

6. Click **OK**.

7. Set the inbound map to **Ext_Quote_To_ProductQuote** and set the outbound maps to contain **Int_ProductInventoryNotification_To_QuoteRequest** and **Int_ProductQuote_To_ProductOrder**.

8. Click **OK**.

Binding the orchestration

We now have all of our ports complete and we are ready to bind the orchestration itself. Click the `Orchestrations` folder in the administration console then right-click the orchestration and select **Properties**. Set the **Host** to **BizTalkServerApplication** and set **IM_Receive_QuoteApproval** as the **Inbound Logical Port** for **QuoteApprovalResponsePort**. Set **IM_File_Send_ApprovalRequest** as the **Outbound Logical Port** for **QuoteApprovalRequestPort** and **IM_Wcf_SendPort_ ItalianMotorOrderService** for **ProductQuotePort**.

We should now be able to start the application and begin to test our solution. We can do this by running the following query against the `AlphaInventory` database.

```
update products set orderstatus = 'Filled'
```

This will cause an XML file to be created in `C:\BizTalk\PRP\ApprovalRequest` which we can view or edit, should we choose to. To reject this order, all we would have to do is move the file to `C:\BizTalk\PRP\ApprovalResponse` and the process would end, updating the product as `Discontinued`.

If we change the `Approved` attribute to `true` then we will see that the order is routed to the web service to place the order and the product's order status is updated to `In Progress`. The product and vendor have their last order date updated to the current date.

Exploring other approaches

Our solution is not perfect as it sits and for all the advantages that SQL notifications can give us, they have several specific drawbacks. One of the largest drawback is that we will never receive notifications for which the location was disabled. This is a problem because we could potentially miss these important notifications. There are two ways we can approach this problem and one is provided by the adapter itself.

Querying for missed notifications

Recall that when we created the notification schema we briefly mentioned the startup event that can be sent by the adapter. This event is intended to inform us that a location has just started and we're ready to receive events on it. The implication is that because the location started there could be records that have changed into a state that would have fired the event had we been listening for it (that is to say the location had been enabled).

We can use this to create a different orchestration or process that will specifically handle these missed records. Fortunately for us, due to clever crafting, our solution will already handle these scenarios. All we have to do is ensure that the notifyOnListenerStart property of the WCF-SQL binding is set to True.

Using the polling method

The polling method is similar to the classic SQL adapter approach of *Chapter 8, The WCF-SQL Adapter and WCF Services*. Our solution is conveniently compatible with changing between the polling approach and notification. This is because we handle the product query outside of the orchestration. The new WCF-SQL adapter actually gives us much greater flexibility in polling and does not require the use for FOR XML in SQL Server.

To use the polling method run the Consume Adapter Service wizard again and follow these steps:

1. Select **sqlBinding** as the binding.
2. Enter **mssql://localhost/sqlexpress/AlphaInventory?InboundId=Inventory Notification** as the URI.
3. Click **Configure**.
4. Go to the **Binding Properties** tab.
5. Change the **InboundOperationType** to **TypedPolling**.
6. Under the **Polling** section of the bindings set the **PolledDataAvailableStatement** to SELECT COUNT(*) FROM Products WHERE Stock = 'Low' AND OrderStatus = 'Filled'.
7. Set the **PollingStatement** to SELECT * FROM Products WHERE Stock = 'Low' AND OrderStatus = 'Filled'; UPDATE Products SET OrderStatus = 'In Progress' WHERE Stock = 'Low' AND OrderStatus = 'Filled'.
8. Click **OK**.
9. Click the **Connect** button on the left side of the screen.
10. Change the contract type to **Service (Inbound operations)**.

11. Mouse into **Category** and hit the **Tab** key.

12. Select **Typed Polling** and **Add** (or double click) to add this operation.

13. Use the **Filename prefix** of **AlphaInventory_**.

14. Click **OK**.

A single schema, `AlphaInventory_TypedPolling.InventoryNotification.xsd`, is created that contains a root element `TypedPolling` and a namespace of `http://schemas.microsoft.com/Sql/2008/05/TypedPolling/InventoryNotification`. The last part of this name corresponds to the `InboundId` we specified in the URI and allows us to have many polling operations against a single database without having name collisions.

If we create a map from `Ext_InventoryNotification_To_ InventoryNotification.btm`, we can transform this typed polling result directly into an inventory notification. All we have to do after deploying the solution is add the map to the receive port `IM_Receive_InventoryNotification` and change the following properties in `IM_WCFSQL_Receive_InventoryNotification` to match the properties we used in the preceding steps for `InboundOperationType`, `PolledDataAvailableStatement`, and `PollingStatement`.

Polling settings

The following settings affect how polling works in the WCF-SQL adapter:

- **PolledDataAvailableStatement:** This is the statement that runs on the polling interval and is expected to return a single column and a single row that is designed to return the number of rows available.

- **PollingIntervalInSeconds:** This setting controls how often the adapter will poll against the target database. The smallest valid amount is 1.

- **PollingStatement:** This is the statement that executes when the `PolledDataAvailableStatement` returns a result. This statement can be a stored procedure or can contain multiple statements separated by a semicolon (as in our example). In this way, we can achieve the locking and updating that we used previously.

- **PollWhileDataFound:** This parameter controls whether the adapter should continue running more queries even if it is still returning results from a previous query. If we have a very low interval and large amounts of data this would result in concurrent reads from the target database.

- **UseAmbientTransaction:** This parameter instructs the adapter to reuse the DTC transaction so that it will send the results to the message box.

A critical issue to remember is that concurrent reads will occur if you have two BizTalk servers in the group each running a host instance that hosts a SQL polling receive location. It is important to either make your reads transactional, so that they do not interfere with each other, or to cluster a specific host, so that only one server runs the location at a given time.

Summary

In this chapter, we learned how to create asynchronous solutions leveraging SQL Broker notifications, polling, continuation, and briefly explored InfoPath and SharePoint options for enriching our processing.

We saw how to explicitly create a correlation exactly like the BizTalk infrastructure does under the covers for every two-way port. We will continue building upon this solution in the next chapters.

13
Performing Parallel Processing and Branching

This chapter will explore the options we have when dealing with parallel and decision scenarios in BizTalk solutions. Several different approaches to common problems are introduced and compared as we continue to expand and refine our inventory management solution.

The following topics are covered in this chapter:

- Broker pattern
- Role-based links
- Parallel actions shape
- Self-correlating shapes
- Scatter gather pattern

Revising solution requirements

All successful software changes; this is a fact of life. Most software that doesn't change is actually a failure because it is so difficult or painful to change that people simply choose to leave it alone and often to write a replacement.

Our solution has been quite successful and we have been asked to make several changes. The first is to send quotes out to different vendors based upon the vendor number in the products table. The first part of this chapter explores different approaches to addressing such a request.

Implementing the broker pattern

This is a fairly common request in integrated solutions and very common in B2B and healthcare scenarios. We need to send the quote request to the specific vendor that supplies that particular product. Our current vendors are Italian Motor Imports, which we're already integrated with, and Japan Racing Accessories. Their vendor numbers in our database are IMI01 and JRA01. They currently both run the same B2B platform so for now, they use the same service, but it runs at different endpoints and the service may change for one vendor in the future. This type of pattern is often called a **broker** because it decides where messages will ultimately be sent.

Using the decide shape

The most obvious solution to this problem is to use the decide shape that we have already used to make decisions. Before we start, make a copy of your `ProductInventory.odx` file. We're going to need this backup soon.

1. Drag a decide shape onto the canvas at the top of the `Yes` branch of the `Is Valid Product Order` shape. Name this shape `Vendor` and rename `Rule_1` to `IMI01`.

2. Set the `Expression` for the `IMI01` branch to: `InventoryNotification.Body.Product.PreviousOrder.Vendor == "IMI01"`.

3. Move `Snd_QuoteRequest` and `Rcv_Quote` to be inside the `IMI01` branch. Right-click the **Vendor** shape and click **New Rule Branch** and name this branch **JRA01**. Set the **Expression** for the **JRA01** branch to: `InventoryNotification.Body.Product.PreviousOrder.Vendor == "JRA01"`.

4. Right-click **Snd_QuoteRequest** and click **Copy** then right-click in the **JRA01** branch and click **Paste**. Do the same thing for **Rcv_Quote**.

We cannot set an expression for the `Else` branch so we will drag a `Terminate` shape into this branch and name it `Invalid Vendor Terminate` and set the `Error Message` property to `The selected vendor is invalid;`.

1. Drag a port onto the port canvas and in the wizard name this port **ProductQuotePortJRA** and click **Next**.

2. Change the radio button to **Use an existing Port Type** and click **Next** again. Be sure to change the port direction to sending. Click **Next** and then click **Finish**.

You will see that the port is created for us and that the operations already exist in it. This is nice in that we can reuse the types and can avoid some work. In order to complete this solution, we will have to repeat this same decision on the actual order placement.

This will involve dragging a new decision shape onto the canvas in the **Yes** branch of the **Approved** decision shape, setting the expression like we did previously and then moving the **Snd_Order** and **Rcv_OrderResponse** into this branch. We will then again have to copy **Snd_Order** and **Rcv_OrderResponse** into the new **JRA01** branch and connect them to the appropriate operation of the **ProductQuotePortJRA** port.

The orchestration will end up looking like the following figure:

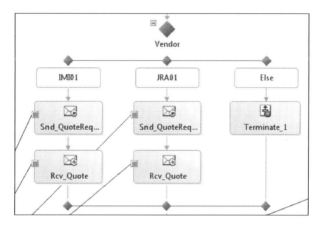

Once we deploy the solution, we will have to bind the orchestration to a new physical port that points to the JRA order service. Since the two companies currently use the same B2B platform we can use the same maps.

Assessing this approach

As you can imagine this is not an ideal approach. If we only have two vendors and will never have more or need to change vendors this is not a terrible approach and the orchestration will certainly accomplish this task, but as we add vendors we have to change our solution at the most internal component; the orchestration. This is a major impediment to business operations that most companies have simply come to accept as inevitable.

We could explore other options like dynamic send ports, but there is a lot of value in the control and visibility that administrators get from the static port approach we have used up to this point. Most administrators really like that part of BizTalk.

Creating a more extensible solution

Ideally we would like to be able to add new vendors without making changes to our orchestration as it is likely to contain a fair deal of our business process. Further, using a different vendor is not really a part of our business process, it is really an implementation detail; a technology detail. Any vendor we use will have to be able to offer us a quote and allow us to place an order. BizTalk does contain an elegant set of tools specifically designed to accommodate exactly these types of variable situations. These tools center around the concepts of **roles** and **parties**.

Understanding roles

As their name implies, roles are placeholders for an actor in a process. That might be a bit of a textbook flowchart explanation, so let's think of them as we would for a play or movie. Not to impart too much animosity into the customer-provider relationship but let's use the analogy of hero and villain. When a movie or play is written, the script is written for the role of the hero and the villain, but the specific actor is not selected until casting time (for us that's runtime).

In this same way, roles play a stand-in for our business process script; that is, our orchestration. Since roles are targeted at business systems and not movies, we replace hero and villain with provider and consumer (or consumer and provider depending on where you sit, again let's keep the animosity to a minimum). Providers implement something others want to use and consumers use it.

Understanding parties

Here's the fun part of the book. No I'm just kidding. Parties are not quite as fun as they may at first sound, but they are incredibly useful and greatly underutilized. Parties are entities that will fill a role. Normally parties are another company or division, but they could be anything. Parties are commonly known as trade partners in the EDI world. In BizTalk, parties are global entities that can be used (or use) certain artifacts in any application in the group.

Improving the broker with role-based links

With our new knowledge of roles and parties, we are ready to improve our current solution. We're going to close the orchestration `ProductInventory.odx` and delete it in Windows Explorer (not in Visual Studio), then rename our copy to `ProductInventory.odx` (I said we'd need it at the beginning of the chapter, so I hope you have kept it).

Implementing role party links

There are two ways to create roles and links. The first is in the orchestration view, similar to how we've worked with multipart messages, the other is by using the Role Link orchestration shape. We will use the latter approach.

1. Drag a **Role Link** onto the port surface of the **ProductInventory** orchestration and a **Role Link Wizard** will start up.

2. Name the link **VendorRoleLink** and click **Next**. Use **the Create a new Role Link Type** option (the default) and enter the name **VendorRoleLinkType** and click **Next**.

3. In the **Role Link Usage**, change to **Consumer Role: I will be sending the first message**.

A new construct that almost looks like a logical port will be added to the port canvas and will resemble the following screenshot:

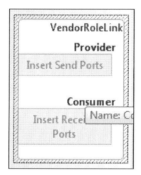

We can see that this shape actually tells us where to drop, send, and receive ports. At first it may appear that the roles themselves are exactly the opposite of what we had just seen in the wizard. We specified that we were the consumer, but send ports go in the provider section. This is because the IDE is showing us the view from the perspective of the orchestration. To the orchestration, the role is being filled by a provider, the orchestration itself is the consumer. To make this clearer, click the **Provider** word in the role link, and change the name to **VendorRoleProvider** in the properties.

All we have to do is drag the port **ProductQuotePortType** into the **Provider** section of the **VendorRoleLink** as shown in the following screenshot:

The last thing we need to do is assign the role link so that it will do a runtime lookup for the party that should fill the role. To do this, drag an expression shape above **Snd_QuoteRequest**, enter the following expression and name it **Assign Vendor**:

```
VendorRoleLink(Microsoft.XLANGs.BaseTypes.DestinationParty) = new
Microsoft.XLANGs.BaseTypes.Party(InventoryNotification.Body.Product.
PreviousOrder.Vendor, "OrganizationName");
```

We can see that this expression uses the new `VendorRoleLink` we created and sets the `DestinationParty` property. In this case, we're using our distinguished vendor field and the `OrganizationName` property to perform the linking. We can now build and deploy the solution.

Creating parties

Before we can run this solution, we need to create the parties that the role will link to in our orchestration. We do this in the BizTalk Administration console.

Right-click the **Parties** node in the BizTalk Administration Console and select **New | Party** as shown in the following screenshot:

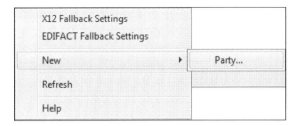

Name the new party **IMI01**. Your configuration should resemble the following screenshot:

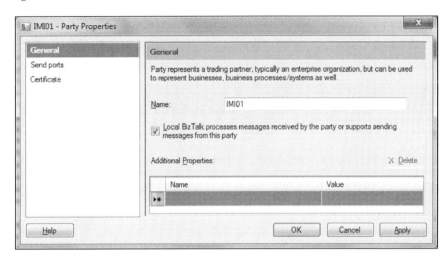

Click on **Send ports** on the left and we will now associate this party with a specific send port. We will select the port **IM_Wcf_Send_ItalianMotorOrderService** as shown in the following screenshot:

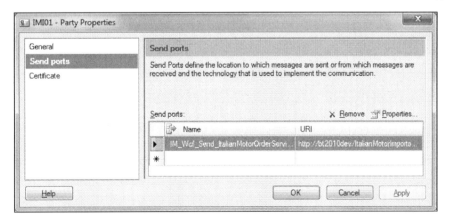

If we look at the bindings for our orchestration in the `InventoryManagement` application we can see that there are not as many as there used to be. The bindings for the WCF calls to the web service are gone, because we now use role party links to bind the logical port to a physical port at runtime.

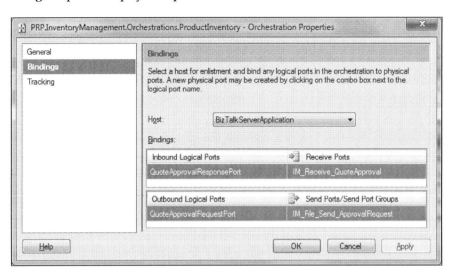

Click **OK** to close the party configuration. We're almost done, but we have one more step to complete the process. We need to tell BizTalk which ports for a party can fill what roles. Click the **Role Links** node in the **InventoryManagement** application and you will see a **VendorLinkProvider** role listed. Right-click **VendorLinkProvider** and select **Properties**.

You are presented with a **Role Link Properties** dialog. Click the **Enlist** button and you will now be presented with a list of parties configured in your environment as shown in the following screenshot:

Check the box next to **IMI01** and click **OK**. You will see a visual cue that this process is not complete yet because there is a yellow warning sign on the party. Click the **Bind** button (be sure to keep the party **IMI01** highlighted) and you are presented with a dialog that allows you to select send ports for this party as shown in the following screenshot:

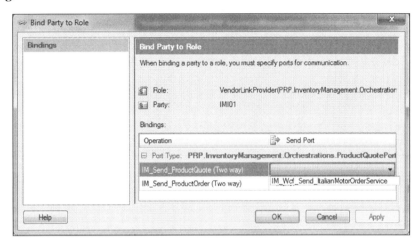

There is only one option in this drop-down, **IM_Wcf_Send_ ItalianMotorOrderService**; select it for both the operations.

There is only one port available because this party only has one port configured with it. If we had multiple ports associated with this party that matched the message exchange pattern (**One way / Two way**) they would be listed here.

You can now run the SQL command that causes this orchestration to fire and it will work as it did before. The following is the command:

```
update products set orderstatus = 'Filled'
```

Adding a new vendor

We now need to create a new send port and party for Japan Racing Accessories. This time the process is much simpler than the previous decision shaped approach; in fact there are no code changes. All we have to do is create a new send port, a party, and then enlist the party in the role. The steps are as follows:

1. Right-click **Send Ports** and click **New | Static Solicit Response Send Port**.
2. Name the port **IM_Wcf_Send_JRAOrderService** and select **WCF-BasicHttp** as the **Type**, then click **Configure**.

3. Set **the Address (URI)** to `http://localhost/JapanRacingAccessories/JRAOrderService.svc` and the **Action** to:

```
<BtsActionMapping xmlns:xsi="http://www.w3.org/2001/XMLSchema-
instance" xmlns:xsd="http://www.w3.org/2001/XMLSchema">
 <Operation Name="IM_Send_ProductQuote" Action="http://tempuri.
org/ItalianMotorOrderService/GetQuote" />
 <Operation Name="IM_Send_ProductOrder" Action="http://tempuri.
org/ItalianMotorOrderService/PlaceOrder" />
</BtsActionMapping>
```

4. Click **OK**.

5. Right-click the **Parties** node and select **New | Party**.

6. Name the party **JRA01** and click **Send Ports** then select **IM_Wcf_Send_JRAOrderService** from the drop-down.

7. Navigate back to the **Role Links** node in the **InventoryManagement** application and right-click **VendorLinkProvider** and select **Properties**.

8. Click **Enlist** and check the box next to **JRA01** (notice how **IMI01** is no longer available as it is already enlisted) then click **OK**.

9. Click **JRA01** and click the **Bind** button and select **IM_Wcf_Send_JRAOrderService** for both the operations then click **OK**.

10. Click **OK** again.

We can now use the application like we did before and we will see that it calls a different web service based on the `LastVendorNumber` of the product. We can test this by running the following query against the `AlphaInventory` database:

```
update products set orderstatus = 'Filled', LastVendorNumber = 'JRA01'
```

We can see where the message was actually sent in the BizTalk Administration console. From here, we can query `Tracked Service Instances`, which was covered in *Chapter 4, Operating BizTalk*. Here we can see all the orchestrations and pipelines that have been involved in the process so far. If you right-click the newest (they default to sort by most recent) `PRP.InventoryManagement.Orchestrations.ProductInventory` orchestration and select **Message Flow** you will see a window that is similar to the following (the following screenshot has been cropped):

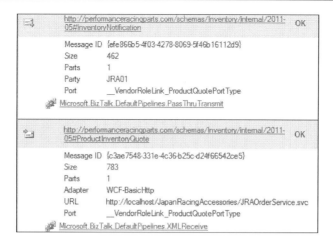

We can see from here that the upper part was a transmit and the lower was a receive (the pipelines tell us this) and both used the vendor role link as the port. We can also see that the lower message has a URL from the Japan Racing Accessories service.

If we approve and complete the request we can also see that the second operation remembers which party we're using and uses the proper port automatically. Our solution is now able to be extended very easily. Even if the vendor used a completely different web service (or an HTTP service or maybe just a SQL query), we can create new external schemas and maps and that is all we would have to change or deploy to interface with the client. None of our core business process is affected.

It is worth mentioning that, despite the fact that one of these solutions is far superior to the other in terms of flexibility and maintainability, they both implement the same broker pattern. The pattern describes their functional action, not their specific implementation. This is really just scratching the surface of parties and role party links. Unlike the traditional publish subscribe model that is driven by the message, parties allow us to add new metadata and constraints at the party level that can be used to drive logic, transport, routing, and encryption. All this sits on top of the publish subscribe model and can be used to deliver rich applications.

Enabling parallel processing

Parallel processing is becoming increasingly important in all software solutions and distributed software in particular. Many business (and technical) processes can be parallelized to decrease how long they take to run. As we move further into the multicore era of CPU architecture, this will become even more significant. Some tasks like our approval and order simply cannot be parallelized, but many others can. We will now expand our solution to perform parallel processing on the product information before we place a quote.

One of our development teams has already written a .NET library that will perform calculations based on basic product information to determine how many of a product we should order. The project for this library has been included in the solution template for simplicity. The primary method for calling these calculations involves calling a static .NET method with one of three enumeration values. The calculation can take a long time as it accesses a large data warehouse. The following is the method signature:

```
public static void ProcessProductMargins(XmlDocument productQuote,
ReorderLotSize reorderLotSize)
```

Passing around `XmlDocument` in an orchestration is a terrible idea, please avoid the temptation to do it and see *Chapter 3, BizTalk Development Guidelines*, for further details.

We need to call this method three different times with different enumeration values. The method uses `System.Diagnostics.Trace.WriteLine` to trace out its progress. We can use `DebugView` to see this trace output.

Solution Instrumentation

`DebugView` is available at http://live.sysinternals.com/ dbgview.exe. `Trace.WriteLine` and `DebugView` are a classic combination for providing visibility into services, but they are no longer a best practice. The BizTalk Solution Instrumentation Framework is now the recommended way to provide tracing for ultra-high performance scenarios as it uses kernel-level features of Event Tracing for Windows (ETW). Since we don't want to make our Product Inventory orchestration overly complicated we will do this processing in a new orchestration that we will call from our current orchestration.

1. Right-click the **Orchestrations** project and select **Add | New Item** and select **BizTalk Orchestration** and name this new orchestration **ReorderCalculations.odx**.

2. Open this new orchestration and switch to the **Orchestration View** and right-click **Orchestration Parameters** and select **New Message Parameter**. Rename the new parameter, which will be named **Message_1**, to **InventoryNotification** and set the **Message Type** to the multi-part message type `PRP.InventoryManagement.Orchestrations.InventoryNotificationType`. Also, change the **Direction** to **Ref**.

> **Orchestration Parameter Direction**
>
> Parameters in orchestrations can be In, Out, or Ref (short for reference). Reference parameters allow for both in and out flows, but can only be used by an orchestration call shape rather than a start shape.

3. Drag an expression shape onto the canvas, name it **Calculate Small Lot** and enter the expression: PRP.InventoryManagement.Library. ProductCalculations.ProcessProductMargins(InventoryNotification .Body, PRP.InventoryManagement.Library.ReorderLotSize.Small);.

4. Repeat this process for the other two enumeration values, Medium and Large.

Your final orchestration will have three expression shapes and will resemble the following image:

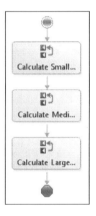

We are now ready to call our new orchestration from our Product Inventory orchestration.

1. Change back to that orchestration and drag a **Call Orchestration** shape onto the canvas above the **AssignVendor** shape. Name this new shape **Call_ReorderCalculations** and set the **Identifier** property to the same value.

2. Double-click this new call shape (which has a red warning next to it) and you will be presented with the following dialog box:

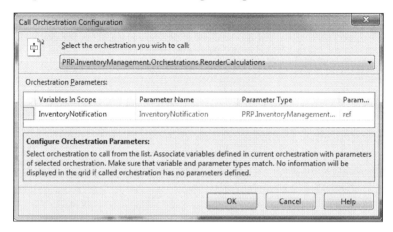

We can see that the orchestration IDE is smart enough to know that the only orchestration we could be calling is `ReorderCalculations` and it fills in all of the information for us.

3. Click **OK** to set these values.

Call versus Start orchestration

Call and Start orchestrations serve a similar role, but function significantly differently from each other. Call orchestration is simply like a method (function) call in .NET; it is a synchronous call that transfers control and context, then returns. Start is different in that it processes asynchronously through the message box. If you start an orchestration, the parent orchestration that called Start will continue immediately and, as a result, you cannot have output or reference parameters in a started orchestration shape.

If we now build and deploy our solution, we will have to bind the new orchestration `ReorderCalculations` to a host, we can use the `BizTalkServerApplication`.

If we start `DebugView` (turn on all capture features except **Log Boot**, then start capture) and run the solution like we did before. By executing that SQL query we can see the trace output in the `DebugView` window:

```
Begin ProcessProductMargins for: Small
End ProcessProductMargins for: Small
Begin ProcessProductMargins for: Medium
End ProcessProductMargins for: Medium
Begin ProcessProductMargins for: Large
End ProcessProductMargins for: Large
```

We can also see the times printed out to the left of this window and see that this part took thirty seconds to execute.

Understanding the parallel shape

We already know these operations can take a long time and don't want this to slow down our processing as it could create long delays that are the aggregated processing time of each operation. We know there is a parallel shape that we can use:

1. Drag a **Parallel Actions** shape onto the canvas of **ReorderCalculations** and name it **Calculate Reorder Size**.
2. Right-click **Calculate Reorder Size** and select **New Parallel Branch**.
3. Drag each of the expression shapes into one of the parallel branches putting small on the left, medium in the middle, and large on the right.

If we deploy and run our solution again we see the exact same output as before. The parallel shape did not parallelize our solution at all. In reality, the parallel shape is not as parallel as we think; it executes from left to right until it hits an operation that goes through the message box (that is, a send shape or a start orchestration).

Many operations we can do could be made parallel even with this in mind. If we needed separate approvals from different departments, or to call multiple services that are not dependent on each other, we can use the parallel shape and reap these benefits. As the first message send to a service occurs, the parallel shape starts executing the next branch on the left.

Imagine if we needed to get quotes from all of our vendors. Just like with our decide shape example before, if we had a static list of vendors, we could use the parallel shape to do this.

Implementing scatter gather

We're going to use the start orchestration shape to process all of these requests in true parallel. This pattern is commonly referred to as **scatter-gather** because we scatter the requests out and then gather the responses back together. To do this we will use a self-correlating direct bound port and another orchestration. First we will add this new port to the `ReorderCalculations` orchestration:

1. In `ReorderCalculations.odx` drag a new port to the port canvas.
2. Name the port `Receive_DirectCalculationPort` and create a new port type named `DirectCalculationPortType`.

3. Set the binding to `Direct` and choose the `Self Correlating` radio button.

4. Rename `Operation_1` to `ProcessCalculation` and set the `Message Type` of the request to `PRP.InventoryManagement.Orchestrations. InventoryNotificationType`.

We now want to use this new port from within a new child orchestration which will be solely responsible for processing and return the results to the calling orchestration (`ReorderCalculations`):

1. Create a new orchestration named `Calculation.odx`.

2. Create a new message parameter named `InventoryNotification`, set the direction to `In`, and the `Message Type` to `PRP.InventoryManagement. Orchestrations.InventoryNotificationType`.

3. Right-click **Orchestration Parameters** and select **New Configured Port Parameter**.

4. Name the port `Send_DirectCalculationPort` and click **Next**.

5. Select **Use an Existing Port Type** and select **DirectCalculationPortType** from the list and click **Next**.

6. Change the direction to **I'll always be sending messages on this port**, change the **Binding** to **Direct** and the select the **Self Correlating** ratio button.

7. Click **Next**, then click **Finish**.

8. Back in the orchestration view, drag a new send shape onto the canvas and name it **Snd_CalculationResult** and connect it to the **ProcessCalculation** operation of the `Send_DirectCalculationPort` port. It will automatically assign the appropriate message, in this case `InventoryNotification`.

9. Right-click **Orchestration Parameters** again, click **New Variable Parameter** and name this variable `LotSize`. For `Type` browse to **<.NET Class>** and then to `PRP.InventoryManagement.Library.ReorderLotSize`.

Back in the `ReorderCalculations.odx` we can now use the `Start Orchestration` shape to execute the calculation. We will need to provide an enumerator variable to do this.

Create a new orchestration variable called `LotSize` and again assign the type `PRP. InventoryManagement.Library.ReorderLotSize`. If we replace the expression in each of our expression shapes (`Small`, `Medium`, and `Large`) with something like the following:

```
LotSize = PRP.InventoryManagement.Library.ReorderLotSize.Small;
```

We will cause ourselves an issue if we try to build that and we'll get a compile-time error similar to the following:

```
'LotSize': if shared data is updated in a parallel then all references
in every task must be in a synchronized or atomic scope
```

Although the parallel shape is not as parallel as we at first thought, it is enforcing parallel access rules to avoid deadlocks and inconsistent updates. It will not allow us to change this variable outside of a synchronized or atomic scope, both of which would re-serialize our solution anyway. This is very similar to how F# works and how it is able to be thread safe automatically.

The way around this is to create three enumeration variables of `ReorderLotSize` and assign them each before we enter the parallel shape.

Delete the expression shapes **Calculate Medium Lot** and **Calculate Large Lot**.

Move **Calculate Small Lot** to above the parallel shape and set the expression to:

```
LotSize = PRP.InventoryManagement.Library.ReorderLotSize.Small;
MediumSize = PRP.InventoryManagement.Library.ReorderLotSize.Medium;
LargeSize = PRP.InventoryManagement.Library.ReorderLotSize.Large;
```

Drag one **Start Orchestration** shape into each of the three parallel branches.

Double-click each start orchestration shape and configure the parameters, being sure to change two of them to be `MediumSize` and `LargeSize` for the last parameter.

Drag three receive shapes after the parallel shape; they can be in any order, and connect them all to the **ProcessCalculation** operation of the **Receive_DirectCalculationPort** logical port. Assign each of these to receive the `InventoryNotification`.

It really doesn't matter what order the receive shapes are in because they will all be received in the message box before they are matched against the instance subscription. If some of these were from different operations or different types they would simply queue in the message box until the specific message that matches the first receive shape is ready.

The completed orchestration will look like the following screenshot:

If we now deploy the solution and run it, again like we did before with the simple SQL query, we can see in DebugView that all three trace statements happen immediately. Perhaps better still BizTalk will distribute this processing (the newly started Calculate orchestrations) over the entire group. If we have multiple servers (or even multiple cores or processors in a single server) we are likely to experience significant performance gains as we are doing true parallel processing.

This is a great improvement over what we had before because we have cut down processing time significantly, but again we have the same problem we had with the original approach to the broker solution: any changes will require orchestration-level changes and recompilation / deployment. Again we have a solution with a hard-coded limitation. In an effort to strive for a more flexible solution, we will now refactor this to be a true scatter-gather solution.

Improving scatter gather

We would like to create a solution that is free to change how many requests are scattered out, without the need to recompile the orchestration and one that is not as limited as with a hard-coded set. This turns out to be relatively easy and can help us turn our BizTalk group into a very powerful parallel processing platform.

We're going to use loops to make our solution more flexible. Since we're using looping we're going to need a counter and we're also going to use an enumerator to control the looping.

1. In the `ReorderCalculations` orchestration create an orchestration variable named `ScatterCount` of type `Int32` and set the `Initial Value` to `0`.

2. Create a variable named `Enumerator` and browse to the .NET type `PRP.InventoryManagement.Library.ReorderLotSizeEnumerator`.

3. Rename **Calculate Small Lot** to **Enumerate Values**.

4. Drag a **Loop** shape below **Enumerate Values**, name the loop **Scatter Loop** and assign the expression **Enumerator.MoveNext()**.

5. Move the **StartOrchestration_1** shape into this loop (you can really use any of the start shapes) then delete the **Calculate Reorder Size** parallel shape and the shapes that remain in it.

6. Drag another loop below the **Scatter Loop** and name it **Gather Loop**. Set the expression to **ScatterCount > 0**.

7. Move **Receive_1** into the **Gather Loop** and delete the other two receive shapes.

8. Set the expression in **Enumerate Values** to: `Enumerator = PRP.InventoryManagement.Library.ProductCalculations.ListReorderLotSize();`

> We're making use of some of the `System.Collections` features in .NET to make this application more extensible. One way is by using a method to return all the possible enumerations as an enumerable object and the other is by using an enumerator class that implements `IEnumerator`. This is because any .NET type used in an orchestration must be decorated with the `Serializable` attribute, which `IEnumerator` is not.

9. Drag an expression shape to the top of the scatter loop, name it **Assign Lot Size - Increment** and use the following expression:
   ```
   LotSize = (PRP.InventoryManagement.Library.ReorderLotSize)Enumerat
   or.Current;
   ScatterCount = ScatterCount +1;
   ```

10. Drag one last expression shape into the **Gather Loop** named **Decrement Count** and use the expression `ScatterCount = ScatterCount -1;`.

The orchestration is now complete and will resemble the following screenshot:

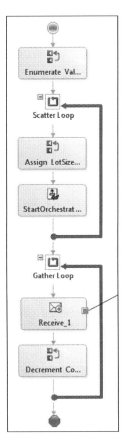

We can now run this solution and again see that it executes very quickly, just like before. To prove the extensibility, all we need to do is add another value to the enumeration ReorderLotSize. Add a Mega value to the enumeration with a value of 3 so the enumeration looks like the following code listing:

```
public enum ReorderLotSize
{
    Small = 0,
    Medium = 1,
    Large = 2,
    Mega = 3
}
```

We can now GAC this assembly, like we did in *Chapter 9, Expanding the Solution with Services and Rules*, and restart the BizTalk host instance. We will see that, instead of three processing requests, there are four.

Not all of these techniques are BizTalk specific; in fact half of our extensibility is the use of .NET enumerators. It is always important in BizTalk solutions to find extensibility points and leverage them; in this case some of them were .NET specific. A common alternative is to use a query, perhaps of all vendors to send a quote request to every vendor. Another is to use something in the message itself to control looping, such as the individual products in the request.

Lastly, this was a trivial example and we really didn't do anything with the resulting messages, but we certainly could have. We could even store them all in a .NET list or collection for use later. Another common approach for scatter gather is to wait for multiple approvals.

Summary

In this chapter, we have learned to use the decide shape as well as how to use role party links with parties to make our solution more extensible and flexible when implementing the broker pattern. We then learned how to use the parallel actions, call and start orchestration shapes to compose complex processes through smaller and simpler parts, which make our solutions easier to understand and maintain. Finally, we used self-correlating direct bound ports and loops to create an extensible parallel processing application that implements the scatter-gather pattern. The next chapter will cover convoy processing.

14
Processing Message Convoys

The final chapter in this book addresses complex issues related to sequencing events and messages. Commonly in integration scenarios we must react to a series of events that span different time and message exchange patterns to create a unified process. When multiple messages are treated together as a single process, the pattern is normally called a **convoy**. This chapter presents different types of convoys through specific examples as we continue to build on our inventory management application.

The following topics will be covered in this chapter:

- Uniform sequential convoys
- Zombies
- Non-uniform sequential convoys
- Parallel convoys
- Dealing with zombies

Creating a sequential convoy

Our solution is working great, but we now need to be able to batch together inventory notifications to be used for reconciliation. Our requirement is to gather all notifications every day and send a single reconciliation message that our users want.

To accomplish this, we are going to create a new orchestration that uses a convoy to collect messages until the end of the day; then use an envelope and send pipeline to combine the messages into a single batch message. A process where many messages are received one after another is called a **sequential convoy**. If all the messages in the convoy are of the same type, as in this case, the convoy is said to be **uniform**.

To create this solution, we will need to create an envelope, a pipeline, and an orchestration. These steps are performed in the next sections.

Creating the envelope

Back in *Chapter 10, Envelopes, Flat Files, and Batching,* we disassembled XML messages using an envelope; now we need another envelope in order to use the pipeline for assembly. In this section, we will create a new XML envelope:

1. Create a new schema named `InventoryNotificationEnvelope.xsd` and rename the `Root` element to `ProductBatch`.

2. Set the schema's `Envelope` property to `Yes`.

3. Right-click **ProductBatch** and select **Insert Schema Node | Any Element**.

> The schema element `<xs:any />` functions like the name implies, it allows any element to take the place of it. This element can be a complex type with elements and attributes of its own. This makes it a sort of wildcard in the XSD toolset; like all wildcards it should be used sparingly. The argument that it provides future support is greatly weakened by the side-by-side versioning capabilities provided by BizTalk.

4. Set the Body `XPath` of the `ProductBatch` root element to `ProductBatch`.

Creating the pipeline

Since we're going to be assembling many messages into a single message, we will need a send pipeline as opposed to the receive pipeline we used before. We need to create the actual pipeline (`.btp`) file that will be used. Again, we follow the solution structure guidance and put this pipeline into a project of its own:

1. Right-click the `Internal Pipelines` project and select **Add | New Item** and create a new **Send Pipeline** named `XmlAssemblerSend.btp`.

2. Drag an **XMLAssembler** onto the **Assemble** stage of the pipeline.

3. Set the **Document schemas** property to include the schema `PRP.InventoryManagement.InternalSchemas.InventoryNotification`.

4. Set the **Envelope schemas** property to include the message `PRP.InventoryManagement.InternalSchemas.InventoryNotificationEnvelope`.

We now have the base messaging components that will be used by our solution.

Creating the orchestration

At this point, we're ready to create the actual orchestration that will implement the convoy itself. In order to use the pipeline we just created from within an orchestration, we must use the `SendPipelineInputMessages` class from the `Microsoft.XLANGs.Pipeline` namespace. This will function as a container in which we can load the messages for the `XmlAssemblerSend` pipeline we created in the previous section.

Using pipelines in orchestrations

One of the keys to this is a class in the BizTalk framework `Microsoft.XLANGs.Pipeline.SendPipelineInputMessages`. We'll need to add a reference in the orchestrations project to the assembly `Microsoft.XLANGs.Pipeline.dll` to use this class. This assembly is in the BizTalk root directory, normally `[Drive:]\Program Files\Microsoft BizTalk Server 2010\`.

We will now create the orchestration that processes this message convoy:

1. Add a new orchestration to the inventory management application named `OrderAggregator.odx`.

2. Create a new orchestration message named `InventoryNotification` and set the message type to `PRP.InventoryManagement.Orchestrations.InventoryNotificationType`.

Notice how we can reuse message and port types between orchestrations. This is very useful, but can also introduce inter-orchestration dependencies that surface during refactoring. Some developers like to put all their message and port types in a single orchestration that solely serves this purpose.

3. Create a new multi-part message type named `InventoryNotificationBatchType` with a part named `Body` set to the schema `InventoryNotificationBatch` and a new message using this type named `NotificationBatch`.

4. Create an orchestration variable named `Aggregator` and set its type to the .NET class `Microsoft.XLANGs.Pipeline.SendPipelineInputMessages`.

5. Create another orchestration variable called `Complete` of type `Boolean` with an `Initial Value` of `False`.

6. Drag a receive shape onto the canvas named `Rcv_InitialNotification` and set the `Activate` property to `True`. Set the message to `InventoryNotification`.

7. Drag an expression shape below the receive shape and name it `Add Message`. Set the expression to: `Aggregator.Add(InventoryNotification);`.

8. Drag a loop below the receive shape named `Aggregate Loop` and set the expression to `Complete == false`.

9. Drag a listen shape into this loop and name it `Message Listen`.

10. On the left branch of the listen, drag a receive shape named `Rcv_Notification`, setting the message to `InventoryNotification`. Below that, still in the branch, place a copy of the expression shape named `Add Message`.

> Right-clicking a shape will allow you to select **Copy** or **Paste** from the context menu, but you can also use the *Ctrl + C* and *Ctrl + V* keyboard shortcuts.

11. On the right side of the listen shape, drag a delay shape named `Order Delay` and set the delay to `new System.TimeSpan(0,5,0)`.

> I know we're not actually meeting our true requirement here because we're not waiting until the end of the day. If we really wanted this, we would use some time calculation against a `TimeSpan` variable, but that detail is left as an exercise to the reader. If you find yourself in need of this type of functionality, using a .NET Class Library or even the BRE is a good idea.

12. Drag an expression shape after the delay named `Mark Complete` and set the expression to `Complete = true;`.

13. Drag a `Message Assignment` shape onto the canvas after the loop and name the construct (outer shape) `Construct NotificationBatch` and set the `Messages Constructed` property to `NotificationBatch`. Name the inner (assignment) `AssignNotificationBatch` and enter the following expression:

```
Microsoft.XLANGs.Pipeline.XLANGPipelineManager.ExecuteSendPipeline
(typeof(PRP.InventoryManagement.InternalPipelines.XmlAssemblerSend
),Aggregator,NotificationBatch);
```

In this step, we are using another utility class form to actually execute the `XmlAssemblerSend` pipeline. The parameters are: the type of the pipeline to execute, the aggregated messages to be used as input to the pipeline, and the output message that will be populated with the results of the pipeline (which is passed by reference).

14. Drag a send shape named `Snd_NotificationBatch` onto the canvas and set the message to `NotificationBatch`.

Your completed orchestration layout should resemble the following image:

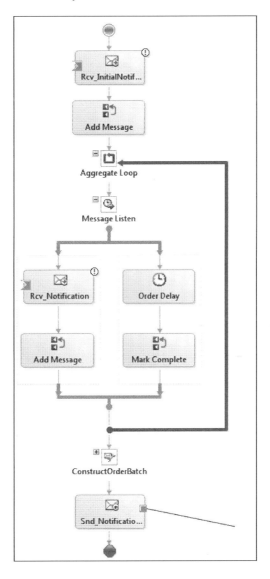

This completes the basic orchestration flow layout and we're ready to fill in the details.

Creating the convoy correlation

The convoy needs a way to relate the messages together. We know from experience that we can use correlation sets to accomplish this. Normally, in sequential convoys you want something even more generic than the quote number we used before (which would correlate all messages with that quote number) so it is common to use Receive Port Name or something similar. If you do use Receive Port Name you should be aware that you are limiting the ability of your operations staff to rename the port without recompiling the application. If many orders could be part of a batch with a specific batch number that would be a natural fit for a convoy correlation:

1. Create a new `Correlation Type` and use the properties `BTS.SPName` and `WCF.Action` to correlate on. Name this correlation `NotificationCorrelationType`.

   > Notice how we are able to use multiple properties when creating a correlation type. A correlation type can contain up to three different properties that are used to create a specific correlation. Although this may sound limiting it is actually quite expressive.

2. Create a new correlation set with the identifier `NotificationCorrelation` using the `NotificationCorrelationType`.

3. Create a new port named `OrderAggregatorPort` and a new port type named `OrderAggregatorPortType`. Make this port One-Way and change the binding to direct. Set the request message type to `PRP.InventoryManagement.Orchestrations.ProductQuoteType`.

4. Set the `Rcv_InitialNotification` shape's `Initializing Correlation Sets` property to `NotificationCorrelation`.

5. Set the `Rcv_Notification` shape's `Following Correlation Sets` property to `NotificationCorrelation`.

6. Create a new port named `ProductOrderBatchPort` with a port type `ProductOrderBatchPortType` that is a One-Way send port with the "specify later" binding and connect the `Snd_ProductOrderBatch` shape to the single operation of this port (we're ignoring proper names for brevity).

7. Build and deploy the solution.

Binding the solution

We're now ready to bind the orchestration in the BizTalk Administration console. Bind the orchestration to the host `BizTalkServerApplication` and for the logical send port binding, click the drop down and under **Send Ports/Send Port Groups** click <**New send port...**> which is shown in the following screenshot:

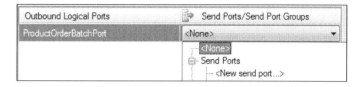

Name the port `IM_File_Send_NotificationBatch` and set it to use `FILE` as the **Type** with the destination folder set to `C:\BizTalk\PRP\PlaceOrder`.

Right-click the **InventoryManagement** application and select **Start**.

Running the sequential convoy

Run and approve an order by running the query `update products set orderstatus = 'Filled'` against the `AlphaInventory` database like we did before; then setting the `Approved` attribute to true in the file created in `C:\BizTalk\PRP\ApprovalRequest`.

 If you created or downloaded the InfoPath form you can simply click the **Approved** checkbox and click **Save**, then move the form to `C:\BizTalk\PRP\ApprovalResponse`.

If you look in the `All In-Progress Service Instances` view of the BizTalk Administration console, you will see an active (or dehydrated) `OrderAggregator` instance.

Run and approve (or reject) a second order and the aggregator will also add that order to the aggregator. Now take a break and have some tea or coffee because we have a five-minute timer in that orchestration so you have a little time to relax. After that five minutes you will see a file output to `C:\BizTalk\PRP\PlaceOrder`. If we open this file we can see a message that resembles the following XML:

```xml
<?xml version="1.0" encoding="utf-8"?>
<ns0:ProductBatch xmlns:ns0="http://PRP.InventoryManagement.
InternalSchemas.ProductOrderEnvelope">
  <ns0:InventoryNotification xmlns:ns0="http://performanceracingparts.
com/schemas/Inventory/internal/2011-05">
```

```
      <IsValidProduct>false</IsValidProduct>
    </ns0:InventoryNotification>
    <ns0:InventoryNotification xmlns:ns0="http://performanceracingparts.
  com/schemas/Inventory/internal/2011-05">
      <Product>
        <CatalogNumber>1234</CatalogNumber>
        ...
      </Product>
      <IsValidProduct>true</IsValidProduct>
    </ns0:InventoryNotification>
    <ns0:InventoryNotification xmlns:ns0="http://performanceracingparts.
  com/schemas/Inventory/internal/2011-05">
      <Product>
        ...
      </Product>
      <IsValidProduct>true</IsValidProduct>
    </ns0:InventoryNotification>
  </ns0:ProductBatch>
```

As can be seen, there are in fact multiple notifications inside this file. We can even see that the first has `IsValidProduct` set to false because it is a side effect of the notification solution we built in the last chapter.

Improving our solution

This solution is not perfect as it sits and there is one common and subtle change that you may need to make. Recall that we use the `<xs:any/>` element in our envelope schema. This wasn't because I wanted to show you a bad practice; it is because when using a send pipeline within an orchestration this turns out to be a necessity. Importing or including the `InventoryNotification` schema like we did before would result in the following error when the pipeline executes:

```
Error details: "Token StartElement in state Epilog would result in an
invalid XML document."
```

The problem is that the `<xs:any>` element makes mapping just about impossible unless we want to use XSLT. This error is unique to orchestrations and I cannot say I truly know the cause, but I do have a solution. All we need to do is create a second schema to represent the batch record we are interested in. Name this schema `InventoryNotificationBatch.xsd` and rename the `Root` node to `NotificationBatch`.

Import the `InventoryNotification.xsd` schema into this new schema.

Create a child record under `NotificationBatch` name and set the `Data Structure Type` to `ns0:InventoryNotification (Reference)` and set the `Max Occurs` property to unbounded.

 When setting the `Max Occurs` property, you can simply type in
* (asterisk) and the IDE will replace it with the word unbounded.

The last thing we need to do is use a map inside the orchestration that will transform from one format to the other, and this can be done with the transform shape. We will need only one Functoid, the Mass Copy, and the map will resemble the following image:

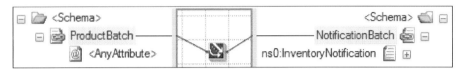

This solution allows us to aggregate messages the way we want to and still have the flexibility and separation of concerns enabled with maps and strong typing of messages.

Dealing with zombies

They're not just in B-movies anymore; zombies are an unfortunate side effect of some convoy scenarios. The convoy we have just created may be a uniform sequential convoy, but it is also a non-deterministic one. This is because it uses a delay to end the collection of messages. This makes it possible that a message could be received and matched with the convoy subscription just as the delay shape is executing, and thus breaking the listen loop. BizTalk would then try to deliver the message to the orchestration instance which would now be terminated (or be in the process of terminating). The result is a zombie, a message that has already been accepted by the message box, but now has nowhere to go.

This will result in a failed instance in the message box with an error like the following:

`0xC0C01B4C` The instance completed without consuming all of its messages. The instance and its unconsumed messages have been suspended.

The good news is that we can use failed message routing like we did in *Chapter 7, Leveraging Orchestration* or even use a WMI script and need to filter only on `ErrorId` = `"0xC0C01B4C"`.

This error code is a change from the error code used in previous versions of BizTalk.

Creating a parallel convoy

We have been asked to create a vendor on boarding process. When vendors join our network, three distinct things must happen before we can do business with them:

- They must have a vendor application filled out
- We must have a credit report run on them
- We perform a bank account validation procedure

Currently these three things all happen independently and a user must coordinate their execution to get a vendor added to the AlphaInventory database.

A scenario that involves multiple, possibly different, messages that must all be collected before processing can continue is called a **parallel convoy**. We will use a parallel convoy to handle vendor on board.

The three schemas that will be used for this process are all included with the project template and can be added by right-clicking **Internal Schemas** and selecting **Add | Existing Item**. The three schemas are:

- BankValidation.xsd
- CreditReport.xsd
- VendorApplication.xsd

Since our goal is to gather all of this information together, we will also create a new vendor information schema that is a composite of the three schemas introduced above.

Creating the VendorInformation schema

We will quickly create our composite schema before we go any further:

1. Add a new internal schema named VendorInformation.xsd. Rename the **Root** element to **VendorInformation**. Click the **<Schema>** folder above the root then change the **Target Namespace** property to http://performanceracingparts.com/schemas/inventorymanagement/internal/2011-06.

2. Set the **Root Reference** to **VendorInformation**.

3. Click the ellipses in the **Imports** property. At the **Imports** dialog change the dropdown to **XSD Include** then click **Add** and browse to the **CreditReport** schema.

4. Include the **BankValidation** and **VendorApplication** schemas as well.

5. Right-click the **VendorInformation** node and select **Insert Schema Node | Child Record** then change the record's **Data Structure Type** to **BankAccount (Reference)**.

6. Add another child record and change its **Data Structure Type** to **CreditReport (Reference)**.

7. Add a final child record for the data type **VendorApplication**.

We now have our source and destination messages and can being tying the pieces together. Promoting the correlated data. The first step in creating a convoy of any type is to decide what data will be used for correlation. All three schemas contain the same core identifying piece of information: Tax Identification Number. Each schema has a slightly different name for this element, but they all represent the same core data. We will create a promoted property for this data and then promote the element in each of the three schemas.

There are two parts to promoting elements. The first is to create a property in a property schema that can be used for promotion. The second is to promote the data in each schema using this property.

Creating the promoted property

In the schema `InventoryManagementProperties.xsd`, which came with the solution, right-click the **Schema** folder and select **Insert Schema Node | Child Field Element**.

Name the element `TaxIdentificationNumber`.

Save and close the property schema so that we can use the property in the other schemas.

Promoting the elements

In the schema `BankValidation.xsd`, right-click the element **TIN** and select **Promote | Show Promotions**:

1. Click on the **Property Fields** tab on the right side of the dialog, then click the folder icon on the upper-right to add a property schema and navigate to the schema **PRP.InventoryManagement.InternalSchemas. InventoryManagementProperties** under the **Schemas** node as shown in the following screenshot:

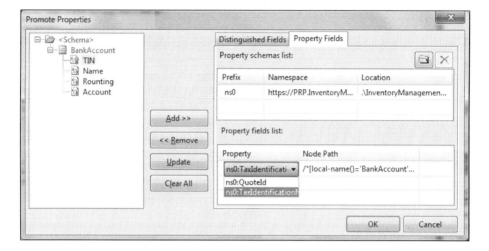

2. Click **OK**.

3. Click **Add >>** and change the drop-down on the right to **TaxIdentificationNumber** then click **OK**. Save and close the `BankValidation.xsd` schema.

4. Repeat this process for `CreditReport.xsd` using the element `TaxIdNumber` and on `VendorApplication.xsd` using the `TaxId` element.

5. Build the solution so that the new types will be visible in the orchestration project.

Creating the orchestration

We will now create the orchestration that will implement the convoy:

1. Add a new orchestration named `VendorOnboarding.odx` to the orchestrations project.

2. Create a new multipart message type named `BankValidationType` and name the default part `Body`. Click the **Type** property then choose **Schemas** and **<Select from referenced assembly>** and click **PRP. InventoryManagement.InternalSchemas** on the left and then **PRP. InventoryManagement.InternalSchemas.BankValidation** on the right.

3. Repeat that step for `CreditReportType`, `VendorApplicationType`, and `VendorInformationType` and their corresponding schemas.

4. Create four orchestration messages `BankValidation`, `CreditReport`, `VendorApplication`, and `VendorInformation` that each correspond to their similarly named multi part message types.

5. Drag a parallel actions shape onto the canvas and name it `Receive Vendor Documents`.

6. Right-click **Receive Vendor Documents** and select **New Parallel Branch**.

7. In the left branch, drag a receive shape named `Rcv_VendorApplication`, set the `Message` property to `VendorApplication`, and set the `Activate` property to `True`.

8. In the middle branch, add a receive shape named `Rcv_BankValidation`, set the `Message` property to `BankValidation`, and set the `Activate` property to `True`.

9. In the right branch, add a receive shape named `Rcv_CreditReport`, set the `Message` property to `CreditReport`, and set the `Activate` property to `True`.

10. Drag a transform shape onto the canvas after the parallel shape and it will automatically create the transform nested inside a construct message shape (just like the assign message shape does). Name the construct message `Construct Vendor Information` and the transform `XForm_VendorDocuments_To_VendorInformation`.

11. Double-click the transform shape and it will bring up the transform configuration dialog. Set the **Source Variable Name** to **BankValidation. Body** and then set two more sources for **CreditReport.Body** and **VendorInformation.Body**. The configuration should resemble the following screenshot:

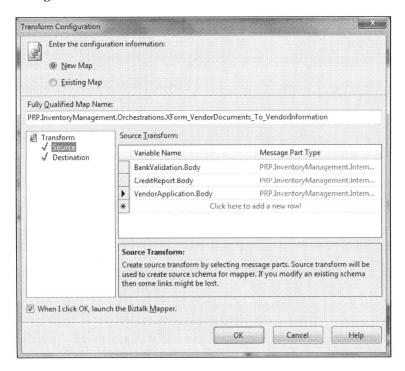

12. Finally, set the **Destination's Variable Name** to **VendorInformation.Body** and click **OK**.

Mapping in orchestration

As useful as this map is, it has one very serious drawback. Since there are many sources used, the messages are all loaded into the DOM behind the scenes. Using this technique with large messages or very high volumes will hurt your memory footprint.

You will notice that a new map has been created for us. The left side of this map is a schema named **Root** that has three children **InputMessagePart_0**, **InputMessagePart_1**, and **InputMessagePart_2**. Each of these records has a child node that corresponds to the specific message types as shown in the following screenshot:

Fortunately for us we only need to map three nodes to make this entire map:

1. Drag **BankAccount** from the left to **BankAccount** on the right and click **Link by Name**. Do the same for **CreditReport** and **VendorApplication**.

 Recall that because this matches both name and structure you could really use either option.

2. Save and close the map.
3. Drag a send shape named **Snd_VendorCreate** onto the canvas and assign **VendorInformation** as the message.

The orchestration should resemble the following screenshot:

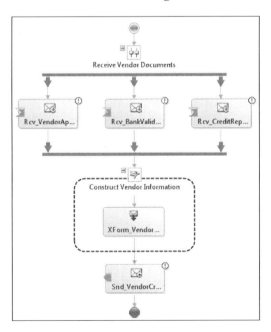

We're done creating the orchestration layout and control flow.

Wiring up the orchestration ports

We now need to connect logical ports in the orchestration to allow our solution to be bound to the outside world. We can do this with the following steps:

1. Drag a port onto the port canvas and complete the wizard to create a port with the name `ReceiveVendorDocumentsPort`, the type `ReceiveVendorDocumentsPortType`, and communication pattern `One-Way` and communication direction of `receive`.

2. Rename **Operation_1** to **ReceiveBankValidation**.

3. Right-click the port **ReceiveVendorDocumentsPort** and click **New Operation** then rename the new **Operation_1** to **ReceiveCreditReport**.

4. Create a final operation named **ReceiveVendorInformation**.

5. Connect the receive shapes to their respective operations.

6. Drag a new port onto the port canvas and name it **CreateVendorPort** with a new port type named **CreateVendorPortType.** Set the communication pattern to **One-Way** with a direction of **Send**.

7. Rename **Operation_1** on the **CreateVendorPort** port to **IM_Send_ VendorCreate** and connect the send shape **Snd_VendorCreate** to it.

Creating the correlation

Now that we have all the pieces in place, we're ready to create the actual correlation itself:

1. Create a new correlation type named `TaxIdentifierCorrelationType` that uses the correlation property `PRP.InventoryManagement. InternalSchemas.TaxIdentificationNumber`.

2. Create a new correlation set named `TaxIdentifierCorrelation` that uses this new correlation type.

> On smaller screen resolutions it may be hard to see the full names. Mouse over and you will see them. This one happens to be last in the list.

3. Set the `Initializing Correlation Sets` property of each of the three receive shapes to `TaxIdentifierCorrelation`.

Build and deploy the solution.

Binding the solution

We have now built and deployed our solution and we need to bind the orchestration inside the BizTalk Administration console:

1. Click the **Orchestrations** node under the **InventoryManagement** application then double-click the new orchestration (it's the only one that will be unbound and red).

2. Set the **Host** to **BizTalkServerApplication**.

3. Click the drop-down next to **ReceiveVendorDocumentsPort** and create a new receive port named **IM_Receive_VendorDocuments** with a receive location named IM_File_Receive_VendorDocuments that uses the URI C:\ BizTalk\PRP\VendorDocuments*.xml and the XMLReceive pipeline.

4. Click the drop-down next to CreateVendorPort and create a new send port named IM_File_Send_CreateVendor that uses the URI C:\BizTalk\PRP\ CreateVendor\%MessageID%.xml.

5. Start the application via the BizTalk Administration console.

Running the parallel convoy

Although this solution did not come with a **UnitTests** project, it does have the test data directories. The folder InventoryManagement\UnitTests\TestData\External contains three example XML files; BRCBankValidation.xml, BRCCreditReport. xml, and BRCVendorApplication.xml that can be copied to C:\BizTalk\PRP\ VendorDocuments either all together or one at a time. The first processed will create a new instance of the orchestration and the others will join this instance.

Creating a non-uniform sequential convoy

The parallel convoy we implemented above was not the only possible solution to our requirement. We could also implement the convoy as a non-uniform sequential convoy; which means that it is still sequential, but the messages within it may be different. Suppose we already knew that the vendor application would always arrive first. If that were the case, we could create a new orchestration and copy the four messages from VendorOnboarding.odx by using *Ctrl + C / Ctrl + V* to copy them from and paste them to the Messages folder of the orchestration view. We could then do the same thing with the three receive shapes, placing Rcv_VendorApplication first. From here, we could copy the ports and the transform / message construct in the same way. As we paste in the pieces (the ports in particular) all the shapes will connect to the ports and the warnings will go away. This is very useful for refactoring orchestrations.

The resulting orchestration would resemble the following diagram:

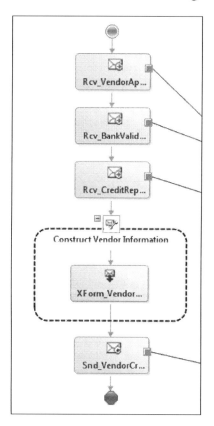

The primary difference between this convoy and the parallel convoy is that any of the three receive shapes can activate an instance of the parallel convoy orchestration. With a non-uniform sequential convoy the first shape must execute first or the other messages will not be routed correctly (in this case that's the vendor information message). After the first message the other messages can arrive in any order if they're all using the same correlation set and BizTalk will simply queue the messages in the message box until their respective receive shapes in the orchestration execute. In this example, even if the credit report were to arrive before the bank information it would be delivered to the correct instance, but it would sit in the message box awaiting consumption.

Using advanced correlations

So far what we have seen are fairly simple correlations, but they need not be so. If our vendor had many branches and we wanted to identify them by postal code and tax identification number we could use both properties together to have concurrent convoys for each office that were separate.

Understanding when and where to use convoys is also important. Like every system, features come at a price and the price for convoys is message box space and zombies. There are situations where it is better to use a database to store records until processing is complete, but it is really more guidance than a hard and fast rule.

All of the convoys that we built in this chapter are actually examples of the **Aggregator** pattern. An aggregator combines multiple messages into a single message. Although one used multiples of the same message type and the others used different types, they are still all technically aggregators.

We can even expand this pattern to create a re-sequencing aggregator debatch messages in a pipeline (ideally at a receive location) and aggregate subgroups within orchestrations. This is fairly common in situations where files can contain transactions from multiple batches. We don't have space to cover a re-sequencing aggregator, but you have all the tools you need to create one.

A note about orchestration development

This chapter, perhaps better than any other, demonstrates a common and effective pattern for orchestration development. The following steps are generally used to build orchestrations:

1. Determine messages and required patterns.
2. Create orchestration messages.
3. Layout shapes.
4. Create logical ports.

Although not all orchestration development (or developers) will follow these steps, I think they work best with the toolset as they start at the edges (messages) and work their way inward, ending in connecting the specific pieces.

Summary

In this chapter, we have learned how to use advanced features of the orchestration engine in BizTalk to help us overcome timing and delivery issues through the use of convoys. We also learned how to call pipeline components from within orchestrations. We have also tied together the last of our inventory management changes and seen how advanced correlations can make our solutions even more expressive and flexible.

Appendix

XML for BizTalk development

XML has become a nearly ubiquitous format for data exchange over the last decade, but many developers still do not know that much about it. Fortunately for us, most of the process of working with XML is abstracted away with tools that make our jobs easier. This section will provide a very brief introduction to XML that can serve as a basic guide in the event that you have had no XML experience. I would call it a rough survival guide at most.

A brief history of XML

Extensible Markup Language (XML) is a syntax for describing information; originally text documents. XML documents primarily consist of markup and content. Markup describes and organizes the content within it; content is, well, content. Importantly, XML itself doesn't actually do anything; it is merely a format that enables us to do things with it. XML documents are basically hierarchical structures that layout information in an extensible tree. XML has been designed from inception to be compatible with international languages through UNICODE text encoding and thus removes a major impediment to many internationalization challenges that had plagued previous formats. Part of this benefit comes at the cost, or feature, depending how you view it, of being quite verbose.

Understanding parts of an XML document

The following is an example of a very simple XML document. We will examine the parts of the XML document in the following sections:

```
<?xml version="1.0" encoding="utf-8"?>
<Order>
  <Number>1234</Number>
  <Date>2011-06-11</Date>
  <Item Number="4432" Quantity="1" />
</Order>
```

Declaration

Generally, the first thing in an XML document is the XML declaration. This line states that the following document is in fact XML and states the version of XML as well as the text encoding used in the document. The declaration in the preceding XML document is: `<?xml version="1.0" encoding="utf-8"?>`.

The preceding declaration specifies that version 1.0 is used with a UTF-8 encoding for this particular XML document. Most BizTalk schemas will use UTF-16 encoding, but BizTalk can handle either.

Elements

Elements are one of the two types of markup that are available within an XML document. An element contains an opening and closing tag and is enclosed in angle brackets, similar to HTML.

In our example, we can see the `Order` element has an opening tag `<Order>` and a closing tag `</Order>`. Notice that the end tag has a / character after the opening angle bracket.

Elements can have other elements nested within them and can also have attributes, which are covered below.

Attributes

Attributes are markup that describes the element to which they belong. In our preceding example, the `Item` element has two attributes: `Number` and `Quantity`. Attributes cannot have children, as there is no place to place them, but they generally describe or enrich the element to which they are attached.

Root elements

Every XML document has one and only one root element which immediately follows the declaration (if there is one). This is a markup element that specifies the actual document in question. Since XML is a tree it must, like all trees, have a single root.

Importantly, an XML document must start with either a declaration or an opening element; anything else, including whitespace and comment lines, is illegal. This is a subtle, but important constraint on XML; one of few constraints.

Namespaces

Although not shown in the preceding example, most XML documents will actually resemble the following one:

```
<?xml version="1.0" encoding="utf-8"?>
<Order xmlns="http://wmp/schemas/quote">
  <Number>1234</Number>
  <Date>2011-06-11</Date>
  <Item Number="4432" Quantity="1" />
  <Item Number="5532" Quantity="2" />
</Order>
```

In this example, we can see that an attribute named `xmlns` has been applied to the root element. This particular attribute actually specifies that the XML document in question uses a specific namespace to qualify the `Order` element. This allows us to define multiple order elements in different parts of the document without ambiguity. In complex XML documents, namespaces can be defined at multiple levels, but basically the namespace is a qualification mechanism. Often you will see named or prefixed namespaces that will qualify particular elements within a document. This is the reason you will often see an element defined like the following: `<ns0:Number>`. This tells us that the `Number` element is defined within the `ns0` namespace, which will have a declaration in the root element similar to the following: `xmlns:ns0="http://wmp/schemas"`. Again, it is important to remember that this is primarily a name/identity resolution technique. We could use the `xmlns` attribute on any given element to specify its namespace, but this can become very verbose as our previous example with the `Number` element would result in the following `<Number xmlns ="http://wmp/schemas">`. Finally, sometimes you will see documents where every element has a prefix, for example `ns0`. These documents have their **element form** set to qualified; the other setting is unqualified which is the default (as in our preceding example).

Understanding XPath

As we have seen, XML documents are basically trees. We can identify specific elements within the tree that is an XML document with a path, referred to as an **XPath**. An XPath is the path to a specific node (or set of nodes) in an XML document. These paths work in a manner similar to paths on a file system or queries in SQL. The simple path to our `Number` element that we looked at before is `/Order/Number`. This tells us that `Number` is a child element of the `Order` element, which happens to be the root.

XPaths do not need to result in a single node and normally do not. In our example, the XPath `/Order/Item` identifies, or selects, a node set; zero or more nodes. In our specific example, this node set consists of two nodes. We can identify specific instances within a node by using a familiar array indexing nomenclature: `[n]` where `n` is the one based index of the set. To select the first `Item` we could use the XPath `/Order/Item[1]`.

Attributes are distinguished from elements by using the `@` sign. In our preceding example, we could select all the `Number` attributes of the `Items` with the XPath `/Order/Item/@Number`.

Finally, there are different wildcards and query capabilities we can use in XPath to identify specific elements. For example, `//Item` would select all the `Item` elements anywhere within the document and `//Item[@Number = '5532']` would select all the `Item` elements that have a `Number` attribute that equals `5532`. Suffice to say that XPath allows us tremendous expressive capability when dealing with XML documents.

The rest of XML

When people say XML they generally mean three related components: schema, instance, and transform that correspond to three specific technologies: XSD, XML, and XSLT.

XSD or schema is the specific format an XML document adheres to and is much like a database schema. A schema describes what constitutes a legal (as in valid) document. An XML document itself conforms to a specific schema, or should. This schema will prescribe what elements, attributes, and values are valid for every part of an XML document. If you are not using XSD schemas, which can really be thought of as data contracts, then you are not making full use of XML. XML without XSD is basically an angle bracket-delimited text file and does not bring many benefits with it, but does incur many costs.

Schemas are covered further within the text, but they can define both structure and data type; much like a database schema defines tables, columns, and column types. Elements and attributes can not only be strongly typed, but their order can be dictated as well as instance requirements such as optional, one, or many (or even an arbitrary number or range).

Understanding equivalence

XML, as the name implies, is extensible, but this extensibility means that a particular XML document can conform to multiple different XSD schemas. This actually gives us a bit of leeway when we deal with schemas that were designed outside of our control. In our example, we could use the schema that defines the example XML document we have seen and add further restrictions such as Quantity must be greater than zero or that Item must exist once, but no more than ten times in any Order. Our specific XML document could conform to both of these schemas because it currently meets both sets of rules.

Troubleshooting guide

The following sections provide a brief troubleshooting guide for BizTalk solutions.

Nothing happened—what now?

This section is a troubleshooting guide to help you get through some of the more subtle (and at times frustrating) parts of BizTalk development. Whether you've already read through the text and are now developing your own solutions, or are skipping ahead to search for answers to other issues, this section will probably be one of frequent reference for many readers.

Perhaps, the most frustrating and difficult part of BizTalk for developers new to the platform is knowing where to look when things go wrong. Being a distributed system by nature, there isn't always a single centralized place to look for all the answers. This is largely a byproduct of the distributed nature of the platform; proving once again that everything comes with a price. The Administration Console does go pretty far in accomplishing this goal, but even within the console there are many places to find specific information:

- Check the BizTalk Administration console for **All In-Process Service Instances** or **Messages**. This is probably the most common location for errors and there may be a failure there you need to see (some only appear in **Messages**).

- Check the **Application** event log. Often BizTalk writes here for warnings and errors. Be sure to check the event log on all machines in the group if this is a multi-server environment. This can be critical to helping operations teams track down issues as some errors will only occur on specific nodes.

- Check **Tracked Service Instances** and **Tracked Message Events** and sort by most recent. If you've turned on failed message routing, this can help you see an error being routed out that you've forgotten about.

- Be sure all your Host Instances, Send Ports, and Receive Locations are started and enabled. If BizTalk reaches an error threshold on any of these, they may shutdown or become disabled. This will certainly cause undesired results.

- If you're calling an IIS hosted service (that is, something running in the Isolated Host) check the IIS Logs. These contain detailed information about every request made to a server and can help you see some errors that happen before the actual call to the message box.

- Consider connecting to the BizTalk Server with **DebugView** to see if any traces are active. If you've followed the advice in this book, you will have embedded, helpful, and low overhead trace statements throughout your solution. This will aid in debugging complex issues. The BizTalk CAT Instrumentation Framework provides even better support for logging and is much more optimized; it is the preferred logging method for high volume scenarios.

- Restart the Host Instances. Especially on older or unpatched systems, this may be required. Some of the older software, custom components and adapters may not be fully optimized. If you're not versioning your BizTalk assemblies, in the .NET sense, then new versions will not take effect until the hosting processing (the host instance) is restarted.

- Reboot the server (yes this is not pleasant, but sometimes necessary, although I've never had to do this in a production environment). This mostly comes up with older versions of BizTalk and the Visual Studio integration. This has gotten much better with the 2010 platform alignment, but it still could happen. A few minutes for a reboot on your development machine can save hours of trouble.

- If you get really desperate break out Ethereal or Netmon (or any other network sniffer). This is getting pretty hardcore, as these tools can be complex, but are extremely powerful. If you really want to know what's going on "on the wire" this is a great way to find out.

I dropped my message and it didn't get picked up

Check that the receive location and the host instances that host it are started. This can be slightly embarrassing when it happens, but even monkeys fall from trees. Also, check the mask if this is a file or FTP receive. Finally, check the event log because there could be security issues associated with any receive location. The devil is certainly in the detail here. Two of the most common causes are user permission and files being marked as "read only".

I dropped my message and it disappears, but does not go where I expect it to go

This is often the result of an erroneous subscription and can be compounded by the use of Failed Message Routing. The Tracked Messages / Tracked Service Instances views should help you see what is happening. Often messages will end up in some sort of error or logging location that someone has set up and forgotten about (or failed to share).

What is coupling?

The following section describes, as succinctly as I could manage, the concept of loose coupling; types of coupling, their impact / cost, and how they pertain to distributed systems / middleware.

Every developer of the last decade knows that coupling in software is bad. It is an anti-pattern, an example of what not to do. Yet if you ask developers what loose coupling is they mostly give examples, not a definition. I myself couldn't create a clear definition until I first wrote on the subject, and as you'll see, it's still not that clear.

Part of what makes coupling so difficult to understand or spot in your own projects is that there are actually many different types of coupling. The following are all examples of coupling:

- Contract/Interface
- Transport
- Location
- Time
- Platform (should be less of an issue in SOA, but it's still there)

Some of these are obvious: transport and location represent clear concepts that services are designed to help alleviate. Others are a little more complex. Consider contract coupling. Contracts can couple in obvious ways, like types, and less obvious ways. Recall that one of the principles of a good service is that it has an explicit contract. XSD does a great job making contracts explicit and enforceable: it allows for strong type definitions, complex types, and type validation. One thing XSD cannot address, however, is implicit coupling. I often see two distinct forms of implicit coupling: untyped messages and implicitly ordered contracts.

Untyped messages

This is one of my favorites as there is almost a good reason behind it: namely flexibility. Generally, it is believed that by using an untyped message (string or `xs:any`) a service interface can be changed at will without the normal planning (or pain) required. This anti-pattern service will often expose a method called Execute or something similar and take a string parameter of the XML payload or just `xs:any`.

This sounds like it might actually provide easy changeability and low maintenance, but there are two fundamental flaws with untyped messages: first consumers have no way to know what is legal to send. They have to ask, for example, payloads or a separate schema file outside of the service definition. This means the service is not well encapsulated. Worse, they only know if their message is correct once they actually send it.

The second issue is that untyped messages accomplish nothing. Just because you can change this vague implicit contract without the cooperation of your consumers does not mean they can now use this service. Remember, they'll be sending what they thought was the correct message before this contract update. Now they will just be sending the incorrect, old format and not know why it doesn't work the way they expect.

I've seen some reputable software companies take this approach, and I've never seen it work out well. There is a difference between extension points in a schema and untyped messaging. As my friend Phil Boardman pointed out, 'Untyped messaging is basically an angle bracket delimited text file'. (Phil does admit he didn't think of this, but I heard it from him).

Implicitly ordered operations

This is a much more subtle, and perhaps more dangerous, type of coupling. This is where implicit rules or restrictions work their way into a service. Imagine a service with operations like these:

- Login
- Add item to basket
- Validate order
- Place order

This should look funny to begin with for a few reasons. First of all, this looks a lot more like an API than a service, and second, you can see there is probably some sort of order expected for these operations, but it is not clearly defined. You would need a separate `readme` document to tell you that you must first call the Login operation, then Add item to basket, then Validate order before calling Place order. WS-Policy is one way to solve the order of operations, but it would only mask the problem (mostly because it is not widely adopted or understood).

This example service also violates other principles: Autonomy and Statelessness. By requiring multiple separate operations to be sent in a specific order, this service implicitly contains state within it (if it didn't, it wouldn't know about your shopping cart or the items in it) and it forces consumers to understand its internal working (the order of operations). These are bad signs as changes to the service will almost certainly impact the consumer. Let's suppose your service now needed to calculate tax or shipping. This type of service would have no real place for them.

This service should really exist as one operation: Place order. In the implementation of this service, the validation and login should all take place together in one unit of work or transaction script.

The continuum of coupling

Service design is a series of trade offs; the impacts of which are not always immediately clear. Thus coupling is really a continuum and where your services fall on this continuum will vary with every implementation based upon these trade offs. For instance, the goal of flexibility is in direct opposition with the goals of validation and control. This is why service design deserves careful attention before you begin implementation. This is the essence of contract-first development, and it is a good idea both in code and in services. Test Driven Development really shines here because you will get to know what your services are like before you are stuck with their legacy implementations.

Definition of loose coupling

When I alluded to that definition of loose coupling I would probably break it down like this: Something is loosely coupled if its interactions are separated by abstractions of type, transport, platform, and state.

So, how can you tell if a service (or code for that matter) is loosely coupled? This part is strangely simple. If it is difficult to test a service, class, or method, then it is probably not loosely coupled. Inversely, code that can be easily tested without major setup and teardown is loosely coupled. To be clear when I say test, I mean effective, completely automated tests. It's very easy to make tests that are almost useless without realizing it. A test suite for even a single service should cover all the major expected scenarios for valid and invalid service invocation.

This is one of those *Code Smells* Martin Fowler writes about in *Refactoring* and you should be aware of it. When you start to realize your setup and teardowns are very large and cumbersome, your code is slipping into tight coupling. This is the same for services and code in general (which is normally service implementations). This is probably the last warning sign that you're about to have major maintenance problems; unless you don't have adequate tests, in which case you'll end up with major production problems.

State

This section outlines the coupling inherent in state.

What is state?

State is the current configuration and settings of a system at a given point in time. When I put my laptop down on the table, it remains there until I move it; it maintains state. When I save this document I am writing it stays that way until I work on it next; it too retains state. On a more technical level, when I set a variable to a value that code now has state. State is a very natural concept for software developers and one they learn early on. The fact that state is constant in all our human activities probably exacerbates the issue.

Back to my previous shopping cart example, adding items to a cart is creating state. When multiple operations are part of a single task they share state in that the task is only complete when all the operations happen. Most often these operations must be in a specific order and the operations must share data to accomplish their task. This data and order are part of the state of this task. The more operations and data are shared, the more state there is and the management of it will become more cumbersome.

Anytime, two or more operations (meaning requests) are composed into a single unit of work (or are required to perform a single task) state is necessarily involved. This is because the requests are somehow related and someone will have to pay the penalty for correlating them; that is to say matching the first request with the second.

Many developers who "came of age" (in the programming sense) during the client server era have state mentality deeply ingrained and will fall back on it when tackling newer problems. This is a dangerous path into stateful, tightly coupled code.

Why is state expensive?

So what is wrong with all this? Why is state bad? State is bad because it is complicated by its very nature. State involves several parts moving in unison in order to work correctly. The separate operations must be coordinated and the progress tracked (normally on both the client and the server); this is most often done through the use of sessions. Sessions are conduits through which this data passes and the mechanism for connecting separate operations into the single task. Any time you open a database connection, or even a terminal screen, that is a session. Sessions must do a lot of coordination in order to facilitate the work being performed. They must match multiple requests from the client to the appropriate session that is in progress (normally a specific thread of execution). Most frameworks do this for us, but the fact of the matter is that as we scale sessions become far more cumbersome.

Even this quasi-automatic matching of requests to specific sessions, often called session affinity, becomes an issue as you scale because if the session is provided in a web server process every request from that user, for that session, must go to the same web server. Alternatively, the session could be stored in a shared resource, like a database, but this will slow every operation as the session is loaded back into process by the application (the web server).

Then it actually gets worse, as besides simply coordinating requests and data, there are issues around session lifetime management. How long should a session be valid? What should be done when a session is no longer valid? Who will clean up whatever resources the session used when it expired? For some older client server applications this was easy, when the application closed the session was over. This shows how tightly bound the application was to its session. In the distributed world, this is a much more difficult problem to solve. Unless you're using a single open, persistent TCP/IP connection there is not a definite lifetime for a session.

How does state relate to coupling?

Finally, the sequence of steps and data exchanged creates a type of coupling we discussed in loose coupling. This prescribed sequence of operations and data exchanges create glue that makes our programs stay in a specific form. This is an implicit contract, perhaps the worst kind, because it is not expressed via the service itself, but normally through outside documentation.

So state is complicated and heavy with great amounts of overhead and it makes it harder to change our services and applications. You can't just create a new mandatory middle step without coordinating with all of your consumers. That would break their existing applications. State affects coupling—generally more increases it, less decreases it.

There are many technical reasons as to why state is bad, but for now let's just stick with the fact that it's complicated and requires a lot of resources and overhead, as well as creating an implicit contract.

Why do people feel like they need state?

More often than not the perceived need for state is actually misplaced. State is obviously useful; all human interactions are built around it. When I'm shopping online, I want to see what's in my cart as I add things. This cart is state, but a careful distinction must be drawn between services and applications. Services are used by applications, applications are used by people. People do not directly use services. Using a web portal to tie together services to provide an e-commerce experience is a great idea, but there is a distinction that must be made between what functionality resides in the services and what resides in the web portal. In our example, the stateful shopping cart definitely belongs in the web portal application, the submission of an order really belongs in a service.

How can you avoid state?

There are several strategies one can use to avoid state in services and they work better in specific situations. The easiest, perhaps, is to defer to the consumer. This is what classic client-server applications did. The client was responsible for tracking and taking care of its own session. This does work and our shopping cart example would fit this type of state deferral pattern. The web portal must keep its own shopping cart and when the user is ready submit it to the Order service.

Another popular technique is to defer to the ultimate destination application that the service is a conduit to. This is less desirable, but also an option. I say less desirable because the service will likely need to carry through information that really has nothing to do with the service itself; perhaps a session ID or token of some sort. If you must go down this route, you should really consider using a custom SOAP header for this information, rather than simply placing it in your request message bodies. The reason is twofold: first, this information has nothing to do with the operation you are providing, it is a technical detail. Second, it is likely to be needed on all your operations, so creating a SOAP header for it saves you from having to put this information into every one of your operation input messages.

Often the best approach is to simply design your services to not need state at all. This can be done by making messages more coarsely grained and requiring them to carry more information in their payload than would be the case of stateful services. This can be paired with bunching operations together and thinking in more coarse grained terms.

Where does all this fit into services?

Statelessness is critical to service orientation because of the unpredictable nature of networks and distributed computing in general. We may take this for granted; especially on smaller scales, but large distributed systems feel this impact as transient errors, slow performance, and difficulty in change.

Services of all flavors are built on the premise and success of HTTP (that is, the web). HTTP is perhaps the most successful protocol ever created. It can effectively be argued that the very success of the Internet is largely due to the HTTP protocol's stateless nature. This has allowed the web to grow in the way that it has.

This can really throw off a lot of people, even technical people, because almost everything we do on the Internet these days appears to have state. The best designed and most scalable services and applications actually do not really have much state.

Index

Thank you for buying
Microsoft BizTalk Server 2010 Patterns

About Packt Publishing

Packt, pronounced 'packed', published its first book "Mastering phpMyAdmin for Effective MySQL Management" in April 2004 and subsequently continued to specialize in publishing highly focused books on specific technologies and solutions.

Our books and publications share the experiences of your fellow IT professionals in adapting and customizing today's systems, applications, and frameworks. Our solution based books give you the knowledge and power to customize the software and technologies you're using to get the job done. Packt books are more specific and less general than the IT books you have seen in the past. Our unique business model allows us to bring you more focused information, giving you more of what you need to know, and less of what you don't.

Packt is a modern, yet unique publishing company, which focuses on producing quality, cutting-edge books for communities of developers, administrators, and newbies alike. For more information, please visit our website: www.packtpub.com.

About Packt Enterprise

In 2010, Packt launched two new brands, Packt Enterprise and Packt Open Source, in order to continue its focus on specialization. This book is part of the Packt Enterprise brand, home to books published on enterprise software – software created by major vendors, including (but not limited to) IBM, Microsoft and Oracle, often for use in other corporations. Its titles will offer information relevant to a range of users of this software, including administrators, developers, architects, and end users.

Writing for Packt

We welcome all inquiries from people who are interested in authoring. Book proposals should be sent to author@packtpub.com. If your book idea is still at an early stage and you would like to discuss it first before writing a formal book proposal, contact us; one of our commissioning editors will get in touch with you.

We're not just looking for published authors; if you have strong technical skills but no writing experience, our experienced editors can help you develop a writing career, or simply get some additional reward for your expertise.

SOA Patterns with BizTalk Server 2009

ISBN: 978-1-847195-00-5   Paperback: 400 pages

Implement SOA strategies for Microsoft BizTalk Server solutions

1. Discusses core principles of SOA and shows them applied to BizTalk solutions

2. The most thorough examination of BizTalk and WCF integration in any available book

3. Leading insight into the new WCF SQL Server Adapter, UDDI Services version 3, and ESB Guidance 2.0

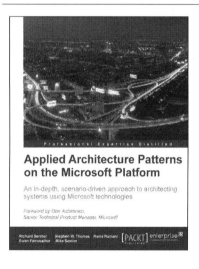

Applied Architecture Patterns on the Microsoft Platform

ISBN: 978-1-849680-54-7   Paperback: 544 pages

An in-depth scenario-driven approach to architecting systems using Microsoft technologies with this Applied Architecture Patterns

1. Provides an architectural methodology for choosing Microsoft application platform technologies to meet the requirements of your solution

2. Examines new technologies such as Windows Server AppFabric, StreamInsight, and Windows Azure Platform and provides examples of how they can be used in real-world solutions

3. Considers solutions for messaging, workflow, data processing, and performance scenarios

Please check **www.PacktPub.com** for information on our titles

Microsoft BizTalk 2010: Line of Business Systems Integration

ISBN: 978-1-84968-190-2   Paperback: 536 pages

A practical guide to integrating Line of Business systems with Microsoft BizTalk Server 2010

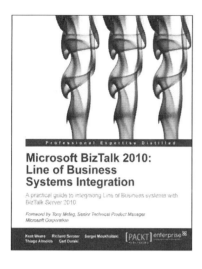

1. Deliver integrated Line of Business solutions more efficiently with BizTalk Server 2010

2. Obtain pre-requisite ERP and CRM knowledge that will make your integration project successfu

3. Examine ways to integrate with leading Enterprise Resource Planning (ERP) systems like SAP and Microsoft Dynamics AX 2009

4. Study techniques used to integrate with leading Customer Relationship Management (CRM) systems like SalesForce.com and Dynamics CRM 2011

Business Process Execution Language for Web Services 2nd Edition

ISBN: 978-1-904811-81-7   Paperback: 372 pages

An Architect's and Developer's book and eBook guide to BPEL and BPEL4WS

1. Architecture, syntax, development and composition of Business Processes and Services using BPEL

2. Advanced BPEL features such as compensation, concurrency, links, scopes, events, dynamic partner links, and correlations

3. Oracle BPEL Process Manager and BPEL Designer Microsoft BizTalk Server as a BPEL server

Please check **www.PacktPub.com** for information on our titles

14765696R00211

Made in the USA
Lexington, KY
21 April 2012